"Rebecca Hamilton has catalogued—realistically, soberingly, and most impressively—the successes and shortcomings of the Darfur advocacy movement from its inception to the present. Her work highlights the challenges for citizens and policymakers alike of adapting their actions to mass atrocities less overtly clear than a Holocaust or Rwanda. But above all Hamilton is the model of an 'upstander,' one whom raises her voice and acts when people—whether near or far, Western or African—are most in need of help."—LGen. the Honourable Roméo A. Dallaire (Ret'd), Senator

"A masterful feat of original research and reporting, *Fighting for Darfur* is an authoritative account of the impact of the first sustained citizens' movement against genocide. With Hamilton's fierce determination to get beyond self-congratulatory slogans and taken-for-granted assumptions about what is required to save lives at risk, she provides insights that will be invaluable for concerned citizens, human rights advocates, and policymakers alike for years and years to come. Essential reading for anyone who wants to help build a better world."—Jody Williams, Nobel Peace Prize Laureate, founding coordinator of the International Campaign to Ban Landmines

"The lack of political will to act is the bottleneck where the best intentions of the international community to stop genocide get stuck. Political will is never there spontaneously; it has to be created, nurtured, and transformed into action by the concerted and committed efforts of citizens confronting their governments with their own stated values and ideals. Rebecca Hamilton's brilliant case study of the efforts to stop the carnage in Darfur and of its limitations combines passion and intelligence to offer a valuable blueprint for a 'movement of conscience' to protect the next population at risk of genocide."—Juan E. Méndez, Special Advisor to the UN Secretary-General on the Prevention of Genocide (2004-2007)

"Moving between American college campuses, the halls of the UN and African Union, the policy battles within Washington, DC, the International Criminal Court in The Hague, and Darfur itself, *Fighting for Darfur* is a vivid account of how a vicious conflict in a forgotten part of Africa came to define an international movement to stop mass atrocity. Herself one of the earliest and most influential of Darfur activists, Rebecca Hamilton poses tough questions for Darfur advocacy movement and the ambition of a global citizens' movement against genocide, which it has spawned."—Alex de Waal, co-author of *Darfur: A Short History of a Long War*

"Bec Hamilton, an intrepid reporter and researcher, has collected and analyzed an impressive amount of original material about one of the least understood foreign policy stories of the past decade: how the world failed to prevent genocide in Darfur. She shrewdly assesses the role of all the major actors including the Sudanese government, the international community, and, most of all, the new citizens movement that pressured officials to stop the killing. Hamilton's account will be of great interest to anyone who wants to know how his or her voice can make a difference."—Mike Abramowitz, director of the genocide prevention program, U.S. Holocaust Memorial Museum

"Rebecca Hamilton captures brilliantly the passion and commitment of the Save Darfur movement but is also cool and clear-headed about what went wrong. She is especially strong on the ever-present risk for any mass campaign organization of oversimplifying multidimensional and ever-changing situations. Complex solutions for complex problems don't make good bumper stickers, and getting what you wish for doesn't always address the real issues. This is 'lessons learned' writing at its best, compelling reading for policymakers, community activists, and anyone anywhere ashamed at our inability to stop mass atrocity crimes and determined to make the now almost universally accepted responsibility to protect principle a universal reality on the ground."—Gareth Evans, author of *The Responsibility to Protect: Ending Mass Atrocity Crimes Once and for All*

"Rebecca Hamilton's book is the authoritative account of the world's response since 2003 to mass atrocities in Darfur—and why the best intentions of grassroots activists, U.S. government officials, the United Nations, other international actors, and the news media have fallen so short. It is a story of missed opportunities and unintended consequences. It is also a timely call for more realistic and more effective approaches—by policymakers and citizen activists alike—as Sudan enters a turbulent transition that threatens the people of Darfur and beyond."—Jon Sawyer, Executive Director, Pulitzer Center on Crisis Reporting

"Rebecca Hamilton offers a compelling and sober assessment of advocacy networks' efforts to stop genocide in Sudan. This highly readable birds-eye account should be required reading for students and practitioners of public policy."—Graham Allison, Professor of Government at Harvard's John F. Kennedy School of Government and author of *Essence of Decision: Explaining the Cuban Missile Crisis*

"Is mass revulsion to mass atrocities sufficient to change American foreign policy? *Fighting for Darfur* tells you why 'It ain't that simple' in a multipolar world with a divided U.S. government. A gripping personal and societal tally of lessons for advocates about how to do better the next time that we face a 'never-again' crisis."—Thomas G. Weiss, Presidential Professor of Political Science, the CUNY Graduate Center, and author of *What's Wrong with the United Nations and How to Fix It*

"*Fighting for Darfur* is the story of a citizens campaign designed to move governments to save millions of lives in Sudan. It is written by a courageous and resourceful human rights activist who was one of the central players in launching that endeavor. Rebecca Hamilton commendably maintains a measured sense of political realism while still inspiring and encouraging citizens in democracies to fight for the rights of those who are suffering in oppressive societies. A compelling read."—Justice Richard Goldstone, author of *For Humanity*

FIGHTING *for* DARFUR

PUBLIC ACTION AND THE STRUGGLE TO STOP GENOCIDE

REBECCA HAMILTON

Preface by Mia Farrow

palgrave
macmillan

FIGHTING FOR DARFUR
Copyright © Rebecca Hamilton, 2011.

All rights reserved.

First published in 2011 by
PALGRAVE MACMILLAN®
in the United States—a division of St. Martin's Press LLC,
175 Fifth Avenue, New York, NY 10010.

Where this book is distributed in the UK, Europe and the rest of the
world, this is by Palgrave Macmillan, a division of Macmillan Publishers
Limited, registered in England, company number 785998, of Houndmills,
Basingstoke, Hampshire RG21 6XS.

Palgrave Macmillan is the global academic imprint of the above companies
and has companies and representatives throughout the world.

Palgrave® and Macmillan® are registered trademarks in the United States,
the United Kingdom, Europe and other countries.

ISBN: 978–0–230–10022–0

Library of Congress Cataloging-in-Publication Data

Hamilton, Rebecca, 1977–
     Fighting for Darfur : public action and the struggle to stop genocide /
Rebecca Hamilton.
       p. cm.
     Includes bibliographical references and index.
     ISBN 978–0–230–10022–0
       1. Sudan—History—Darfur Conflict, 2003—Moral and ethical
aspects. 2. Sudan—History—Darfur Conflict, 2003—Civilian relief.
3. Genocide—Sudan—Darfur—Prevention—International cooperation.
4. Humanitarian intervention—Sudan—Darfur. 5. Humanitarian
assistance—Sudan—Darfur. 6. Darfur (Sudan)—Foreign public opinion.
I. Title.

DT159.6.D27H36 2011
962.404'3—dc22   2010023220

A catalogue record of the book is available from the British Library.

Design by Newgen Imaging Systems (P) Ltd., Chennai, India.

First edition: February 2011

10 9 8 7 6 5 4 3 2 1

Printed in the United States of America.

For those who will lead the multigenerational effort to challenge traditional foreign policy formulation.

And for Ben Batros.

"The only real nation is humanity."

—Paul Farmer

CONTENTS

PREFACE

In 1918 Henry Morgenthau, U.S. ambassador to the Ottoman Empire, wrote of the Armenian genocide: "I am confident that the whole history of the human race contains no such horrible episode as this. The great massacres and persecutions of the past seem almost insignificant when compared to the sufferings of the Armenian race in 1915."[1]

Tragically, we have learned nothing since the first genocide of the twentieth century when the Turks killed more than a million Armenians.

Throughout the past hundred years there has been an almost unbroken chain of genocides and mass murders leading up to today: In the 1930s and 1940s the Japanese killed millions across Asia; in the Soviet Union, more than 8 million perished in the Gulag camps and beyond; from 1941 to 1945 the Germans slaughtered 6 million Jews; in 1945 the U.S. president Harry Truman chose to drop nuclear bombs on two Japanese cities killing 300,000 defenseless civilians; in the 1950s and 1960s the communist Chinese killed approximately 30 million people; during the 1970s, the Khmer Rouge killed 1.7 million Cambodians, 20 percent of that country's population; then came Bosnia, Rwanda, and, today, Darfur.

In the last century there have been 100 million victims of genocide and mass murders. We, the international community, have been bystanders—again and again and again.

A Polish lawyer, Raphael Lemkin, who lost 49 relatives in the Nazi Holocaust, felt there needed to be a word for what Churchill called "a crime that has no name" and an international law to punish the crime. In 1944 Lemkin introduced the word *genocide* and became a one-man crusade to create a convention against the crime of genocide at the United Nations.

In the face of enormous events, our own feelings of helplessness are our worst enemies. It is crucial to remember that we who live in a democracy have a voice, a responsibility, and a role to play. In order for genocide and mass murder to take place, certain key components must be present. In every instance there is a leader or small group of leaders who are able to use people's existing fears, grievances, convictions, or prejudices to convince them that another group poses a threat to their own futures and well-being. Details are organized and put into action. Ordinary people choose to participate. Those with the power to halt the killing choose to do nothing.

If, by chance, we are blessed to live in a place where it is safe and possible to meet our basic needs and where our human rights are respected, what then is our responsibility to others who happen to be born where there is hunger, thirst, bloodshed, terror?

My own family mantra is "with knowledge comes responsibility." It is precisely this—the weight of a powerful "knowing" that has brought me to this point in my life, to a place so far from where my life began in Beverly Hills, California. It has carried me away from many things, even from people. It is taking me on a journey I never could have anticipated or envisioned. A journey that requires everything.

I think this chapter of my life began with Rwanda.

How can we not be haunted by the Rwandan genocide of 1994? Its components define us, condemn us, demand better of us, and pose profoundly wrenching questions. What were we in the United States doing while as many as 800,000 people were slaughtered? Many of us were watching the O.J. Simpson murder trial. My country, my church, the United Nations, and all the nations of the world did nothing to halt that hundred-day rampage. Collectively and individually, we must bear the burden of our profound and abysmal failure.

In that context, a *New York Times* piece in 2004 took my breath away. On the tenth anniversary of the Rwandan genocide I learned that another genocide was unfolding in a place I had never heard of—Darfur. The Sudanese government, in tandem with their proxy militia known as Janjaweed, were launching coordinated aerial and ground attacks on the ethnic tribes of that remote and disenfranchised Sudanese region.

With knowledge comes responsibility. And so it was that in 2004 I first went to Sudan.

Darfur in 2004 was an inferno that no words can adequately convey. Dante himself would surely shudder. Bombings and attacks upon villages were ongoing. Families were on the run, sheltering under scrubby trees, dazed, terrified, and surrounded by their attackers. I traveled from camp to camp where traumatized survivors were eager to tell their stories of loss, torture, terror, and rape; of beloved homes and carefully tended fields ablaze, of lives destroyed. These stories are with me always.

In one of the camps I met a woman named Halima. She insisted that I accept one of several amulets hanging from her neck, "For your protection," she said. Halima had been wearing the amulet on the day her village was attacked. Without warning the morning skies had filled with attack aircraft, which rained bombs upon families as they slept, as they cooked breakfast, as they were walking out to tend their fields, as they prayed. Halima tried to gather her children, and with her infant son in her arms, she ran.

But "from all directions, on camels and horseback" men swarmed the village, shooting and shouting racial epithets. They caught Halima as she ran, and before they raped her, they tore her baby from her arms and bayoneted him. Three of her five children were similarly killed on that day, and her husband, too. "Janjaweed," she said, "they cut them and threw them into the well." Then she clasped my hands and said, "Tell people what is happening here. Tell them we need help. Tell them we will all be slaughtered." As we were speaking, the camp was invaded by men on camels. Halima and the other women scattered while I jumped into a UN vehicle and sped across the sand toward a waiting helicopter.

I don't know if Halima is still alive. To this day, I wear her amulet around my neck, and my promise to her has become my moral mandate.

I do know that after six years, no adequate protection has come for Halima or anyone in Darfur.

The only message we have sent to the people of Darfur is that they are completely dispensable.

On the plane heading home I tried to process all I had seen and learned. The family mantra, "with knowledge comes responsibility," took on new meaning. An inescapable knowledge of atrocities and immeasurable suffering was now mine. But what could *I do?* At that point I knew only that I must honor my pledge to Halima and other courageous survivors and do my utmost to "tell the world what is happening" in Darfur, with the hope that good people everywhere, if only they knew, would rise to put an end to the killing.

I had no idea then what my utmost would mean. I couldn't know it would take me back to the Darfur region 13 times; that I would write scores of articles and that they would actually be published; that my photographs of Darfur would appear in exhibitions and in print around the world; that I, who had shirked interviews all my life, would give interviews in the thousands; that I, who know nothing about money business, would immerse myself in a divestment campaign. And when it was announced that Beijing would host the 2008 Olympic Games, I saw that as a window of opportunity to press China to use its relationship with Sudan to end the killing and to admit UN peacekeepers with the necessary capacity. I am daily discovering what my utmost can be.

My deepest conviction is that we have both a responsibility to remember and a responsibility to protect. Genocide is not inevitable or unstoppable—unless we choose to let it happen.

I had the great privilege of spending time with Miep Gies who, for two years in Amsterdam, risked her life to hide Anne Frank's family and four others—eight people in all. I wanted to understand what it was within her that caused her to do these extraordinary things. Why Miep Gies? Why Raul Wallenberg? Why Oskar Schindler? And most importantly, why not everyone?

Miep shed no light on her decisions. "Of course it was not easy," she told me. "But what else could I do?" The profundity of her response lies in its simple ordinariness. For Miep, there were no other options. She could not have done otherwise.

I have a Rwandan friend who survived the 1994 genocide but lost most of her family and was witness to unimaginable atrocities. Based on what took place in her country, she calculates that "95 percent of people can pick up a machete and kill strangers and friends alike for 90 days. This we know. Three percent, they don't want to kill, they will run away."

My friend's words dropped me into the bleakest silence. But eventually I thought, 2 percent! That's not zero! We have something to build on.

Miep Gies always insisted, "I am not a hero. There is nothing special about me." I respectfully disagree. Miep Gies was among the 2 percent who set the bar, show us the way, and help us all feel more hopeful about being human.

As Elie Wiesel wrote of the Holocaust: "The victims perished not only because of the killers, but also because of the apathy of the bystanders. What astonished us after the torment, after the tempest, was not that so many killers killed so many victims, but that so few cared about us at all."[2]

Two percent.

The responsibility and the choice are ours.

—Mia Farrow

AUTHOR'S NOTE

Over the past four years I have conducted more than 150 interviews with policymakers in the U.S. government, the United Nations, and, thanks to a fellowship from the Open Society Institute, I was able to travel to interview officials from the Sudanese government, the African Union, and the Arab League. Through these interviews I was able to piece together what took place inside the corridors of power while citizen advocates rallied outside. Aspects of the picture that emerged from these interviews with respect to U.S. decision making on Sudan were further sharpened by U.S. government cables and other contemporaneous documentation that, with the help of the non-governmental organization, the National Security Archive, I managed to get declassified through the Freedom of Information Act. Equally important were scores of interviews with those Darfuris who survived the attacks on their villages and had managed to reach relative safety in the displacement camps in Darfur, the refugee camps in Chad, and the poorest suburbs of Cairo.

Then there is the citizen advocacy movement itself, which I was completely immersed in until 2006 when I took a step back in order to conduct this research. While I have spent hundreds of hours communicating and interacting with those at the core of the movement, for the purpose of this book I have filtered the story of the movement through four individuals: Omer Ismail, Sam Bell, David Rubenstein, and Gloria White-Hammond. I chose these four advocates because they provide a window into different aspects of the movement. They are not perfectly representative of the whole; Ismail can no more speak for all Darfuri diaspora than White-Hammond can speak for all African Americans involved in the movement. But I believe that their voices, taken together, provide a sense of the hopes, assumptions, motivations, and frustrations recognizable to many who have been involved in Darfur advocacy over the past six years. Each of these advocates gave me hours of their time, in multiple interviews, from 2006 to 2010. Any quotes of theirs that are not sourced in the notes come from these interviews.

August 2010

INTRODUCTION

"**N**gere," he said, giving his chin a nod upward. "Rebecca," I said, taking his outstretched hand with both of mine. "Ah," said Mr. Ngere with a smile, "same as Dr. John's wife." It was the summer of 2004 and my first time in Sudan.

The "Dr. John" Ngere referred to was John Garang de Mabior, commander of the Sudan People's Liberation Movement/Army (SPLM/A). After a 21-year war with the Sudanese government, the SPLM had almost concluded negotiations on a peace agreement that would give the people of southern Sudan a stake in the government and the wealth of their land for the first time in history. In the south, an unfamiliar optimism was taking hold. Under the terms of the agreement John Garang would, on July 9 the following year, assume the mantle of first vice president of Sudan.

By the time I returned to Sudan a second time, in August 2005, Garang was dead, just three weeks after being sworn in as the second most powerful man in the land. Southerners mourned the loss of someone who had long since transcended his position as a rebel commander. His death under suspicious circumstances temporarily overshadowed his mixed history with its fair share of violations, and it heightened his already iconic status as the first person to force Sudanese president Omar al-Bashir's Islamist generals in Khartoum to give away any power.

The peace agreement achieved under Garang's leadership was followed carefully by rebel groups in Darfur—a region in the west of Sudan—whose attempts to attract attention to their own marginalization in every aspect of life had seen al-Bashir's government unleash a genocidal campaign against their people. When I had first met Ngere, while southern Sudan was brimming with promise, Darfuris were being killed in horrific numbers.

That first summer in Sudan, Ngere was my translator—formally of language, but in practice of everything about the unfamiliar world in which I found myself. We walked up to six hours a day through a landscape without roads, electricity, running water, or any of the other basic necessities that so many people take for granted. Our purpose was to visit different camps of displaced southerners who had been driven from their homes and villages by years of fighting. Humanitarian organizations that had started to think through what development could be delivered once the peace agreement was signed wanted to know where these people would want to live if peace were realized.

In our travels, Ngere and I met Kana, age six, carrying her three-year-old sister on her waist. Kana explained to me, "This land is not for us. We are not from here." Roda, eight months pregnant, said she wanted nothing more than to get back to her home village before she had her baby. She had miscarried twice during her time "in the forest." She knew her village had been destroyed, but she felt this baby would have a better chance of survival if born "at home."

Like many students from wealthy countries who, without too much difficulty, obtain funds to work in developing countries between semesters or degrees, I left Sudan in 2004 with a visceral connection to people living in circumstances that, through the sheer randomness of birthplace, I would never experience firsthand. A little less common was that I would take those connections into the first week of Harvard Law School. For Ngere, the precise details of where I would be studying were immaterial. To him what counted was the country. On the day of my departure, as we sheltered under an acacia tree, discussing our last interviews, Ngere suddenly went quiet. I looked up from my notes and found him staring directly at me. "You are going to America?" he said. I nodded, not really sure where this was going. "In America you have a voice. In America you can speak about what happens here and they can do something about it. Here, if we speak about what is real we will be detained, tortured. Here we have no voice. But in America, it is different."

I remembered Ngere's words as I stood engulfed in the swirling unreality of the welcome for incoming law students in Cambridge, Massachusetts, on September 3, 2004. As caterers dressed in crisp white shirts offered us, the class of 2007, an unending stream of wine and canapés and the who's who of the academic glitterati spoke of the opportunities that lay ahead, I had a distinct urge to bring the whole spectacle to a standstill.

How could it be that I was standing there with the option of saying no to a third glass of wine while Martha, whom I had interviewed in Sudan, was worrying about whether she would be well enough to make the long trek to the nearest borehole for water? There was no way to make sense of it. I thought of Makur, age 14, who told me his biggest wish in the world was to go to secondary school—there wasn't one within walking distance of the displaced persons' camp that served as his home. Ngere had commented that Makur was actually quite lucky—he at least had two years of primary school studies. Meanwhile here was I, about to embark on my sixth year of higher education.

As I stood hearing various professors indulge us with commentary on how we had worked so hard to get to Harvard, all I could think was that whatever contribution I had made to my present state of being was nominal compared to the critical factor of not having been born into a society where preventable disease kills more than 100,000 people annually, where almost 50 percent of the population have no access to safe drinking water, and where one in ten children don't make it to their fifth birthday. Of course, I knew all this before I went to Sudan—but having the two experiences, of displacement in rural Sudan and entry to Harvard Law, placed side by side in time, suddenly made the whole issue both very personal and completely inescapable.

Martha, Kana, Makur, Roda, and I are, in all important respects, the same. The biggest differences in our lives are not a result of who we are as people but merely the consequence of where we happened to be born. And while I have a platform through which to talk about this deep inequality, Martha, Kana, and the others I spoke with in Sudan do not. And so began the journey of working out how I was going to put Ngere's words into practice.

Six days after Harvard's welcome, U.S. Secretary of State Colin Powell declared that the situation in Darfur constituted genocide. It was the first time a government had ever declared "genocide" while violence was ongoing. His words became the catalyst for the formation of a citizen-based Save Darfur movement that was able to mobilize and sustain unprecedented numbers of Americans intent on pushing the U.S. government to stop the killings.

Save Darfur has been called the biggest social movement in the United States since the campaign against apartheid. Along with hundreds of thousands of others, I have been deeply involved in this movement, initially urging Harvard to become the first of scores of universities to divest from companies whose business ventures in Sudan help fund the Sudanese government's military budget, and then speaking to groups across the United States about all the actions we could take to make a difference. I was one of many who were convinced that if only we raised our voices loud enough about what was happening in Sudan, the U.S. government would ensure Darfuris received protection.

But when I began my final year of law school, the situation in Darfur was unresolved, and the peace agreement between the government and the SPLM was faltering. I had questions that needed answering. Chief among them was what accounted for the mismatch between the efforts advocates were putting in and the results on the ground?

I began researching the impact of the mass movement for Darfur over the summer of 2006. I was driven by a need to ascertain the meaningfulness of the advocacy efforts so many were involved in. If we were wrong in believing our actions could make a difference, then I wanted to know. If we were becoming unnecessarily despondent about the role we were playing, then it was important to know that too. Most of all, I felt that by understanding what influenced U.S. government decision making on Darfur—the first genocide to have prompted such sustained public action—I could start to understand how ordinary people like me might be able to help prevent genocide and mass atrocity in the future.

FIGHTING FOR DARFUR is the story of what happened when regular citizens adopted as their own concern the human rights of people in a remote region of the world that most Americans will never see and demanded that their elected representatives do the same. Year after year, they held rallies, lobbied congress, harangued newspaper editors, wrote letters to world leaders, and undertook an array of creative online activities to bring Darfur to the attention of those in power.

At the beginning of the citizen movement for Darfur the key, and somewhat uncomfortable question, was whether the American public, so derided overseas for its parochialism, cared enough about a crisis in Africa to put in the work required to move the behemoth U.S. political system to action. Six years later, this question can be answered resoundingly in the affirmative. While many millions of Americans still do not know about the atrocities that have taken place in Darfur, many millions do—and a meaningful segment among them have taken that knowledge, expanded on it, and turned themselves into tireless and increasingly sophisticated lobbyists for the cause. As one U.S. government official told me, citizen advocates turned Darfur into a domestic issue, an achievement that cannot be overstated.

But now there are new, even less comfortable, questions to be asked. What effect has this remarkable citizens' movement had on the policy options pursued, and what effect have these policies had on Darfuris and their nation?

As the Darfur movement gained increasing media attention, many a commentator fell into the trap of attributing any policy decision—good, bad, or otherwise—to advocates. But advocacy, even at its most influential, is just one of the many drivers of a system as complex as foreign policy formulation. In starting this research, it was readily apparent that to try and understand what, if any, impact advocacy had on policy, I would need to look at the policy process as a whole and learn about all the other factors influencing policy at any given time, rather than just looking at what advocates were doing. To date, Darfur advocacy has been both blamed and credited for things that were not the consequence of its actions alone or, in some cases, of its actions at all. Part of the motivation for writing this book was to balance the excesses on both sides of this policy influence matter.

The Darfur movement is just one case of a citizen movement, and only time will tell whether its lessons can be generalized. Moreover, the most interesting questions usually butt up against a counterfactual that cannot be known—namely, what would have transpired in the absence of the Darfur movement. Nevertheless, the questions I attempt to answer are: Given what we know about the history of U.S. government responses to genocide and mass atrocity, is there reason to believe that the citizen movement led the U.S. government to do anything beyond what we would have expected in the movement's absence? If not, why not? If so, did these U.S. government actions lead to improvements on the ground in Darfur? And if they did not, then why not and what could have?

Addressing these questions led me into a second layer of issues that were not in the minds of those of us who, at the start of this new century, pinned our hopes for an end to genocide and mass atrocity on the outcry of an engaged American public: What are the options for stopping genocide when—as in Darfur—the U.S. government alone does not have enough influence over the state committing the crimes to stop them? What is the future of a U.S.-based citizen movement against genocide and mass atrocity in such a scenario?

The basic structure of the book is chronological. The story takes us from the Darfur massacres of 2003 (when mainstream media and global attention was focused solely on the peace negotiations underway between the north and south of Sudan), to the seismic shift in focus to Darfur, and finally to the aftermath of the Sudanese national elections in 2010 when the international spotlight again returned to the south of Sudan, leaving Darfur in darkness. Individual chapters tackle the policy decisions that commentators have attributed to the Darfur advocacy movement. The final chapter stands alone as a summary of what government action was and was not attributable to advocacy, what impact those actions had on the situation in Darfur, and what the Darfur story suggests might be needed to move toward a world without genocide and mass atrocity.

The chapters are grouped into four parts that roughly track the life of the advocacy movement from nonexistence in 2003, to emergence in the shadow of lessons from the 1994 genocide in Rwanda, and then rapidly to substantial influence in the U.S. political realm. But by late 2006 the advocacy movement began to flounder as advocates realized that the United States alone could not "save Darfur" and began to seek other channels through which to pressure Khartoum. Then finally, advocates shifted from focusing on Darfur in isolation to looking at problems between the north and south of Sudan in advance of a referendum, scheduled for January 2011, to determine if southern Sudanese want to become an independent nation.

TODAY IN DARFUR, 2.7 million people remain stranded in displaced camps. After rigged Sudanese elections in April 2010 in which most of Darfur's displaced persons were unwilling or unable to vote, those most responsible for the destruction of their communities have an even greater grip on power than they did at the height of the massacres in 2003 and 2004. To that extent, *Fighting for Darfur* falls into the bleak body of work that documents the repetitive occurrence of genocide and mass atrocity and the equally repetitive failure to stop it. This time, the story came with a twist, as thousands of regular citizens did their utmost to change this depressing trajectory. But in no way can Darfur be seen as a "success story." So is this the point at which we all throw up our hands and dismiss as idealistic any hope that mass murder will not continue into the future as it has throughout the centuries? Actually, *Fighting for Darfur* offers a small silver lining.

Until Darfur, the persistent failure of the U.S. government to protect civilians from genocidal violence could be all-too-easily attributed to and justified by the absence of a politically relevant outcry from citizens. The insufficiency of that alibi has now been revealed. By telling the story of what happened when citizens did create an outcry, *Fighting for Darfur* enables us to take the next step and begin to understand the other missing pieces of the genocide prevention puzzle.

ACRONYMS

AJWS	American Jewish World Service
AMIS	African Union Mission in Sudan
AU	African Union
CPA	Comprehensive Peace Agreement
DPA	Darfur Peace Agreement
DPKO	UN Department of Peacekeeping Operations
GI-Net	Genocide Intervention Network
ICC	International Criminal Court
IDP	internally displaced person
JEM	Justice and Equality Movement
MSF	Médecins Sans Frontières
NCP	National Congress Party
NGO	non-government organization
PDF	Popular Defense Forces
R2P	Responsibility to Protect
SLA	Sudan Liberation Army
SPLM/A	Sudan People's Liberation Movement/Army (SPLM refers to the political wing, and SPLA refers to the military wing of the rebel movement)
UN	United Nations
UNAMID	United Nations/African Union Mission in Darfur
UNMIS	United Nations Mission in Sudan
USAID	U.S. Agency for International Development

PART I

BEFORE THE OUTCRY

CHAPTER 1

AN UNGOVERNABLE LAND

"**O**ur village now is only a name. They burnt everything. When our village existed it had about 100 houses. From those 100 houses, there are no men left. All the children are without fathers now. My children—all of them were male, so all of them were killed." Miriam averted her gaze. "I don't know what they do to the women, but the women cry all the time."[1]

It was August 2008, and I was sitting in a refugee camp in Chad under a makeshift cover of triangular cloth strung between two sticks and a mud-brick wall. As the midday temperature hovered around 115 degrees, Miriam told me how she managed to survive the attack by government-backed militias, known as Janjaweed, that destroyed her home across the border in Sudan some five years earlier.

"I was sitting in my kitchen, making food for my children. It was 2 p.m., just after prayer time. A neighbor ran into my home and said that Janjaweed were surrounding our village. I ran outside my house and I saw horsemen shooting guns. I was afraid for my children, and so I ran back inside, but aircraft started bombing," she explained.[2]

Miriam described a pattern of attack that was central to the Sudanese government's counterinsurgency campaign to destroy Darfur's non-Arab villages. The campaign was the latest chapter in a series of atrocities conducted under the watch of General Omar al-Bashir, who has run Sudan, geographically the largest country in Africa, since a 1989 military coup. His regime initially hoped to create an Islamic state but subsequently abandoned the plan in favor of staying in power by any means necessary. To quell a rebellion in Darfur, those means included sending Janjaweed, recruited from predominantly landless Arab tribes as its proxy militia; the Janjaweed attacked on the ground as the Sudanese air force bombed from above. The targets were people like Miriam, whose only "crime" was being from the same non-Arab ethnic groups that most of the Darfuri insurgents were from.

"There were four Antonovs [Russian-made airplanes]," Miriam remembered. "One was a camouflage color, and the other three were white. The Janjaweed had control of our village. They killed the men and took our animals. Everyone tried to run toward the mountains to escape, but the Janjaweed chased us. It was a terrible time. I cannot explain how it was to you. We couldn't even take the wounded with us—we just had to run." Miriam readjusted the bright yellow cloth of her headscarf, waited for my translator to finish, then continued. "Those of us who managed to escape walked through the night. Finally we arrived at Abu Leha, but all we found was dead bodies, everywhere."³

"On our journey we used donkeys to carry our children. We had some few grains of sorghum but that was all.... There were about 45 of us in the group. The journey took us nine days. We would walk only at night, and during the day we hid ourselves in the bushes."⁴

When Miriam first reached Chad in 2003 there was no refugee camp set up to provide her with shelter, nor was there any humanitarian operation equipped to respond to the thousands of dehydrated, wounded, and traumatized like her, who were scattered across an inhospitable desert terrain. The regime that bombed her village and gave weapons to the militia that killed her children was in the midst of negotiating, with the support of the international community, a peace agreement that would stop a different war, one that had been fought for two decades in the south of the country. Experts hailed the agreement as a chance to bring a democratic transformation across the whole of Sudan. And so none of the world powers said a word about Darfur and the thousands of people like Miriam.

SUDAN HAS BEEN in a state of almost continuous civil war since it became the first country in sub-Saharan Africa to gain its independence from the British in 1956. One consistent source of conflict has been over what makes a person Sudanese.⁵ The debate over race, religion, culture, language, and ethnicity defines who is included and who is excluded from the wealth and power of the country.

The struggle for consensus over national identity can be intuited just by looking at a map. Sudan's sprawling territory borders nine countries, from Egypt and Libya in the north to Uganda and Kenya in the south—or, imagined differently, from the Arab world to the African world. Sudan's rulers, who have always governed from the north of the country, have typically defined Sudan as an Arab nation, thereby disenfranchising those who affiliate themselves with an African identity.

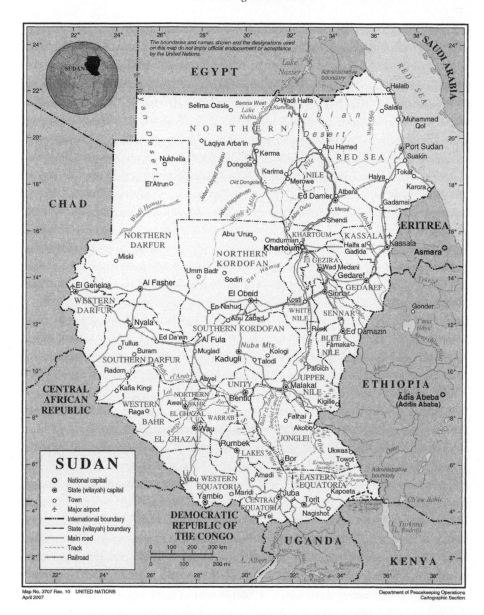

The various layers of Sudanese identity, however, run along more than just an Arab-African divide. For example, Sudanese also draw a distinction between the Sudanese Arabs from around the Nile River (known as the riverine Arabs) and those who are not. The latter tend to be nomads, centered in the eastern and western areas of northern Sudan, while the riverine Arabs have traditionally been traders. For as long as anyone in modern-day Sudan can remember, the three ethnic groups that make up the riverine Arabs have held political power and thus had the upper hand in defining what it means to be Sudanese.[6]

The result has been the marginalization of vast areas of the country. In the south, the east, the far north, and the western region of Darfur, where Miriam comes from, Arabs and non-Arabs alike have suffered economic and political discrimination under the minority rule of the riverine elite.

These present-day governance problems have their origins in the period well before Sudanese independence.[7] In 1899, Britain and Egypt jointly ended a four-year insurgency against Turco-Egyptian rule, which had been instigated by the Mahdi, a Sudanese Islamist whose initial support had come from Darfur.[8] The two nations agreed to share sovereignty over Sudan. But because Egypt had itself been occupied by Britain for a decade, the agreement amounted to British rule.[9] Twenty years later Egypt revolted against British occupation, and by 1922 Britain had granted Egypt its independence. The British feared that the newly independent Egyptians would foster nationalist aspirations among Sudan's educated elite, so they tried to counter this with a new system of governance in Sudan called Native Administration.

Native Administration meant that local areas were governed by so-called tribal leaders. In many areas tribal leadership as the British envisaged it did not exist, but this did not deter them from simply creating it by giving honorific titles to men who had not previously played a leadership role. The British preferred to bestow leadership upon uneducated locals than on the newly educated class who might seek independence from Britain.[10]

The aspirations of educated Sudanese were not the only threat that the British perceived. Remnants of the Mahdi's movement repeatedly challenged their rule, leading the British to worry about Islam as a mobilizing force. To try and reduce the threat, the British instituted a policy of physical segregation, with permits required to cross between the north and south of the country.[11] And while development projects progressed in the northern area that the British ruled from, the south was economically neglected.[12] In the subsequent decade, the separatist policy went further still, enforcing a system of religious and linguistic segregation. By dividing the country and effectively outsourcing any responsibility for the provision of education and welfare services in the south to Western missionaries, the British hoped to create an English-speaking Christian population in the south that would be isolated from Islam.[13]

The British segregation policy was not cut from whole cloth; during the Turco-Egyptian period (1821-1885) the slave trade was run by northerners who viewed southerners as inferior and therefore enslavable. Economic discrimination also was entrenched long before the British arrived, with rulers predating the Turco-Egyptian period viewing the peripheral areas of the country as places to be exploited in order to sustain growth in the northern area where they ruled. British policy institutionalized these distinctions, contributing to the identity gap among Sudanese citizens. And after solidifying these fractures, the British abruptly left Sudan to fend for itself.

At the end of World War II, largely to counter Egyptian claims over Sudan, Britain advocated Sudanese self-determination—a concept favored by the newly formed United Nations.[14] But by 1952, a change in leadership meant that Egypt no longer wanted Sudan and so encouraged the Sudanese to call the British bluff.[15] By 1953 the British had been cornered into agreeing to Sudanese self-determination. The next year "Sudanization" began, and 800 governmental positions held by British and Egyptians were transferred to Sudanese; just six of those posts went to southerners. As one southerner described it, "our fellow northerners want to colonize us for another hundred years."[16] With "Sudanization" effectively being "northernization" a mutiny began in the south. As the mutiny escalated, Britain refused to deploy forces to diffuse the situation, fearing that British intervention would encourage Egyptian intervention.[17] Instead, the British brought forward the date for independence, seeking to extricate themselves from problems they had helped create.[18]

The 1955 mutiny became a 17-year war between southerners and the northerners to whom the British handed over control of the country at Sudan's independence. The deal that ended the fighting, the Addis Ababa agreement, granted southerners semi-autonomy with a southern regional government.[19] The deal was enshrined in Sudan's 1973 Constitution, which also stated that Sudan was a secular state with sharia (Islamic law) governing only personal matters between those who were Muslim.[20] However, the agreement was deeply unpopular among some northern political factions, particularly the Muslim Brothers, a group that advocated the creation of an Islamic state with sharia law enforced nationwide.[21]

In 1983 the peace unraveled. To preempt what he feared would be an attempt by the Muslim Brothers to overthrow him, Sudanese president Jafaar Nimeiri dissolved the southern regional government by dividing the single southern region into three blocs; with southern political power emasculated, he then imposed sharia across the country, including for non-Muslims in the south.[22] In response, a group of southerners formed the Sudan People's Liberation Movement/Army (SPLM/A), with a military base in Ethiopia, led by U.S.-educated southerner John Garang.[23] Sudan returned to civil war.

At the time, the Sudanese armed forces consisted of just 60,000 men—not enough for Nimeiri to be victorious; he looked for a way to strengthen his hand.[24] Like the rest of Sudan, the south was diverse, and local disputes often broke out between different groups, particularly over access to land for farming or grazing. Seeking to bolster his limited military capacity, Nimeiri began exploiting these tensions by arming nomadic Arabs from the border region between the north and south to conduct raids against the key ethnic groups from which the SPLM/A gained support.[25] The raids by the government-sponsored militia, known as *mujahedeen*, followed a common pattern—one that would be repeated against Darfuris like Miriam two decades later. When a village was attacked, the men would be killed, the women raped, and the livestock looted.[26]

In 1985 Nimeiri was ousted. A Transitional Military Council took control of Sudan and, remarkably, allowed democratic elections in 1986, bringing to power the Mahdi's great-grandson Sadiq al-Mahdi.[27] But not for long. By 1989 with the war ongoing, Prime Minister al-Mahdi came under pressure to reach a political settlement with the southerners and arranged a meeting with the SPLM/A leader John Garang. The Muslim Brothers, who now called themselves the National Islamic Front, feared that an agreement with Garang would undermine their goal of securing Sudan as an Islamic state; a few days before the scheduled meeting they overthrew al-Mahdi.[28]

In the years immediately following the 1989 coup, General Omar al-Bashir was the public face of the new regime. Behind him were key figures from the National Islamic Front: Ali Osman Taha and his mentor, an Islamist intellectual and lawyer named Hassan al-Turabi.[29]

I interviewed al-Turabi at his sprawling home in the Sudanese capital, Khartoum, in 2009. He told me that his only concern in the overthrow was to deliver democracy to the Sudanese people. It was an improbable spin on events given that the overthrown government had been democratically elected. When pushed, al-Turabi attempted to justify his statement by arguing that what "the people" really want is an Islamic state—thus, if democracy delivers anything other than an Islamic state, it must be due to a flaw in the democratic system.[30]

Once the National Islamic Front came to power, "the people" had very little say. Al-Bashir issued a dizzying number of antidemocratic decrees, banning political parties, dissolving trade unions, and prohibiting demonstrations.[31] Meanwhile al-Turabi began implementing his long-held plan to make Khartoum the global center of an Islamic revolution.

In the aftermath of the 1991 Gulf War, al-Bashir's regime declared that no "Arab brothers" would require a visa to enter Sudan, and al-Turabi formed a Pan-Arab Islamic Congress to support Islamic revolutionaries in 50 different countries.[32] The most notorious of his efforts involved hosting Osama bin Laden in Sudan. Bin Laden was just one of many Islamist militants whom the National Islamic Front supported throughout the early 1990s, leading the U.S. State Department to designate Sudan a state sponsor of terror.[33]

Al-Turabi's scheme came to an abrupt end in 1995 after he and Taha sponsored a failed assassination attempt on Egyptian president Hosni Mubarak, who was facing internal opposition from Islamists backed by al-Turabi. The story captured world headlines, and the UN Security Council responded by sanctioning Sudan for its role as a state sponsor of terrorism.[34] In a subsequent effort to regain a veneer of legitimacy, al-Bashir authorized the formation of political parties, changed the name of the National Islamic Front to the National Congress Party (NCP), and in 1996 expelled Osama bin Laden.[35] Nonetheless, al-Bashir's attempts to curry favor did not change perceptions in Washington.

In 1997 President Bill Clinton issued a wide-ranging executive order prohibiting all trade with Sudan.[36] The following year, after terrorist attacks on U.S. embassies in East Africa were linked back to Sudan, the United States bombed a pharmaceutical factory they believed was manufacturing chemical weapons in Khartoum.[37] By this time, Washington had downgraded diplomatic relations with Sudan and no longer had an ambassador posted in Khartoum.[38] Yet, throughout this period of drastically deteriorating U.S.-Sudan relations, one branch of the U.S. government stayed heavily involved with the war-torn south of the country.

SUDAN'S CONGRESSIONAL CHAMPIONS

In April 1989 Republican congressman Frank Wolf traveled into a remote part of southern Sudan to meet John Garang. The meeting—the first between the SPLM/A leader and a member of the U.S. congress—went well, continuing late into the night until Wolf finally fell asleep on an old mattress in the bombed-out shell of an abandoned building. Roger Winter, who accompanied Wolf on the trip, says the congressman became committed to the plight of the southern Sudanese. And Wolf was not alone.

The summer of 1999 marked Democratic congressman Donald Payne's fourth trip into southern Sudan—this time the former head of the Congressional Black Caucus brought two Republican representatives with him: Congressman Tom Tancredo and Senator Sam Brownback. In a mud-walled church, Tancredo stood before a congregation of hundreds of southerners displaced in the ongoing war and told them how he first heard about their suffering at his church back in Colorado. Tancredo had been alerted to the scale of the human crisis by a coalition of evangelical Christian and African American advocates who subsequently formed a group called the Sudan Campaign. Senator Brownback assured the southern Sudanese congregation, "The three of us are members of Congress, and we will be carrying the message of your cause back to the United States. You are not forgotten."[39]

Decades of war had decimated the southern Sudanese population. Atrocities were committed by all sides, and some of the worst crimes were committed by southerners against southerners.[40] But the bulk of the responsibility for the loss of an estimated two million southern lives and the displacement of four to six million more lay at the feet of the predominantly riverine Arab rulers in Khartoum.[41] For the northern elites, the south was *dar al-harb*, land of war.[42] Torture, slavery, starvation, and forced conversions to Islam were just some of the crimes committed against those who survived the massacres of their communities.[43]

After Payne's group returned from Sudan they pushed the U.S. congress to condemn al-Bashir's regime "for its genocidal war in southern Sudan."[44] In the years ahead, the connection these congressmen felt to Sudan and the efforts they had made to learn about the governance of the country would become critical to the influence of the Save Darfur movement.

A NEW VISION FOR SUDAN

John Garang, or "Dr. John" as he was known among southerners, was not your run-of-the-mill insurgent. His parents died when he was a child, and a relative sponsored him to attend secondary school in Tanzania, where he excelled and earned a scholarship to study for a Bachelor of Economics in the United States. Returning to Sudan, he joined his fellow southerners in the ongoing war against the government, just a year before the 1972 Addis Ababa peace agreement was signed. As part of the agreement, he and other southerners were integrated into the Sudanese army and received training at Fort Benning, Georgia. He rose to the rank of colonel before taking leave to complete a PhD in agricultural economics back in the United States. With these experiences under his belt, he was by 1983 ready to form the SPLM/A.[45]

Unlike many of those he fought alongside, Garang did not seek an independent southern Sudan. His vision was larger and in many ways much more ambitious. Garang dreamed of a unified, democratic, secular Sudan, where the marginalized people across the entire country would have representation at the center of government and where the historical trends of economic and social discrimination would be reversed. He called this country the New Sudan.[46]

In 1999 the U.S. chapter of the SPLM arranged for Garang to speak of this vision of the New Sudan to an invited audience in Washington, D.C. In the crowd listening to Garang was a 41-year-old Darfuri refugee, Omer Ismail. Garang's talk of a democratic and just Sudan for all Sudanese resonated deeply for Ismail, and afterward he turned to his friend, Suleiman Giddo, a fellow Darfuri, saying, "We are not less than this. We have some ability and now we are in a better place." Ismail had been a refugee in the United States for almost a decade following al-Bashir's coup; that night he and Giddo decided that the time had come to found an organization to advocate for the people of Darfur.

Sitting with me in Washington one morning in 2009, Ismail described the place where he was born, a place that he had not seen for 20 years. Plain language would not do; he recalled instead a poem by a famous Darfuri poet: "Greater el-Fasher, sleeping on a hill, flirting with the stars,"[47] he recited with reverence. "That is my hometown. When you sit on top of one of the sandy dunes, el-Fasher looks like an oasis of trees."

Ismail's first memories are of a home filled with lots and lots of people. "I know I'm number three—so there could have only been two ahead of me...but there were more," he puzzles for a moment. There were more because his father, Gamareldin, took in nieces and nephews from rural village areas, supporting them through schooling in el-Fasher, Darfur's capital. And after his father died, his mother continued the practice. "I call every week and it's someone different who picks up the phone. But they all hear my voice and they say, 'Omer!'" he smiles. "A family rich in culture and tradition, though not in money, extended as far as the eye can see," he tells me, conjuring the same sense of awe with which he had recited the poem.

As one of 14 children in addition to the various cousins, Ismail's childhood in a remote region without electricity, hospitals, or roads was poor by Western standards. But his memories contain no hardship. "You learn early to share everything including even your own clothes. Everyone protects the group. There are about 30 kids around your age.... I was small so I became loud and competitive," he says, dimples appearing fleetingly at the sides of his mouth. In a conservative Muslim society, Ismail's memory is of a liberal household, "where choice was the norm and you were always given a chance to say what you think."

Ismail tells me of the time his father gave him a new *djellabya*, the cool flowing robe so suited to Darfur's desert climate. It was a few days before Eid al-Fitr, the Muslim holiday that marks the end of the fasting month of Ramadan, and tradition holds that children are given new clothing to wear for the occasion. "One day before Eid I told him, 'I don't like this'.... He was fasting and a little tired. He said, 'If you don't like it, do what you like.'" Ismail picked up his new clothing, headed over to his grandmother's house, climbed a tree, and began ripping the *djellabya* to shreds. "When you're fasting, you are not supposed to show anger. I suppose I was taking advantage of that. I knew he wouldn't punish me," Ismail says. His father didn't get angry. He told Ismail that he would not punish him but instead would not care if he had to walk around naked on Eid because he had no new clothes. "I said, 'I am a child. When people see me they will not say, Ismail is naked, they will say, Gamar's son is naked!'" His father laughed in spite of himself. "After that, I always wore what I wanted. I was foolish enough to believe I wouldn't get punished—but I paid for my freedom of expression later in life," Ismail concluded.

In the years following Garang's speech in Washington, Ismail and his friend, Suleiman Giddo, founded the Darfur Peace and Development

Organization, "dedicated to a peaceful Darfur that is justly governed and developed in a sustainable manner."[48] When they began their advocacy efforts, the American public had never heard of a place called Darfur. Even among those inside Sudan, few were focused on the tensions that had long been brewing in the western region. "But if you are born and raised in that region, you know what is wrong and what needs to be done," says Ismail.

CHAPTER 2

THE STAGE IS SET FOR GENOCIDE

D arfur, in the west of northern Sudan, is composed of up to 90 different ethnic groups.[1] In the harsh desert terrain, cooperation over land use and resources has been key to the mutual survival of Darfur's different groups over the centuries. Some groups, generally those who are identified by themselves and others as "Africans," "blacks," or "non-Arabs,"* are engaged in farming; others, generally those who identify as Arabs, are engaged in livestock, which, at different points in the year, must be moved from dry to wet areas of the region, crossing farmland on the way.

A traditional system of land ownership and use, established long before Darfur became part of modern-day Sudan, granted ownership rights over discrete areas (each called a *dar*, meaning homeland) to certain leaders, and the group to which that leader belonged would generally establish settlements on that land. The land was granted on the understanding that these leaders would give access rights to nomads who had to bring their herds through the area.[2]

---

*In this context, "non-Arab," "African," and "black" are different ways of referring to the same constellation of people (primarily the Fur, Zaghawa, Massaleit, Dajo, and Tama); however, only the term "non-Arab" will be used in the remainder of this book. This word choice reflects the fact that both Arab and non-Arab Sudanese are, to greater or lesser degrees, racially African or black. Therefore, referring to the Fur, Zaghawa, Massaleit, and other non-Arab groups as African or black should not, in and of itself, distinguish them from Arab Sudanese. Indeed, there are a minority of Arab Sudanese who identify themselves as African. But the fact that the terms African and black have come to be used to differentiate between primarily Arab perpetrators and primarily non-Arab victims in Darfur reflects a more general tendency among Arab Sudanese to deny any African commonality with their non-Arabized Sudanese compatriots. This in turn stems from a view of African or black as inferior and Arab as superior. It is a view subscribed to by those most responsible for the crimes covered in this book and is one that I am keen to avoid perpetuating. See generally, Francis Deng, *War of Visions: Conflict of Identities in the Sudan* (Washington, D.C.: Brookings Institution, 1995).

For the most part this customary system worked well, although tensions would invariably arise when livestock trampled crops. Retaliatory raids on the nomads' livestock sometimes took place. But usually these disputes were settled through local processes, leading to repayment for losses. This limited the extent to which these problems led to any serious polarization between the different groups.[3] Identities remained fluid. Farmers who did well and could afford to buy livestock sometimes adopted a nomadic way of life, assimilating into one of the Arab groups; intermarriage was common.[4]

For centuries Darfur managed to retain its independence from foreign invaders, even sustaining an independent Fur sultanate until 1916, some 17 years after the British took control of the rest of Sudan.[5] As in the south, independence for Sudan did not bring much benefit to Darfuris who had no representative from their region in the central government for over a decade after the British left.[6] Darfur was viewed by the now-Sudanese rulers of Sudan as not much more than a source of cheap labor for the massive industrial development projects being built in the center of the country and as a place to recruit foot soldiers for the Sudanese army (whose officer corps was drawn primarily from the ranks of the privileged riverine Arabs).[7]

DARFUR'S PATH TO CATASTROPHE

In the 1970s, Darfuris began to suffer the effects of the Cold War power-plays taking place around them. The 1969 coup that installed President Nimeiri had been backed by the Sudanese Communist Party. But in 1971 the communists sought to overthrow him. In an effort to secure his leadership, Nimeiri looked for outside support and found a willing partner in the United States, which was all too happy to enlist Sudan as a bulwark against communism in neighboring Soviet-backed Ethiopia.[8] Nimeiri's realignment with the West was not appreciated by Muammar Qaddafi, the leader of Libya, Darfur's northwest border neighbor.

Qaddafi was pursuing an anti-Western agenda that sought to create a pan-Arab belt across the region, and Nimeiri's 1972 Addis Ababa agreement, which gave the non-Arab southern Sudanese a measure of autonomy, threatened to undermine this vision. Qaddafi began supplying arms to Nimeiri's rival, Sadiq al-Mahdi.[9] The supply route for the Qaddafi-sponsored plan to overthrow Nimeiri in Khartoum went through Darfur, and for the first time Darfuris found a supply of AK-47s readily available in their markets.[10] Qaddafi's meddling was also responsible for the increased number of foreign insurgents using Darfur as their staging ground for attacks against the government in neighboring Chad.[11]

Adding to the tensions that the influx of weapons and fighters brought was Nimeiri's decision to dismantle Native Administration and prohibit all political parties in Sudan. From 1971 onward, all local governance issues were to be dealt with by a single party of the government. New administrators, primarily from the riverine Arabs, were brought in to govern Darfur. This left Darfur much more susceptible to escalating violence triggered by tensions that would have, in an earlier day, been diffused by traditional means.[12]

Weaponry was not the only instrument of destruction flowing from Libya into Darfur during the 1970s and 1980s. The ideology of Arab supremacism, which underpinned Qaddafi's plan to create an "Arab belt" across Africa, began to be appropriated by Darfuri Arabs, and it raised the stakes of the local land disputes that were already beginning to spiral out of control.[13]

"The killing started on February 27, 1982," Professor Abul Gasim Seif el-Din told me, revisiting his memories of Darfur in the 1980s, when he lived in Ismail's hometown of el-Fasher. His recollection shows that the roots of the violence that destroyed Miriam's family stretched back more than two decades. "The first sign of a problem was at Awal market, near Kebkabaiya," the professor told me. "Two hundred Arab horsemen cordoned off the market and announced that the Arabs were now going to rule Darfur. They singled out the Fur [Darfur's largest non-Arab group] among all the tribes in the market. They let the others go free, but from the Fur they took all their valuables and they killed three of them. The Arab Gathering issued leaflets and cassettes telling people that the Arabs were coming to rule,"[14] he said, describing the Arab supremacist organization that Qaddafi supported in the Darfur region.[15]

Nature, too, began conspiring against Darfur. While the rock stars of the world were drawing attention to the plight of Ethiopians starving as a result of the devastating 1983-1985 drought, the effects of the drought on Darfuris over the same period were initially unnoticed by the outside world. President Nimeiri, struggling on multiple fronts and keen to at least ensure that foreigners continued to invest in Sudan, refused to acknowledge the existence of the drought. But eventually the numbers became too big to hide. Darfuris who could make it eastward to the capital, Khartoum, did. President Nimeiri ordered the army to round them up and dump them back in Darfur; many managed to stay in squatter camps on the outskirts of the city, where they remain to this day.[16]

The drought hastened the desertification underway throughout the region; usable land became increasingly scarce. This exacerbated tensions around the ownership and use of land. Back when the *dars* were originally granted, Darfur's nomadic Arab groups did not need land ownership rights. While many nomadic groups in southern Darfur were granted areas under their control, the lack of a *dar* among other nomadic groups was not a cause for concern; land was plentiful, and the tradition of granting nomads the access they needed to sustain their livestock was strong. By the time of the drought, this was no longer the case, and those groups without their own *dar*—primarily

Arab nomads from the northern and western regions of Darfur—began agi-
tating for control over land.[17] This made them particularly vulnerable to
recruitment into the *mujahedeen*, which President Nimeiri had started using
to bolster his military power against the rebellion in southern Sudan; the
militarization of Darfur's Arab population was set in motion.[18]

AFTER SUDAN'S 1986 ELECTIONS, the Arab Gathering argued in an open
letter to the new prime minister, Sadiq al-Mahdi, that the Arabs should rule
Darfur—at the time the governor of Darfur was Fur. The letter concluded:
"Should the neglect of the Arab race continue...we are afraid things could
escape the control of wise men...with dire consequences."[19] A brutal Arab-
Fur war ensued.

In 1988 the Arab Gathering issued a directive instructing Darfur's Arabs
to attack what they referred to as the *zurga*—a term that means black but in
this context was used pejoratively to refer to all of Darfur's non-Arab groups.
According to the Arab Gathering's instructions, the *zurga*'s leaders had to be
"eliminated" and conflicts created among them to "ensure their disunity,"
and *zurga* schools should be disrupted "by all possible means."[20] Police records
from el-Fasher in 1989 list the destruction of 4,000 Fur villages, resulting
in the death of more than 2,500 Fur people and 40,000 of their livestock.
Among Arab groups the same police records document a death toll of 500,
with 3,000 head of livestock lost.[21]

Transcripts from an attempt at reconciliation between the Fur and the
Arabs in 1989 reveal how polarized the groups were becoming. The Arab
representative accused the Fur of beginning the war, aiming to create an
"African belt" and "remove all the Arabs from this soil."[22] The Fur representative described the Arabs' aim as "a total holocaust and no less than the
complete annihilation of the Fur people and all things Fur."[23]

Al-Bashir's 1989 coup aggravated matters further. To continue fighting
the war against the SPLM/A in the south, his regime recruited yet more
of Darfur's Arab groups into a government-sponsored militia known as the
Popular Defense Forces and gave them weapons to conduct raids on southern villages. When they were done, they brought those weapons back to
Darfur. In 1994 al-Bashir introduced new land laws in Darfur. The first
of the reforms separated the single Darfur region into three states, using
the division to emasculate the Fur's political power.[24] The second reform
restructured the governance system in Dar Massaleit, the homeland of the
Massaleit, another of Darfur's non-Arab groups.[25] The effect on the ground
was that Arab groups gained unprecedented control of the region, and an
Arab-Massaleit war was ignited.

Diaspora groups reported that Arab militias moved systematically to torch houses in Massaleit villages shortly before crops were due to be harvested, and that the militias sought to "destroy the Massaleit people, expose them to famine, and force them to flee their ancestral lands."[26] More than 100,000 people were displaced from their homes in the fighting, which took place with active support of the government.[27] In 1998 another document associated with the Arab Gathering circulated, this time proposing that Darfuri land be secured for nomads from Sudan, Chad, and the Central African Republic, and setting a target date of 2020 for the completion of this project.[28] By the start of the twenty-first century, Darfur's historically fluid ethnic groupings had become dangerously static and entrenched.[29] This was not the homeland that Omer Ismail remembered growing up in.

IN 2000 AN ANONYMOUS publication dedicated to "the majority of the Sudanese people who still suffer marginalization of power and wealth" appeared on the streets of Khartoum. Known as the *Black Book*, the publication provided formidable evidence, much of it from the Sudanese government's own records, of Sudan's domination by the riverine Arabs. Despite representing just 5 percent of Sudan's total population, the *Black Book* showed that this group had almost consistently maintained 60 to 80 percent of the ministerial positions in the Sudanese government.[30] The undeniable accuracy of the claims threatened al-Bashir's regime[31]; thousands of photocopies were shared both inside and outside Sudan as the *Black Book* became a popular, albeit clandestine, read.[32] One of the authors was subsequently revealed to be Khalil Ibrahim, a Darfuri from the Zaghawa, another one of the region's non-Arab groups, who was a known supporter of Sudan's most infamous Islamist, Hassan al-Turabi.

In 1999, after al-Bashir began to suspect that al-Turabi was plotting to overthrow him, he declared a state of emergency and removed al-Turabi as the head of the NCP.[33] In June 2000 al-Turabi founded his own party.[34] This was the first serious split since the Generals seized power in the 1989 coup. Al-Turabi's former protégé, Ali Osman Taha, who now held the vice presidency of Sudan, sided with al-Bashir, while most of al-Turabi's supporters followed his lead and deserted the ruling NCP.

Historically al-Turabi was believed to have a base of supporters in Darfur, which led al-Bashir to worry that Darfur could become his opponent's launch pad for a coup. In the following months, NCP officials in Darfur once again sought to recruit militias from Darfur's landless Arab groups, this time not to launch attacks in southern Sudan but to prepare to fight any insurgency in Darfur.[35]

AMERICAN PRIORITIES:
NORTH-SOUTH PEACE AND COUNTERTERRORISM

In 2001, as al-Bashir was gearing up for battle in Darfur, the new U.S. president, George W. Bush, a Republican and a committed evangelical Christian, met with a group of evangelical leaders who were part of the Sudan Campaign, which advocated for southern Sudanese.[36] On September 6, 2001, President Bush appointed former three-term senator from Missouri, John C. Danforth, as his special envoy to Sudan, tasked to see what role the United States could play in finally bringing an end to the war in southern Sudan.[37]

Five days after Danforth's appointment, two passenger aircraft flew into the twin towers of New York's World Trade Center, killing nearly 3,000 people. The 9/11 attack had been masterminded by Osama bin Laden: the legacy of al-Turabi's support for terrorism had hit U.S. soil. That evening President Bush, in a live address to the nation, said the United States would "make no distinction between the terrorists who committed these acts and those who harbor them."[38] With the memory of Clinton's 1998 missile strike on the Khartoum pharmaceutical factory still vivid, and Sudan's previous hospitality toward bin Laden now all the more salient, the Sudanese government rapidly began making overtures to the Bush administration, assuring it that Sudan no longer provided safe harbor for terrorists and offering to supply intelligence to assist the U.S. war on terror.[39]

At the same time as the CIA's relationship with Khartoum intensified, Danforth began to engage with north-south peace negotiations that had begun almost a decade earlier at the initiative of countries neighboring Sudan.[40] The peace process finally gained something that looked like momentum in July 2002 when the NCP agreed that following a six-year transition period, southerners could vote on whether they wanted independence, and the SPLM dropped its demand for a totally secular Sudan, agreeing that sharia law could govern the north of the country.[41]

Views differ on why the breakthrough came at this point. Certainly the negotiations had progressed since the United States along with the United Kingdom and Norway began sustained involvement with the process. And in the aftermath of 9/11, moderates in Khartoum saw a window of opportunity to normalize relations—to have Sudan removed from the U.S. State Sponsors of Terrorism list, have all economic sanctions removed, and have an American ambassador posted back to Khartoum—in exchange for counterterrorism cooperation and an agreement to end the war against southern Sudan through a negotiated settlement. The position of these moderates was furthered strengthened in relation to Khartoum's hardliners as a result of internal pressure. Saddled with debt, the country was spending all its income on weapons to fight a war it wasn't winning; northerners returned to Khartoum in body bags, while unemployment rates were rising and civil servants were going unpaid.[42]

At the same time, in the United States political pressure was rising against the Khartoum regime. After persistent advocacy by the congressional champions and the Sudan Campaign, legislation called the Sudan Peace Act was signed into law.[43] It presented the findings of congress, concluding that: "The acts of the Government of Sudan ... [against people in southern Sudan] ... constitute genocide."[44] By the time the act was signed into law, in October 2002, a cease-fire was in place and peace negotiations were underway. Congress expressed strong support for Danforth's involvement in the peace process, and the new law established a list of sanctions that would apply to the government of Sudan if it was found not to be negotiating in good faith.[45]

With the full backing of congress, Danforth maintained involvement in the north-south negotiations over what was now called the Comprehensive Peace Agreement, or CPA for short. In fact, the CPA was rather misnamed; the agreement was solely between the NCP and the SPLM, and it dealt only with southern Sudan and not the marginalized areas in the rest of the country. At the start of 2003 the two parties agreed on the formation of a new government in Khartoum called the Government of National Unity. The new government would have a set percentage of seats for the NCP and the SPLM. At the urging of the U.S. government, the parties also agreed that halfway through the six-year period before southerners had their referendum on independence, there would be a nationwide democratic election, so that those who were not part of the CPA negotiations would get a say in who was to run their country.[46] In late 2003 John Garang and Sudanese vice president Taha decided to conduct negotiations face-to-face.[47] The promise of an end to the war that had left two million dead seemed within reach.

MEANWHILE IN DARFUR

As Khartoum was beginning to make peace with southern Sudan, it was ramping up its counterinsurgency in the west of the country toward genocidal levels. The letter of a political prisoner, Abdel Wahid al-Nur, who would become an important insurgency figure, describes the level of violence in Darfur in August 2002. "The security forces act with virtual immunity, terrorising the Fur people, raiding randomly and arresting people including the elderly and children and detaining them without charge of trial.... The Arab tribes attack their lands, looting their properties and stealing their livestock. Many Fur villages have been completely deserted." He concluded his letter with a plea to "the international community and human rights organisations to intervene to free us and protect the people of Darfur from the aggression of the government."[48] The call went unheeded.

The governor of North Darfur tried to rein in the escalating violence, organizing a reconciliation conference and arresting those he considered to be most responsible for the attacks. Among those arrested was Musa Hilal, who had inherited the leadership of one of Darfur's landless Arab groups and had been organizing his own tribe, as well as enlisting Chadians from across the border, to help attack Darfur's *zurga* population.[49] But the governor's efforts could not touch the source of the violence and of the weapons that made it possible: the central government. In just one example, a Sudanese air force plane dropped 18 bombs on the village of Kidingeer during a single day in October 2002.[50] "Why do we say the government and Janjaweed are one?" a Darfuri responded to one of the first human rights investigators to report on the attacks. "Because they come together, they fight together, and they leave together."[51]

But the limited attention that the global community had for Sudan was focused on the north-south peace process. With Garang and Taha negotiating in person, this was the closest the parties had ever come to ending Africa's longest-running civil war. Moreover, their negotiations were portrayed as holding the promise of transforming Sudan from a dictatorship to a democracy. That government-sponsored massacres were underway in the west of the country was a complication that nearly no one was willing to absorb. Gerard Galluci, sent to run the U.S. embassy in Khartoum in August 2003, was instructed by Washington to focus solely on concluding the negotiations to end the war against southern Sudan and on building counterterrorism cooperation.[52]

NO ONE IS LISTENING

Lack of information was not to blame for the U.S. government's failure to instruct its senior official in Sudan to work on halting the massacre of civilians in Darfur. "In diplomatic circles in Khartoum by the fall of 2003 Darfur was something we talked about at receptions," Galluci tells me.[53] The senior Dutch diplomat in Khartoum at the time remembers the same thing, but says that when he tried to get the message through to the UN Security Council, the United States and United Kingdom "were so concerned about the CPA, they blocked any discussion of Darfur."[54]

Nevertheless, the message that something serious was underway in Darfur did make it through to Washington. USAID, the government development agency, produced charts estimating death tolls reaching into the hundreds of thousands. One of the junior officers receiving cables from Sudan remembers the message, "We have to respond in a huge way or a million people will die."[55] But it wasn't enough to change the basic calculation that relations must be maintained with the Sudanese government so as not to disrupt the north-south peace process. The promise of normalization with the United States was seen as critical to Khartoum's continued participation in the peace talks, and challenging Khartoum over its actions in Darfur might generate doubts over the U.S. commitment to normalization.

I asked Omer Ismail if he remembered the first time he went to lobby a U.S. official about the escalating violence in Darfur. "Almost to the day," he said. In February 2002 Ismail met with Roger Winter, the man who had accompanied Congressman Wolf on his first trip to Sudan and had since begun working for USAID. He told Ismail to try and get Darfur on CNN: Until Darfur attracted media headlines, Winter felt unable to move the crisis up on the administration's agenda.

Throughout 2002 and 2003 Ismail tried, and failed, to get media attention. The only news story on Sudan that received coverage was about the prospect of an end to the north-south war. "You cannot separate the two issues," Ismail struggled to convince journalists. In his view, both the north-south war and the attacks in Darfur were linked to the core problem of how the NCP governed all the marginalized areas of Sudan. But it was a view that had no traction in the public realm. Consequently there was almost no mainstream media coverage of the growing crisis in Darfur and only fleeting clues to publicly indicate that genocide might be underway, despite information about the atrocities being available from some human rights organizations.

In 2003 the Cairo-based Sudan Human Rights Organization began publishing the names and ages of those killed in Darfur and posting them on their website.[56] The International Crisis Group, based in Brussels, dedicated a significant section of its June 2003 report, "Sudan's Other Wars," to the violence in Darfur, noting the potential for "large-scale forced displacement of the Fur and other African peoples in Darfur."[57] These reports gained virtually no U.S. media attention: The *New York Times* was the first newspaper to mention fighting in Darfur, with a single sentence buried in its "World in Brief" section on July 13, 2003.

In November 2003 Amnesty International issued a press release providing the first in-person account of the ethnic dimensions of the violence. Refugees reported that during the attacks on their villages they were told, "As you are black, you are slaves. The government is on our side."[58] The next month, the International Crisis Group released its second report addressing the situation, and this time it was more explicit about the ethnic dimensions of the violence: "Government-supported militias deliberately target civilians from the Fur, Zaghawa, and Massaleit groups, who are viewed as 'Africans' in Darfur."[59]

FORMATION OF AN INSURGENCY

Inside Darfur, people were fending for themselves. With no external assistance forthcoming, non-Arab Darfuris fought to protect their villages. Upon

Abdel Wahid al-Nur's release from prison, he formed an organization eventually called the Sudan Liberation Army (SLA). An alliance of fighters primarily from the Fur, Massaleit, and Zaghawa, the SLA had made its first attack against the government on February 26, 2003, killing government soldiers in the Darfuri town of Golo.[60]

The similarity between the name of the SLA and that of the SPLA, the armed wing of John Garang's movement, was no coincidence. Nor was the timing of its formation. The north-south peace negotiations were heading toward a conclusion that would create a new deal for the division of wealth and power in Sudan, something that Darfuris, Arab and non-Arab alike, needed. But the deal was being done between the NCP and the SPLM alone; Darfuris were not represented. As much as the emergence of the rebellion was linked to the escalating attacks by the government, it was also influenced by the closing window on a historic deal that was about to be concluded without considering the needs of Darfur.[61] Those aligned with al-Bashir in Khartoum viewed the connection in a slightly different light, suspecting Garang's hand behind the formation of the SLA. They believed that the SPLM/A was quietly sponsoring the destabilization of Darfur, and indeed the other marginalized areas of Sudan, to ensure the SPLM/A had a strong military hand if the peace talks failed.[62]

Shortly after the SLA's first attack, another Darfur rebel group announced its formation. This group was founded by *Black Book* co-author Ibrahim Khalil and was called the Justice and Equality Movement (JEM). Although no link between al-Turabi and the JEM has ever been proven, the close links between al-Turabi and Khalil Ibrahim led many of al-Bashir's supporters to believe that this was part of al-Turabi's plan to regain control of the NCP.[63]

The regime in Khartoum monitored these developments in Darfur with increasing alarm, which soon turned to outright panic. On the morning of April 25, 2003, the SLA and JEM mounted a joint attack on the government airbase in el-Fasher.[64] They destroyed seven planes, killed more than 70 government soldiers, and took the commander of the Sudanese air force hostage.[65] Hardliners in al-Bashir's regime decided that the insurgency must be defeated militarily and quickly.[66] The trouble was that the Sudanese army, whose foot soldiers were largely drawn from Darfur, could not be relied upon to crush their own people.

GENOCIDE

The government released Musa Hilal from jail and sent him back to Darfur and fired the governor who had arrested him. Hilal was tasked with recruiting the predominantly landless Arabs into a militia that was now commonly referred to as Janjaweed[67] (literally "devil on horseback," the term traditionally referred to armed bandits, but during the Arab-Fur war of the late 1980s, it began to be used to refer to Arab militias[68]).

With government money, Hilal and others like him set about recruiting thousands of Janjaweed, who were armed and given a salary of 300,000 Sudanese pounds (U.S. $135) a month.[69] "Change the demography of Darfur and empty it of African tribes" was the instruction that Musa Hilal subsequently issued to Janjaweed leaders, copying his instructions to the hardliners in Khartoum.[70] The directive was steeped in the Arab supremacist ideology of Qaddafi's Arab Gathering, which Hilal had been introduced to by the Libyan-sponsored Chadian insurgents based in Darfur during the 1980s. But never before had this underlying racism been given such aggressive government support. "All this is because we are black," explains Idriss, a farmer whose village was destroyed by the Janjaweed in October 2003. "We could defend ourselves against the Arab nomads, but not against the Janjaweed. The government has given them very good guns and [and they attack] with them."[71]

In village after village, coordinated land-air assaults were carried out by the Janjaweed and the Sudanese air force. Villages where primarily non-Arabs lived were destroyed, while neighboring Arab villages were left untouched. Those who managed to flee the initial attacks on their homes would find Janjaweed lying in wait for them on the outskirts of their villages or at water points in the desert. Anything that could be used to support life—livestock, food stores, water sources—was looted or destroyed. Men and boys who were not killed in the initial attacks were rounded up and executed. Women and girls were systematically raped, often multiple times, by a group of men over a period of several days.[72] In Darfur, ethnicity is passed on through the father, so rape was as effective as killing to change the demography of Darfur.[73] Witnesses reported that the women who were raped were told by their Janjaweed attackers that they would have a "free baby" (Janjaweed view non-Arabs as slaves)[74] and that "every woman will deliver red" (Arab skin tone is perceived to be red compared to non-Arabs).[75]

Yet it was not until February 25, 2004, some 12 months after the conflict began, that the genocidal dimensions of the crisis appeared in a major U.S. newspaper, and even then it was not a news report, but an op-ed entitled "Unnoticed Genocide."[76] Its author, Eric Reeves, had written the article in early December 2003, but it had taken him nearly three months to convince the *Washington Post* to publish it.[77] "Late 2003, early 2004 was the worst time for Darfur—and in government circles at that time there was not really any big discussion," recalls the head of United Nations (UN) peacekeeping.[78] "Member states were *very* focused on the north-south peace negotiations," agrees Jan Egeland, the head of the UN's humanitarian operations, recalling the message he was given by the U.S. envoy John Danforth: "Don't rock the boat, we're trying to finish this (north-south peace agreement)."[79]

With no significant pressure from outside, the U.S. government spent 2003 responding to the first mass atrocity of the twenty-first century the same way it had responded to similar situations throughout the twentieth century—with an effort to not respond.

THE PRICE OF SOUTHERN PEACE?

In 2009, sitting in one of the air-conditioned shipping containers that now serve as UN offices in the middle of Darfur's desert, former Sudanese government employee Hussien Adam told me about the first year he spent establishing what would eventually become one of Darfur's largest camps for those who had been forced to flee their villages. "There is something I will never forget," he said, then paused, considering if he really wanted to tell me what it was. "I was talking to the sheiks, and Saeed, who was working with me, pulled me aside. 'We need more coffins' he said. 'We don't have enough coffins to bury the dead bodies.'" Adam paused again. "People were dying in very, very big numbers. I thought, 'Is this the end of the civilization?'"[80] As if seeing the scene before his eyes, he started talking to me in the present tense. "Nobody is sure of what is going to happen in the coming few minutes. They are happy only to survive till now—frightened, puzzled, sick, starving." He readjusted his focus, took off his glasses, and drew in a deep breath.[81]

On the same trip to the Chad-Sudan border that I met Miriam, I also interviewed other Darfuri refugees, the vast majority of them women and girls because the few men and boys who had survived were typically back inside Darfur fighting for the rebels. The day before I interviewed Miriam, I had met a woman who told me she had watched her cousin's 18-month-old son being burnt alive after he was thrown into a burning hut by the Janjaweed that surrounded her village.[82] I heard her. I believed her. And yet there was a level at which I was unable to absorb what she was telling me.

As the days and weeks passed and I met more and more women, the individuality of their stories began to blur. Were it not for my interview notes, I couldn't say whether it was Miriam, or Amira, or Hawa who imitated for me the sound that the helicopter gunships make, or who it was that told me that she had been raped by five government soldiers and left for dead, or whose 11-year-old sister had been held for five days during their journey to Chad by the Janjaweed who found her at a water point; she had walked there at night, hoping that the cover of darkness would protect her. I do remember that the girl, by then 16, had not uttered a word since. Their stories were littered with the recollection of racial slurs, like *zurga* and *abid* ("slave," or the U.S.

equivalent of "nigger"[83]) hurled at them. They were told that this was not their land and that they didn't belong here.

Not until after I left Chad was the guilt of my inability to maintain a personal connection to each and every horrifying detail slowly replaced by something else. Each individual story evoked sadness, but as a collective the devastatingly repetitive features of their stories directed my attention back to the Sudanese government's culpability. With decades of experience using proxy militias to fight in the south, those in Khartoum who supported the policy of using the Janjaweed in Darfur knew what would result. They knew that the animosities built up in Darfur over the years would ensure that the attacks by those recruited into the Janjaweed would be motivated by hatred. They knew that by supporting the Janjaweed, they were writing a death warrant for the non-Arabs of Darfur.

Hussien Adam, faced with the situation of thousands of Darfuris pouring into his makeshift camp to die, and women like Miriam, who had lost their entire families and then walked across the desert in an attempt to find safety in Chad, formed just a tiny fraction of the hundreds of thousands of people whose lives had been ripped asunder. By the beginning of 2004, Darfur was a zone of human devastation. And the governments of the world knew it.

CHAPTER 3

DARFUR ATTRACTS ATTENTION

R wanda cast a heavy shadow over the U.S. State Department following the election of George W. Bush. Under the previous administration of President Bill Clinton, the systematic slaughter of ethnic Tutsi and moderate Hutu in the small east African country of Rwanda had taken place over just 100 days in 1994. Some 800,000 people were killed, most of them hacked to death by machete; it was the most efficient massacre the world had seen since the Holocaust.

In the first term of his presidency, Bush read an article documenting the U.S. government's willful failure to try and stop the killings and scribbled in the margins of the report, "NOT ON MY WATCH."[1] When Lorne Craner became assistant secretary for Democracy, Human Rights, and Labor at the State Department in mid-2001, he remembers Secretary of State Colin Powell instructing him and the assistant secretary of state for African Affairs, "There is not going to be another Rwanda."[2]

Craner was already acutely aware of the U.S. government's poor track record in the face of genocide and mass atrocity. During his first rotation in the Foreign Service in 1989, Craner met career service officer Charlie Twining, director of the Office of Vietnam, Laos, and Cambodia. In 1975, as the Khmer Rouge unleashed its campaign of destruction inside Cambodia, Twining had taken the testimony of fleeing refugees at the border. When Craner was advised he was being sent to Cambodia in 1990, the first U.S. executive officer to be posted there since the evacuation of the U.S. Mission 15 years earlier, Twining took an interest in the young diplomat.

Craner recalls Twining telling him about his experiences on the Thai-Cambodia border and about looking at the refugees and seeing the faces of those fleeing the Holocaust. He recounted to Craner the incredulity with which Washington viewed the firsthand accounts that he sent back of the atrocities that were being committed by the Khmer Rouge, and the guilt he felt for not pushing harder against the administration's unwillingness to comprehend the scale of the violence.[3] The conversations with Twining remained vivid in Craner's mind a decade later as ethnic tensions in Rwanda's neighbor, Burundi, began to flare up.

When viewed from a desk in Washington, Burundi looks like Rwanda's twin. Nestled just below Rwanda, between Tanzania and the Democratic Republic of the Congo, Burundi was also colonized by the Belgians and has a Tutsi minority and Hutu majority. After the Belgians left, Burundi faced decades of civil war and genocide.[4] In 2000 peace accords were finalized, but with two of the main armed groups refusing to sign, the situation remained unstable. "We thought that Burundi was going to be our Rwanda," recalls Craner.[5]

Throughout 2002-2003 the State Department's African Affairs bureau devoted a significant amount of time to Burundi. Under their watch, the United States continued to deploy extensive diplomatic and economic resources in support of Burundi's stability, and by 2003 a cease-fire was brokered between the Burundian government and the largest Hutu rebel movement.[6] Although ethnic tensions continue to be a feature of life in Burundi, the return to genocidal violence did not came to pass. "We really applied the 'no Rwandas' rule to prevent the situation in Burundi from getting any worse," says Craner.[7] The irony was that Craner and his State Department colleagues' diligence on Burundi was taking place as violence was escalating in Darfur.

BEYOND A HUMANITARIAN CRISIS

At 8.30 a.m. each morning, Powell met with his senior staff on the seventh floor of the State Department. Everyone at the level of assistant secretary and above would attend, making for a full room of 40 people. In the fall of 2003 the head of USAID, Andrew Natsios, began ringing the alarm on Darfur in those morning meetings.

Natsios, a bald and bespectacled figure, had a long history with Sudan. He first visited Darfur in 1991 and in subsequent years led the delivery of humanitarian aid to southern Sudan. Having seen the number of lives lost under al-Bashir's regime, he had no difficulty accepting that the information about the scale of atrocities in Darfur was credible. Attendees at these morning meetings recall Natsios' "terrierlike" persistence in making sure everyone understood this was a serious problem that demanded attention. With his USAID hat on, however, Natsios focused on the humanitarian aspects of the crisis.

The United States has always shown a tendency to respond to the massacre of foreigners in humanitarian terms—reacting to the consequences of the crisis by providing food aid and other emergency materials but not trying to address the cause of the crisis itself. This makes sense as a response to a tsunami or hurricane, but it is, at best, an awkward approach to an ongoing crisis caused by a violent group or government. From a political point of view, however, prioritizing food aid over security responses has a certain logic. Funding, let alone deploying, troops to protect another country's citizens from violence is, in diplomatic terms, a confrontational move. It signals that either the government of the country in which the violence is unfolding is incapable of protecting its own citizens or it is actively harming them. Neither bodes well for intergovernmental relations. It was not surprising then that State Department officials in Washington were all too happy to view Darfur as a purely humanitarian crisis, which could be responded to without disrupting U.S. engagement with the Sudanese government on the north-south peace process.

For those inside Sudan the picture was different. The most senior member of the State Department in Khartoum, Gerard Gallucci, kept trying, without success, to convince his superiors to act on anything other than the provision of food aid. "I remember essentially begging my boss in Washington over it," recalls Gallucci who, after spending four months in Sudan, had become convinced that Darfur was not an issue the State Department could sideline in the service of achieving a north-south peace deal.[8]

In December 2003 the State Department issued its first press release on Darfur. It stated that more than 3,000 unarmed civilians had been killed, more than 600,000 had been displaced from their homes, and another 75,000 had made it across the border to Chad. It made no mention of the ethnic dimensions of the violence.[9]

Even as he sat through Powell's morning staff meetings listening to Natsios predict the growing death toll in Darfur, Craner says it was not clear to him that Darfur presented a situation in which they would have to shift into the "no Rwandas" mode of action. Part of the explanation for failing to recognize what he was being presented with was that State Department officials, overloaded with information from the field, fall back on the same information-processing heuristics as everyone else. Situations that match a preexisting schema of what a "typical genocide" looks like garner attention while situations that do not appear to match are overlooked. The identification of Burundi as a potential problem was easy enough given its superficial similarities with Rwanda, which was the genocide schema at the forefront of the minds of State Department officials like Craner. Darfur—a vast desert region with a confusing array of ethnic groups—did not fit this schema so readily.

In addition, those inside government are not immune to the phenomenon that psychologists call cognitive dissonance: the discomfort caused by two conflicting ideas. People typically resolve the dissonance by discounting one of the ideas.[10] Faced simultaneously with information that Khartoum was both set to deliver a historic north-south agreement and responsible for mass murder in Darfur, officials in Washington found it initially easier to discount information about Darfur than to revisit the highly attractive idea that a once-in-a-generation diplomatic breakthrough was about to occur in Sudan. And so, despite substantial warnings to the contrary, Darfur continued to be treated solely as a humanitarian issue, and the State Department saw no need to disrupt its steadily improving relationship with Khartoum.

The first U.S. government official to speak publicly about the ethnic dimensions of the conflict and to highlight the manmade nature of the crisis was USAID's Roger Winter, the man that Omer Ismail had been lobbying since February 2002. Upon Winter's return from a fact-finding trip to Darfur in February 2004, he said to journalists: "The question arises: Is this an ethnic cleansing in motion that is taking place there [Darfur]? . . . I'm not a human rights lawyer, [but] it sure looks like that."[11]

With the United States the largest contributor to the World Food Program and responsible for funding humanitarian flights, it had been relatively easy for Winter to get access to a plane in Darfur. Ostensibly on a World Food Program mission, Winter actually had a broader agenda in mind. He took several State Department officials with him to show them "what was really going on in Darfur." He was worried that they couldn't see past the north-south peace negotiations. So he told the pilot to find smoke. "We came across a village that was actually being attacked—you could get a perspective on what an attack was really like—people fleeing, being chased."[12] It had the desired effect. "We were astounded by what we saw. It was instantly clear that the situation was worse than we imagined, beyond our wildest dreams," one of the State Department officials on the trip later told me.[13] Another of the State Department officials looked at Winter, pointed to his forehead, and said, "Okay, I got it."[14]

The morning after Winter and the State Department officials returned to Washington, Janjaweed militias wearing government uniforms attacked a boarding school in Tawila, North Darfur, forcing 110 Zaghawa girls to strip naked at gunpoint before conducting multiple rapes and then setting the school on fire.[15] Eyewitnesses reported seeing Musa Hilal arrive on the scene in a government helicopter, provide the militia with weapons, and issue instructions.[16]

It was finally becoming clear to Craner and his State Department colleagues that they would have to move away from business as usual on Darfur. Shortly after the Tawila school attack, Craner was walking down the rabbit warren halls of the State Department with Ambassador-at-Large for War Crimes Pierre Richard Prosper. For several weeks, Craner had been mulling over one of the insights he took away from reading a book called "*A Problem from Hell*": *America and the Age of Genocide*. The book documented the failure of the U.S. government to stop genocide across the course of the twentieth century, and it became the framework through which Craner began to filter information about Darfur. "In past genocides, people have used ignorance as an excuse—they have said they did not know even if they did. I started thinking that if we could put the information authoritatively in front of people then no one would be able to deny it,"[17] recalls Craner. He sought Prosper's counsel on what could be done.

Prosper had previously conducted surveys of refugees fleeing ethnic conflict in Kosovo. Prosper and Craner began to discuss whether the same approach could get them the kind of unassailable data they felt they needed from Darfur.[18] So in March 2004 they began to build internal support for the idea of sending a team to conduct a systematic survey of the Darfuris who had fled across the border into Chad.

At the same time, Craner had his staff prepare a report on Darfur that the United States could present at the UN Commission on Human Rights in Geneva. Human rights reports by the State Department are often criticized for underplaying violations committed by states with which the department needs to maintain cordial diplomatic relations. But by March 2004 Craner's superiors had started to treat Darfur differently. "Powell, [Under-Secretary of State] Grossman and [Deputy Secretary of State] Armitage all said to us, 'Don't filter the information—write what you think is true—just tell it like it is,'" recalls Craner.[19]

Despite the attitude of these key senior staff, there had been a deadly 13-month lag between the nominal beginning of the Darfur crisis in February 2003 and the active acknowledgment by State Department officials that this was something that could not be addressed simply through the provision of humanitarian assistance. And the mainstream media were only starting to catch up.

TEN YEARS AFTER THE RWANDAN GENOCIDE

In late March 2004 Pulitzer Prize–winning journalist Nicholas Kristof began reporting from the Chad-Sudan border for the *New York Times*. His first piece, "Ethnic Cleansing, Again,"[20] was followed three days later by a much bolder statement: "The government of Sudan is engaging in genocide against three large African tribes in its Darfur region here."[21] Despite Kristof's stark language, most other media outlets did not pick up on the situation until the first week of April, when commemorations for the tenth anniversary of the Rwandan genocide began to take place around the world. It was these commemorations that finally took the Darfur crisis from a topic discussed among the diplomats in Khartoum into the broader public sphere.

In the six months prior to the tenth anniversary, a total of three articles about Darfur appeared on the editorial pages of the major U.S. newspapers.[22] Six such commentaries appeared within a single week of the ten-year anniversary.[23] Media stories connecting the commemorations to the crisis in Darfur made it nearly impossible for heads of state to acknowledge the Rwanda anniversary without also committing themselves to a position on Darfur.

In a *New York Times* op-ed on April 6, 2004, Samantha Power—the author of *"A Problem from Hell"*—drew the link explicitly with a piece entitled "Remember Rwanda but Take Action in Sudan," chastising the Bush administration for its silence on Darfur.[24] Advocates from Africa Action wrote an article calling for the Bush administration to say that Darfur was genocide: "We should have learned from Rwanda that to stop genocide, Washington must first say the word."[25] They were taking their cue directly from Power's book.

After winning a Pulitzer Prize, *"A Problem from Hell"* had become required reading for current and aspiring human rights advocates. Particularly memorable was the way that Power mocked representatives of the Clinton administration who tied themselves in linguistic knots trying to follow an instruction to refrain from calling what was happening in Rwanda "genocide" for fear that using the word might actually commit the U.S. government to do something.[26] In popular culture, the administration's equivocation over what became coined "the g-word" symbolized the accompanying failure of the U.S. government to take effective action to halt the killings. The lesson drawn was that to stop genocide, the U.S. government must be willing to call it by its rightful name.

In 2001, summing up her research on the U.S. government's response to Rwanda, Power had written that "few Americans are haunted by the memory of what they did in response to genocide in Rwanda."[27] But by the tenth anniversary of the Rwandan genocide this was no longer true; the collective efforts of writers, artists, and filmmakers had steadily built up public consciousness around American abandonment of Rwanda.[28]

Of course, Darfur in 2004 was nothing like Rwanda in 1994. But framing Darfur as a Rwanda-like problem resulted in sufficient guilt-by-association to promote a flurry of political rhetoric. On April 7, 2004, President Bush issued his first public statement on Darfur, condemning the atrocities.[29] Although it seems obvious in hindsight, there was nothing inevitable about this coupling of the Rwandan commemorations with the situation in Darfur. There are other issues that could have been linked to the occasion. If, for instance, Armenian advocates used the anniversary to push for congressional acknowledgment of the Armenian genocide and no one had made an explicit connection to Darfur, the attacks on Darfur's non-Arab population might have remained background noise. As it turned out, the lens of Rwanda was exceedingly effective in attracting attention to Darfur.

U.S. government officials were not the only parties conscious of the link being drawn in the media between failure in Rwanda and the imperative toward action in Darfur. In April 2004 a cease-fire agreement for Darfur was negotiated in the Chadian capital of N'Djamena. The Sudanese government and the rebel groups, SLA and JEM, signed a 45-day humanitarian cease-fire and established a Cease-fire Commission to monitor it.[30] The timing of the agreement, signed the day after the tenth anniversary of the Rwandan genocide, was no coincidence. Vice President Taha, who was leading Sudan's negotiations on the north-south agreement that he hoped would lead to the normalization of relations with the United States, wanted to short-circuit any momentum toward Western intervention in Darfur, which is what some members of the Sudanese government feared would result if Darfur were seen as the "next Rwanda."[31] On the tenth anniversary, the Sudanese government representative at the negotiations in N'Djamena called Taha, requesting more time to finalize the agreement. Taha refused. "We need a signed agreement by tomorrow," he instructed.[32] Allegations of violations began within 24 hours of the agreement coming into effect,[33] but with global media coverage now dominated by world leaders congratulating the Sudanese government on the cease-fire agreement, Taha had what he wanted.[34]

REACHING THE DISPLACED

The Sudanese government put in place a formidable set of restrictions to ensure that as few outsiders as possible reached Darfur; they knew that even those entering on purely humanitarian missions would be witness to the unfolding tragedy. As a result, diplomats and humanitarians alike would battle for weeks to get a travel permit to Darfur, only to have it issued the day before it was due to expire. Despite the thousands displaced, the Sudanese government denied UN humanitarian agencies access to Darfur.

Inside Darfur, Hussien Adam's desperation was growing. Each day, more women and children would arrive at his makeshift camp. After a while the youngest among them would start calling him "Daddy." The men whom the children should have been turning to were all either dead or with the rebellion.

Out of options, Adam made the journey to Khartoum right to al-Bashir's Presidential Palace on the Nile to speak to Vice President Taha, who was in charge of Darfur policy. "Is the government ready to cover the needs of the displaced or will you let me call for the international community to help?"

he asked Taha. The vice president didn't answer the question directly. "Do your best," he told Adam, who understood the message; no outside assistance would be allowed.[35]

The head of the UN's humanitarian operations, Jan Egeland, was also doing all he could to get aid to those displaced in Darfur. In March 2004 he tried to get permission to brief the UN Security Council on the situation but was blocked by Pakistan, which then had the presidency of the Council.[36] When the presidency rotated to Germany in April, he got his chance. "I described, in detail…war crimes, crimes against humanity, scorched earth campaigns, ethnic cleansing and massacres of the worst kind." He was invited back to brief the council again at the end of the month.[37]

Khartoum tried to upstage Egeland's second briefing to the council, claiming it had nothing to hide and finally offering UN Secretary General Kofi Annan access to Darfur. In what was to become a familiar tactic, Khartoum found ways to stall the execution of their offer: "We had information that the Sudanese government intended to postpone any access by anyone for several weeks to let the burning villages stop smoking, as if this would hide their atrocities," recalls Natsios.[38] But finally, in June 2004, Annan visited Sudan. Annan's visit coincided (without coordination) with Colin Powell's first visit to Darfur. Meeting with the Sudanese foreign minister, Powell "affirmed U.S. desire to keep relations [with the Sudanese government] on a positive note" but also said that Darfur "complicated" this objective. Gerard Gallucci, present at the same meeting, told the foreign minister that trying to get access to Darfur was like "trench warfare."[39]

Both Powell's and Annan's visits to Darfur were carefully stage-managed by the Sudanese government, who even went so far as to forcibly relocate a thousand displaced people from a camp that Annan was scheduled to visit, so that he wouldn't witness the conditions they faced.[40] But back in Khartoum, Annan met with a range of officials, including Hussien Adam, who had traveled to the secretary-general's hotel to try and speak with him. "I told him there had to be a way to get the UN agencies in there," recalls Adam, the urgency of his plea still present in his voice when recalling the conversation five years later.[41]

Adam worked with Annan's staff on a proposal to lift the travel restrictions and fast-track the agencies into Darfur. Annan took the proposal to al-Bashir. "I really went there to plead with him that these are his own people," says Annan. "I pushed hard. I said if they are not able to help them, and they refuse help from others, then they will be held to account."[42] Under pressure, al-Bashir agreed to issue a moratorium on the main restrictions on humanitarian agencies' access.

"If you had not had the world media attention, the Security Council considering sanctions, the secretary-general, and Colin Powell there at the same time and apparently keen to swing his club, we wouldn't have gotten the moratorium," says Egeland.[43] More than a year after Hussien Adam had begun struggling to save those who survived the attacks on their villages, some external assistance was finally on its way.

POLITICS

While there was some slow progress on the humanitarian front by mid-2004, there had been almost none at a political level. The U.S. State Department, itself late to the table, was seemingly the only foreign affairs ministry globally willing to talk about anything other than the humanitarian consequences of the crisis.

The vote of the 53-member UN Commission on Human Rights provided an early insight into the relative positioning of the United States and the European nations on Darfur. Armed with Craner's report, "Ethnic Cleansing in Darfur," the U.S. ambassador to the UN commission, Richard Williamson, took to the floor in Geneva on April 23, 2004: "Mr. Chairman, ten years from now, the 60th Commission on Human Rights will be remembered for one thing and one thing alone: Did we have the courage and strength to take strong action against the ethnic cleansing in Darfur?"[44]

The short answer was "no." A resolution jointly drafted by the Africa Group and the European Union (EU) was introduced to "express concern" over human rights violations in Sudan, without making any mention of ethnic cleansing.[45] The United States was the only nation to vote against the resolution.[46]

Five days later, the CBS television program *60 Minutes II* broadcast photographs of U.S. soldiers at the Abu Ghraib prison near Baghdad torturing Iraqi detainees. Within minutes the photographs were posted on websites the world over. The image of a hooded detainee standing on a box with electrical wires attached to his body rapidly became the iconic symbol of America's presence in Iraq. Other photographs and the acts of torture they conveyed were no less horrific. By May 5 U.S. National Security Adviser Condoleezza Rice was on Aljazeera television doing damage control with the Arab world.[47] That same day, Sudan was reelected to the UN Commission on Human Rights for a three-year term, filling one of only 14 vacant seats.[48] Ambassador Williamson walked out of the election meeting in protest. Sudan made the most of the opportunity the confluence of events presented: "The United States delegation, while shedding crocodile tears over the situation in Darfur...is turning a blind eye to the atrocities committed by the American forces against the innocent civilian population in Iraq."[49]

Frustrated by the outcome of the meeting, Craner and Prosper pushed ahead with their idea to gather authoritative evidence from refugees on the Chad-Sudan border. For someone who had given such conscious attention to the history of responses to genocide and mass atrocity, Craner's faith that the evidence would make such a difference seems strangely misplaced. While people who gather evidence find it compelling, those who read the evidence collected by others have all too frequently found ways to minimize the information they receive. Nevertheless, it was a significant departure from business as usual to pursue an initiative that the U.S. government had previously avoided, and Craner genuinely believed that the results could be used to generate the political will needed to resolve the crisis.

During the Clinton administration, the Office of the Secretary of Defense had argued that investigating genocide in Rwanda was dangerous because a positive finding could commit the administration "to actually do something."[50] Had the same analysis been given to Powell, the idea of an investigation may never have seen the light of day. Instead, the State Department's chief legal adviser, William Taft IV, took a different view. Taft's legal analysis of the implications that would flow from calling Darfur genocide focused on Article 8 of the Genocide Convention. Drafted in the aftermath of the Holocaust, the 1948 document states that parties to the convention may call on the UN to take action under the UN Charter to prevent and suppress genocide. Taft's understanding was that if the United States determined genocide was underway, its only obligation would be to present their findings to the UN. On this reading of the convention, the political risks of making a genocide determination were significantly lower than what the Clinton administration had understood them to be.

According to Taft, the legal ramifications of the genocide assessment were seen as the sole domain of the State Department. There was no competing legal advice from the Defense Department, nor, indeed, from any other branch of the government; no one else was consulted.[51] Any concern that the United States would be obliged to take further action following a genocide determination was neutralized by Taft's legal analysis alone.

With the legal obligations dealt with, the next issue was technical feasibility. The Chad-Sudan border is one of the most inhospitable places on earth, even in times of peace. Logistically it is a nightmare for outsiders to deal with due to an almost complete lack of infrastructure and an ever-persistent water shortage. Craner contacted non-governmental organizations (NGOs) with experience in documenting human rights abuses. On June 23, 2004, he brought them together and presented an ambitious proposal.[52] With financial support from USAID, assessment teams were on the Chad-Sudan border a mere two weeks later with a survey instrument to interview a sample of 1,147 refugees—enough to make statistically significant inferences about the type and scale of violence.[53]

The assessment team proposal was a rare example of a decision on Darfur that could be implemented almost entirely within the control of the U.S.

government. By placing the teams on the Chadian side of the Chad-Sudan border, no permission was required from the Sudanese government. And the teams were funded by the United States; the financial support of other countries was not required. Internal support within the State Department was also crucial. Without it, the logistical obstacles could easily have become an excuse, and not an implausible one, for refusing to go ahead with the assessment.

ANSWERING THE GENOCIDE QUESTION

Ever since the crisis in Darfur had entered the media through the lens of Rwanda, journalists had pressured the U.S. government to answer whether or not Darfur was genocide.[54] And while the assessment teams were conducting their survey, the House and the Senate unanimously passed resolutions to say that genocide was occurring.[55]

When these congressional resolutions were introduced, the majority of the American public had only just begun to hear about a place called Darfur; there was no organized interest group for Darfur, let alone anything resembling a mass movement. However, groundwork done by southern Sudan advocates over the preceding decade ensured that some key members of congress were open to believing the worst of Khartoum. A bipartisan group including Frank Wolf, Donald Payne, Tom Tancredo, Sam Brownback, Bill Frist, and Michael Capuano, many of whom had been leaders in the pro-southern Sudan Campaign, had all either met with Sudanese refugees in America or spent time in Sudan themselves. The initiative of these congressional champions on Sudan, rather than any organized public commitment to Darfur, accounted for the introduction of the genocide resolutions in congress.[56]

Yet, for people within the executive branch of the government, congressional interest serves as a proxy for where the public stands on an issue because of the transparent lines of accountability between representatives and their constituents. In reality, "the public" that congress hears from is never a truly representative sample of the American population; issues that benefit from the engagement of organized interest groups are more likely to garner the attention of congress. However, the relative input of congressional initiative and public pressure can be hard to disentangle from the outside, and the unanimous passage of the genocide resolutions served as a powerful proxy for public opinion on the issue.[57]

Given that there was no requirement for the assessment teams' findings to be made public, it would have been easy enough to decide that whatever evidence they brought back was inconclusive and that the matter should be investigated further. Without the congressional resolutions in the Republican-controlled House and Senate, there is a reasonable possibility that this is what would have transpired. Instead, when the refugee interviews gathered by the assessment team reached Washington, they were carefully scrutinized.

Before the data was submitted to Powell, there was a meeting to discuss the results with Taft and other members of the State Department. The key question was whether or not it was genocide. All the attendees turned to Taft, who was the only one in the room who knew the Genocide Convention. In classic lawyerly style Taft stated, "We can justify it one way, or we can justify it the other."[58] With the issue undecided at the end of the meeting, the staff put together a package of the assessment team results along with other sensitive information and passed it to Powell to make the determination.

Powell remembers Taft telling him it was a "close call," but says that upon reflection he decided to call it genocide because he believed that would push the UN Security Council to respond. "I made the judgment call," he says.[59] There was no question that the acts of killing, the destruction of everything needed to sustain life, and the mass rapes against Darfur's non-Arab population could all constitute acts of genocide. The question was whether the stringent legal standard of "special intent" was met—meaning that not only were acts like these committed, but that they were carried out with the intent to destroy all or part of the victim group. "Will Taft told me that others could argue against the genocide determination with a strong legal basis, but that the conclusion on genocide was legally supportable," says Powell.[60]

In light of the defense secretary's opposition to determining genocide in Rwanda, I asked Powell what the Pentagon thought of his decision. "I don't remember discussing it with them," he replied. In fact, Powell never held a meeting with any of the other U.S. government agencies before deciding to publicly call Darfur genocide. And given the gravity of the determination, his consultation with President Bush on the matter was breathtakingly minimal. "My recollection is that Colin Powell came to see the president to say that he was giving this congressional testimony on Thursday—this must have been the Tuesday," recounts Stephen Hadley, then Bush's deputy national security adviser.[61] "I never asked the president, 'Do I have permission to do this?'" says Powell. "I just said that this was what I was going to do."[62]

Hadley says that after meeting with Powell, the president instructed Condoleezza Rice to tell all the principals of the various government agencies that Powell would be making a genocide determination "so they wouldn't be taken by surprise."[63] When I asked Powell about the reaction he got from other members of the administration when they heard he was calling Darfur genocide, he characterized their responses as "somewhere between supportive and indifferent."[64]

On September 9, 2004, Colin Powell testified before the Senate Committee on Foreign Relations that "genocide has been committed in Darfur and that the Government of Sudan and the jinjaweid[65] bear responsibility, and genocide may still be occurring." However, he went on to say that "no new action is dictated by this determination" on the grounds that the U.S. government was already doing all it could.[66] Powell did not put any time limit on his view that genocide "may still be occurring." With no recommendation that his assessment be reviewed after a set period of time, Powell's testimony tied the word "genocide" to the U.S. government's approach to Darfur for the indefinite future.

Powell's testimony marked the first time that the executive branch of any government in the world had labeled a crisis genocide while the violence was ongoing. Human rights advocates who were so conscious of the Clinton administration's refusal to use the "g-word" welcomed Powell's testimony as a sign that the Bush administration was mobilized to support the people of Darfur. Little did they know just how insulated Powell's decision had been from the rest of the U.S. government.

Gerard Gallucci, reading the secretary's testimony from his office in Khartoum, was cynical. "By the time the administration tried to correct its image about having done nothing in Darfur, the cheap and straightforward thing to do was call it genocide."[67] Gallucci's skepticism was echoed by those who had heard the news from their offices in Cairo and Addis Ababa. Explaining to me why he believed that Powell had determined the situation was genocide, the head of the Arab League, Amr Moussa, said, "At that time there were very tense relations between the U.S. and the Arab and Muslim world."[68] Moussa's special envoy to Sudan was more forthright. "Let us speak frankly," Salah Halima told me. "The Bush administration was against the Sudanese government, against their political system, against the Islamic system. They didn't show us any evidence which convinced us it was really genocide."[69] At the African Union the reaction was similar, with lead staff describing Powell's statement as "political"[70] and made "under pressure."[71] Six months since photos of U.S. soldiers torturing detainees at Abu Ghraib had gone public, the determination of genocide was viewed cynically by the very people that Powell and Craner had hoped would be compelled to act.

PART II

BUILDING THE OUTCRY RWANDA NEVER HAD

CHAPTER 4

CITIZENS HEED
THE CALL

In the aftermath of the Holocaust the world powers issued a series of declarations about the kind of human behavior they would not tolerate. The horror of the footage from the liberation of Nazi concentration camps sustained unprecedented negotiations between powerful states to reach agreements on principles, like the UN Declaration on Human Rights, and to sign onto commitments, like the Convention on the Prevention and Punishment of Genocide, which for the first time elevated the well-being of people over the interests of states. But this prioritization of human rights remained largely aspirational. Occasionally powerful states acted to support the rights of peoples other than their own, but these exceptions tended to occur only when such actions coincided with the intervening states' own interests.

During the Cold War, a model of advocacy that focused on documenting and exposing human rights violations showed some success in reorienting powerful states toward the interests of people under threat. Helsinki Watch and Americas Watch, precursors to the NGO Human Rights Watch, effectively pointed out the contradictions in a U.S. foreign policy that simultaneously condemned abuses under communism while sponsoring proxies to conduct similar abuses in the name of fighting communism. Amnesty International put a spotlight on prisoners of conscience and in 1977 was awarded the Nobel Peace Prize.

By the end of the Cold War, human rights advocacy had transitioned from being the prerogative of a handful of impassioned volunteers to a professional industry, with associated costs and benefits. Human rights organizations were now accepted as a legitimate part of the U.S. policy world. With robust budgets, they conducted research in hot spots across the globe, and the information they gathered was often integrated into the universe of data used by the government to make foreign policy decisions. But as the twenty-first century began, there was increasing disquiet over what this documentation model had not been able to accomplish.

One idea that started gaining traction was the marketing of human rights to regular citizens in order to move the human rights conversation from the elite hallways of power out to "the churches and the shopping malls."[1] And when it came to genocide, the crime that inspired the original slew of human rights pronouncements, it seemed that the U.S. government would continue to be a bystander to its occurrence—unless, the new thinking went, citizens themselves created an outcry that levied a political cost on inaction in the face of atrocity.[2]

In declaring that Darfur was genocide, Secretary of State Powell had hoped to shock the governments of the world into responding; instead, ordinary Americans were catalyzed into action.

SAM BELL

Sam Bell was one of those ordinary Americans. In the fall of 2004, Bell was 21 years old and in his final year at Swarthmore—a small liberal arts college in Philadelphia. A fellow student, Mark Hanis, had followed the crisis in Darfur during his summer internship and had since been pestering Bell and others in their class to start paying attention to Darfur. For Hanis, the grandson of four Holocaust survivors, the responsibility to become an "upstander" against genocide was clear.

In his childhood Bell attended Hebrew school each week and read "many, many" books about the Holocaust. He remembers that in around fifth or sixth grade, when he and his classmates were starting to become more conscious of their parents' expectations, his friends' parents talked about them becoming lawyers. At the time, Bell's mother was the lead attorney on two major cases against American gun manufacturers. And when Bell, age 12, asked about his parents' expectations, his mom replied, "We raised you to lead the Warsaw ghetto uprising if you had to."

By the time he reached college Bell was interested in politics. Throughout the fall of his senior year he worked on a voter registration project for the upcoming presidential election. He was skeptical, however, about the value of rallying people around any single cause: "The thing I liked about voter registration was that you brought people in to participate in their world—it was not about pushing any one issue," says Bell.

After the presidential election, Bell was sitting in the cramped basement of Swarthmore's library with Hanis and another classmate, Andrew Sniderman. "We were in these little cubicles—two computers to each. Mark kept pestering me to start reading up on Darfur, and I said, 'I can't, I gotta catch up on work.'" But by January 2005 the cumulative impact of Powell's statement, his classmate's persistence, and the moral indignation of a speaker who came to campus led Bell to turn himself into an issue advocate for Darfur.

The campus speaker was Eric Reeves, an English professor and scholar of Shakespeare and Milton. Whenever Reeves speaks, he exudes a sense of moral righteousness. To this day he carries his draft card from the Vietnam War in his wallet; its status box is marked "1-0"—conscientious objector. After reading about southern Sudan in a 1998 report on the world's most underreported humanitarian crises, he became obsessed with the country. In subsequent years he transformed himself into a tireless advocate, got involved with the Sudan Campaign, and was one of the first among the southern Sudan advocates to raise the alarm on Darfur with his *Washington Post* op-ed. "Eric was clearly gripped with the issue," recalls Bell. "So many speakers come to campus and they don't really care. This was different."

With Reeves' encouragement, Bell, Hanis, and Sniderman began organizing a congressional lobby day for Darfur. Reeves put them in touch with Congressman Donald Payne's office, who was thrilled to see a group of college students interested in a country that Payne had long been committed to. Not all representatives were like Payne though, and Bell remembers his frustration at trying to get meetings with other members of congress and always being passed off to low-level staffers.

Other student groups were also starting to mobilize in response to news of genocide. Five days after Powell's testimony, Lisa Rogoff, a student intern at the U.S. Holocaust Memorial Museum who was also from a family of Holocaust survivors, organized a presentation on Darfur for students. Concerned by what they heard at the event, students from Georgetown University banded together to form an organization they called STAND, Students Take Action Now for Darfur. They believed that by raising their voices they could push the U.S. government to stop the atrocities in Darfur quickly, viewing their activism as "an activity for the fall semester."[3] Little did they imagine that in the coming years their organization would not only become permanent, but would grow until there were more than 750 chapters of STAND on college campuses across the country.

Bell and his classmates began to work with STAND. They also put their energies into a novel approach that was inspired by the book *Shake Hands with the Devil*, written by Lieutenant-General Roméo Dallaire, a Canadian who led the UN force deployed to Rwanda to monitor the peace accords that preceded the outbreak of genocide in 1994. Before the genocide began, Dallaire had warned the UN of the impending massacres and fought hard to have his small contingent of peacekeepers strengthened. But, once the genocide started, concerned about the risks to their own troops, the powers on the Security Council instructed Dallaire's contingent be drawn down to a meager 270.[4] Dallaire believed that with the right mandate and just 5,500 troops, he could have stopped the massacres.[5] Analogizing to Rwanda, the Swarthmore students became convinced that they could help protect civilians in Darfur if they could just get resources to the peacekeepers that had started to deploy there.

There was an obvious candidate for outside help. The task of monitoring the fragile April 2004 Darfur cease-fire between the Sudanese government and the SLA and JEM had been delegated to the African Union (AU), a regional body that had technically been in operation for less than two years and whose organizational structure had just been finalized.[6] Born of disillusionment with the corruption and weakness rife in its predecessor, the Organization of African Unity, the vision statement of the newly minted AU spoke of an Africa that "cannot afford to wait until tomorrow to have its problems resolved."[7] This could not be truer for the people of Darfur, and in 2004 hopes were high that Darfur would be a successful test case of the AU's ability to find "African solutions to African problems."

By June 19, 2004, the AU had deployed a cease-fire commission accompanied by 29 AU peacekeepers to the North Darfur capital of el-Fasher.[8] The operation was called the African Union Mission in Sudan (AMIS). With no funding of its own, AMIS relied entirely on contributions from donor countries to finance its operations. The UN struggles to get countries to provide the funds they owe for ongoing UN peacekeeping operations, and these contributions are at least forecast in each country's annual budget.[9] By contrast, funding for AMIS had to be begged and borrowed from other sources on an ad-hoc basis. The result was that the small AMIS contingent that arrived in Darfur had neither the manpower nor equipment to cope with the massive violence.

This problem of a regional organization like the AU having to secure funds for peacekeeping on an ad-hoc basis had already been recognized by the UN. Secretary-General Kofi Annan had commissioned a report on strengthening the UN in the twenty-first century that recommended the UN peacekeeping budget rules be amended so the UN could use its assessed contributions scheme to finance regional peacekeeping operations on a case-by-case basis.[10] Published in 2004, the recommendation was not (and at the time of this writing has still not been) taken up.

The AU was stuck with going around, cap in hand, which in many ways made it the ideal organization for the Swarthmore students to start raising money for. "The original idea was to get resources to people who are there trying to make a difference. It was the Dallaire model that we had in mind," says Bell. So as 2005 began, the students started to hold movie screenings and host house parties to raise money for AMIS. "Eric Reeves wrote this piece about how aid workers were literally passing a hat around to collect funds to buy the AMIS peacekeepers boots. That was the image I had in my head—if we could just get them those funds," says Bell.

DAVID RUBENSTEIN

At six foot two, with a lean frame and graying hair, 52-year-old New Yorker David Rubenstein resembles John Kerry, the senator who contested George W. Bush for the presidency in 2004. But unlike Kerry, who comes across as aloof and unemotional, Rubenstein has a tendency to wear his heart on his sleeve. After a stint in telecommunications, he spent most of his career in the non-profit sector within the United States. But in 2003 the break-up of his marriage propelled Rubenstein to do volunteer work with poor rural communities in Guatemala. Returning stateside later that year, he began looking for a new project.

He found it on the day he read a column about Sudan in the *New York Times*. "It began for me on May 29, 2004," recalls Rubenstein. The article, one of Nicholas Kristof's many on Darfur, criticized Bush and others for a lack of leadership. Kristof's final salvo read, "We have repeatedly failed to stand up to genocide, whether of Armenians, Jews, Cambodians or Rwandans. Now we're letting it happen again."[11] Between reading Kristof's piece and the first meeting of the soon-to-be-named Save Darfur Coalition in New York six weeks later, Rubenstein scanned news articles and read reports by Human Rights Watch to educate himself on the situation.

The idea for a New York meeting arose during a three-party conference call with Rubenstein, Ruth Messinger, head of the American Jewish World Service (AJWS), and Jerry Fowler, director of the U.S. Holocaust Memorial Museum's Committee on Conscience. Rubenstein had no institutional affiliation with either the Holocaust Museum or AJWS, but during an event on Darfur for the museum, he had attracted attention by asking rather bluntly why the museum could not start lobbying policymakers instead of just putting up exhibits.[12] Messinger proposed that a statement should come out of the meeting and produced a first draft. She also suggested that the groups that came to the meeting might think about working together as a coalition. As Fowler recalls it, "the original name was something that was a little unwieldy." So he suggested making the name of the proposed coalition "more succinct, and focus on what we hoped to accomplish, which was to save lives in Darfur, or even more succinct, Save Darfur."[13]

Attendance at the meeting in New York was predominantly Jewish, reflecting the common constituency of the organizers. The outcome of the meeting was a Unity Statement, which listed four goals: ending the violence against civilians, facilitating adequate and unhindered humanitarian aid, establishing conditions for the safe return of displaced people to their homes (the requirement that returns were "voluntary" was subsequently added), and holding the perpetrators accountable.[14] Individual organizations with representatives at the meeting could then decide whether or not they wanted to sign on.

"I would not say that the coalition was created with a strong strategic vision," reflects Fowler.[15] Rubenstein also remembers that at that time there was no thought of a long-term structure. But after the meeting Rubenstein started sending out e-mails updating the attendees on current events in Darfur. Seeing that this information sharing was useful, he looked for a way to do it more systematically. Sending off a grant proposal through AJWS, he secured a retainer and $5,000 in expenses to set up a website. With just 100 e-mail addresses (three-quarters of which were his personal friends and acquaintances), Rubenstein began sending information on Darfur to a list that would subsequently grow to more than one million.

A month after their first Save Darfur Coalition meeting in New York, Fowler e-mailed Rubenstein, noting that one of his interns was wearing a "Livestrong" yellow rubber wrist band, which raised funds for cancer research. Given the rate that the Livestrong bands were catching on among students in particular, he suggested they try the same thing for Save Darfur. Rubenstein ordered 1,000 green wristbands, then upped the number to 5,000, before finally confirming the order at 10,000. They sold out within one week of delivery. "There was all this ferment growing around the country; people were spontaneously organizing events," recalls Fowler. "And because the Save Darfur Coalition had the brand name, people started gravitating toward it."[16]

The ferment Fowler was referring to, with community groups and religious organizations around the country starting to bring in speakers and raise funds for Darfur, was bolstered by a coincidental piece of timing. Hollywood had released the feature film *Hotel Rwanda* just two days after Powell's testimony. Ten-and-a-half years after the Rwandan genocide, it was the first time a mainstream American audience saw the tragedy portrayed on the big screen. Audiences left theaters across the country wondering what they had been doing as 800,000 people were massacred, and some drew a connection to what they had started to hear about Darfur.

CATALYSTS TO ACTION

By using the word *genocide*, Powell had, in the minds of many Americans, elevated Darfur from "just another" crisis in Africa to a different level of gravity. The label pushed Darfur beyond elite advocacy circles and closed government doors to capture the attention of ordinary citizens. The word alone may not have had such an effect but for a couple of key ideas that had gained traction in the years immediately preceding Powell's testimony.

One idea that became important to the emerging U.S. movement for Darfur was called the Responsibility to Protect (R2P). The term had been coined by an international commission that had looked at the role of sovereignty heading into the twenty-first century. The commission concluded that each country has a responsibility to protect its citizens; however, if a country is unable or unwilling to carry out that function, the country abrogates its sovereignty, at which point both the right and the responsibility to remedy the situation fall to the international community. This notion, that sovereignty is contingent upon a country's responsibility to protect its citizens, was the core of the R2P doctrine.[17]

The leaders of the growing citizens movement believed that R2P heralded the beginning of a fundamental shift in the way the international community thought about countries hiding behind the shield of sovereignty. They hoped that in the new century countries would assume the responsibility to intervene in situations like Darfur, rather than turn a blind eye to the massacre of another country's citizens. And, because of another salient idea that was gaining currency around the same time, they believed that it was within the power of regular citizens to ensure their political leaders undertook such interventions.

In a radio interview immediately after the Rwandan genocide, the late Senator Paul Simon had argued, "If every member of the House and Senate had received one hundred letters from people back home saying we have to do something about Rwanda, when the crisis was first developing, then I think the response would have been different."[18] The quote gained a wider audience after being recorded in *"A Problem from Hell,"* which concluded with a call to action: "American leaders have been able to persist in turning away because genocide in distant lands has not captivated senators, congressional caucuses, Washington lobbyists, elite opinion shapers, grassroots groups, or individual citizens. The battle to stop genocide has thus been repeatedly lost in the realm of domestic politics."[19]

The leaders of the new Save Darfur Coalition spread this message as they began speaking to people in their communities about what was happening in Darfur and what ordinary citizens could do to help people half a world away. Within a matter of months it became an article of faith within the Darfur advocacy community that in order for government to take genocide or crimes against humanity seriously, "there needs to be a politically salient constituency of citizens raising its voice."[20]

GLORIA WHITE-HAMMOND

Unlike Bell, Rubenstein, and most of the other citizens who were becoming activists on Darfur, Gloria White-Hammond had been involved with Sudan for several years before Powell's genocide determination. An African American pastor, White-Hammond first visited southern Sudan in the summer of 2001 after hearing reports of modern-day slavery. She had been told that southern

Sudanese were being abducted by northern raiders, used as slave labor, given Arabic names, and forced to convert to Islam. An NGO called Christian Solidarity International had begun sending money into Sudan to pay slave-owners for the freedom of the enslaved, a controversial practice known as redemption.[21] White-Hammond went to witness slave redemption firsthand.

"I remember seeing a long line of redeemed slaves and being blown away by how surreal it all looked," she told me, recalling the scene vividly almost ten years later. An attractive woman with close-cropped hair, sparkly eyes, and a well-worn voice, White-Hammond was 50 years old and running a hectic schedule that combined her religious duties with her work as a pediatrician at a Boston community medical center when she first heard about slavery in Sudan. She says that she used to wonder what her ancestors might have thought about their own enslavement. "I think they were thinking about people like me. They were thinking that if they could hold on, maybe there would be some-body like me who would have degrees from wonderful institutions of learning, who would have titles and live in a nice house and see her responsibility to do everything she could to see that such things don't happen again."[22]

It was the rainy season when White-Hammond and her husband arrived in the undeveloped terrain that dominates southern Sudan. It was a place like none she had ever seen. They pitched a tent for shelter as the wind howled and the rain came down in torrents. After a sleepless night, she spent the next day watching a redemption event and talking to those newly freed. She was struck by how stoic the women were, even as they presented their injuries for medical examination. "There was this woman who had, her eyeball was— I'm not even using the medical term—but it was just turned around, and she talked about it so matter-of-factly."

By the time of Powell's testimony, White-Hammond had made another four trips back to Sudan. In 2002 she founded an organization called My Sister's Keeper, to support girls' education in the village of Akon, the first place she had been to in Sudan. In 2003 My Sister's Keeper raised funds back in Boston to provide supplies to an outdoor girls' school that the women of the Akon had started. That project grew as My Sister's Keeper committed to support the women's idea of building a proper structure for the school. "When an old man in the village heard about it he said, 'People always make promises,'" recalls White-Hammond. "If it's what you do we will celebrate you. If you fail we will defame you," the man told her. I asked her how she responded. "We rolled up our sleeves."

With each visit back to Sudan, White-Hammond's commitment to the Sudanese women she met grew, as did her understanding of the broader polit-ical context for their experiences. During a visit to Akon in 2004, there had been some discussion among the women about whether Darfur should be included in the north-south peace agreement—something that diplomats had already ruled out. Tramping through the dense brush, White-Hammond heard the arguments debated back and forth on either side. But the one comment that remained in her memory when she returned to Boston was that of a woman who said, "We can't be free until all of us are free."

So back in the United States, White-Hammond began to get involved in Darfur advocacy. But she soon found that coming into the Save Darfur Coalition through a southern Sudan lens made her an anomaly within the new movement. "The people who came into this were ahistoric—they heard 'genocide' and 'Darfur,'" she says. Trying to put the whole picture together for herself, White-Hammond traveled to Darfur for the first time in February 2005. It was one month since the north-south peace had been formalized with the signing of the Comprehensive Peace Agreement. The CPA stated that in January 2011 southerners would get to vote on whether they wanted to become an independent country. In the intervening six years, however, it was agreed that both the NCP and the SPLM, now partners in a new Government of National Unity, would do everything possible to make the unity of the country attractive by leading Sudan through a process of democratic transformation.

There was much to be done. Wealth-sharing and power-sharing protocols were to be implemented, and under an interim constitution Sudanese citizens were guaranteed basic human rights, including freedom from torture and slavery, freedom of expression, and equality before the law. A national democratic election would be held partway through the transformation period to allow those outside the agreement, like Darfuris, to participate in the governance of their country.[23] But for those White-Hammond spoke with in Darfur, this peace agreement seemed very abstract.

White-Hammond focused her time in Darfur on speaking with women who had been displaced. Among her memories of the visit was meeting Karima, a woman who had given birth just two weeks before the Janjaweed attacked her village. Through a translator, Karima told White-Hammond what had happened. Then she stopped talking and simply lifted up her shawl to show White-Hammond the thick scars over her back, arms, and legs; the physical reminders of how the Janjaweed whipped her after they had raped her. "*Ana asif*," White-Hammond whispered, "I'm sorry." She and Karima began to cry.[24]

To White-Hammond's ear, the stories that the displaced Darfuri women were telling her sounded desperately familiar. "In so many ways it was the same scenario I had heard the women in the south talk about with the *murahaleen*,"[25] she says. On her return to Boston, she felt still further detached from the growing Darfur movement. "What was astounding to me was that people didn't know so much [about the south] and weren't making the connection," she recalls. "People weren't getting that you couldn't siphon off Darfur. It was like saying in the civil rights movement, 'Well you can deal with civil rights in Mississippi, but not Chicago'—it doesn't make sense."

SAVE DARFUR

It was the involvement of regular citizens who were new to human rights advocacy, and new to Sudan, that distinguished the emerging efforts for Darfur from the preexisting organizations on the human rights landscape. While this was not true of everyone involved, and exceptions like Eric Reeves, who had been a southern Sudan advocate for many years prior stood out, it was certainly the case that most citizen activists had joined the Darfur movement without any background knowledge of Sudan. The mobilization of thousands of citizens as first-time advocates was one of the movement's great strengths, but it was not without its costs.

In July 2005, when SPLM leader John Garang was inaugurated as first vice president of Sudan—a position awarded to him under the CPA—Khartoum's streets overflowed with emotion. Literally millions of regular Sudanese citizens turned out to welcome Garang to the capital. Residents of Khartoum's neighboring city, Omdurman, walked to the airport to see his plane land because there was not enough transportation to get there any other way.[26] Across the city the diverse mix of Sudan's population was on display, dancing, singing, and cheering.[27]

To those steeped in the history and policy challenges of Sudan, this was a seminal moment. A U.S. official in Khartoum remembers watching the scene with amazement. "I saw Garang dance and reach out to all the people at the inauguration event, and I finally perceived his thinking; Garang honestly believed he could be elected president of Sudan, uniting the marginalized groups in the east, north, and west with the south."[28]

But not everyone saw it in this light. Late that night, as trains rattled above the basement office that housed the Swarthmore students' fund-raising efforts, Sam Bell was reading the news coverage of the scenes in Khartoum. "The journalist was arguing that in order to sustain that optimism the international community would have to work to implement the CPA, and suggesting that this should be the highest priority in Sudan," says Bell, who remembers being dumbfounded by what he was reading. "I was outraged that a genocide was happening in Darfur and someone was saying there was a higher priority!"

The people who started turning up to Darfur events were not those already on the mailing lists of traditional human rights organizations like Human Rights Watch. In many cases they were people who had never advocated on a human rights issue before. This constituency was not one of elite actors, the professional human rights advocates who have inside access to lobby policymakers. It was primarily a citizens' corps of ordinary Americans—volunteers who didn't pay their rent with a salary from a human rights organization.

"It is in the realm of [U.S.] domestic politics that the battle to stop genocide is lost,"[29] was the key message from the mammoth research Samantha Power had undertaken into the genocides of the twentieth century. It was a mantra that could be seen scribbled on Post-it notes on Darfur advocates' desks and added as the sign-off to their e-mails. The citizens who started to join the growing movement for Darfur believed that the power to make "never again" meaningful was in their hands, that if they created a loud enough outcry, they could generate the political will needed to get their political leaders to save Darfuri lives.

CHAPTER 5

WHO WILL DELIVER JUSTICE?

C ondoleezza Rice stood immaculately dressed in a primrose-colored suit to the left of the podium from which President Bush announced he was nominating her to replace Colin Powell as secretary of state. It was November 2004, and Bush had just been reelected president. Powell's deputy had commented that by 2004 he and Powell were "about as influential as a couple of potted plants."[1] However, Rice was widely described as Bush's most trusted and loyal adviser.

Rice's confirmation hearing marked 636 days since Bush had donned a full flight suit to sit co-pilot on a Navy Viking jet as it landed him aboard the USS *Abraham Lincoln* to declare "mission accomplished" in the U.S.-led invasion of Iraq. Two years later, with the invasion looking increasingly like a quagmire and the Bush administration widely condemned for its flagrant abuse of human rights in both Guantanamo and Abu Ghraib, relations with even those few European allies who had initially supported the war were strained. Rice's first order of business was to rebuild those relations, and she announced a trip to Europe the day she took office.[2]

Darfur, in particular the question of who should adjudicate crimes committed in Darfur, was Rice's first test case for transatlantic relations. European countries were committed to seeing the recently created International Criminal Court in The Hague take on the task. But the United States was a staunch opponent of the new court. And the embryonic constituency of citizen advocates was too preoccupied with building their new organizations to enter into the debate over who should deal with justice for Darfur.

THE BATTLE FOR THE ICC

The concept of an international criminal court can be traced back to the 1948 Genocide Convention created in the aftermath of the Holocaust. Drafters of the convention assumed that a court with jurisdiction over the crime of genocide would soon be in existence.[3] The onset of the Cold War, however, delayed the creation of such a court for 50 years. Throughout much of the twentieth century, individuals who committed a single murder were much more likely to be prosecuted and receive a serious sentence than those responsible for the murder of millions. So it was a genuinely historic development when in 1998 a treaty to form the International Criminal Court (ICC) was signed in Rome. In 2002 this "Rome Statute" came into effect, and by 2005 one hundred countries had joined the court. The birth of the ICC brought much hope that in the twenty-first century leaders would no longer be able to assume that they could get away with mass murder.

The ICC was designed as a court of last resort; it can only adjudicate allegations of genocide, crimes against humanity, or war crimes if the relevant domestic court is unable or unwilling to do so. In this respect, its design reflects the notion of the Responsibility to Protect that had gained such a following among the new Darfur advocates. If (but only if) a sovereign state abrogates its fundamental responsibilities, the international community must step up to the plate.

Although the United States had signed the Rome Statute in December 2000, President Clinton showed no urgency in getting the treaty approved by the Senate—a prerequisite for U.S. ratification of international treaties.[4] And once the Bush administration came into office, the United States formally expressed its intention not to join the ICC. John Bolton, who would later become Bush's ambassador to the UN, described his rescinding of the American intention to ratify the Rome Statute as "the happiest moment in my government service."[5] The U.S. view stood in stark contrast to the many countries in Europe and Africa that rushed to join the court. Most European and African countries were as strongly in support of the ICC as the United States was opposed. And these proponents of the ICC were determined that the court would survive what they saw as American efforts to kill it.

U.S. foreign policy has always oscillated between internationalism and isolationism, but even during its most outward-looking phases, there has been a philosophical wariness of subjugating U.S. sovereignty to binding international commitments. The United States did not ratify the Genocide Convention until 1988, and it retains the dubious distinction—along with Somalia—of being one of the two countries in the world not to have ratified the UN Convention on the Rights of the Child.

By and large, the United States does not dispute the bulk of the substance of the various international treaties that it refuses to join. Rather, it objects to the idea of being bound to any forum over which it does not exercise control, preferring instead to conform as a matter of choice. It seems to remain impervious to other countries' criticisms of its à la carte approach to international law, and there has always been a striking willingness to suffer the wrath of the international community over what is often more of a philosophical than substantive objection to international legal treaties.

In addition to its philosophical bias, the United States also had specific policy objections to the ICC. Chief among these was a concern that the court could charge U.S. military personnel with war crimes. The ICC can examine crimes committed on the territory of a country that has joined the court or by a national of a country that has joined the court. The exception is if the UN Security Council refers a situation to the court, in which case the court can examine crimes committed in any country (by its nationals or others) regardless of whether or not that country has joined the court.[6] As the United States has not joined the ICC and has a veto on the Security Council, there is no prospect of the court investigating any activities on U.S. soil. The United States, however, remained concerned that its citizens could be prosecuted for crimes committed on foreign soil.[7] Opposing the ICC became a favorite pastime for many members of congress and for the Bush administration, which even implemented a policy of withdrawing military assistance and certain economic aid from any country that joined the court.[8]

Sudan also was not a member of the ICC, and thus the crimes committed in Darfur could not be investigated by the court in the absence of a UN Security Council resolution. Unlike the United States, however, Sudan was not a permanent member of the council and so had no veto with which to shield itself from investigation. The key question in relation to whether the ICC would adjudicate the Darfur case was whether the American desire to undermine the court would lead it to veto a Security Council resolution giving the court jurisdiction.[9]

POWELL'S LEGACY

The first article of the Genocide Convention places two obligations on countries that ratify it: to prevent genocide and to punish those who commit genocide.[10] Having said genocide had been committed in Darfur, Powell believed he had taken steps toward the obligation to prevent further genocidal acts by referring the situation to the UN Security Council. But just as the United States had been unwilling to act on information gathered by others and instead sent its own team to investigate, so too the UN wanted its own data source. Nine days after Powell's testimony, the Security Council established an International Commission of Inquiry to investigate the atrocities in Darfur.[11]

The Commission of Inquiry would soon become relevant to the obligation to punish, with U.S. officials anticipating, correctly as it turned out, that the commission would want Darfur referred to the ICC. John Danforth, previously Bush's special envoy to Sudan, had been appointed as the U.S. representative to the UN in June 2004. But in January 2005 he retired from government. Before he left, he wrote Rice a memorandum, referring to the likelihood that the commission would recommend ICC involvement in Darfur as the looming "train wreck."[12] Danforth's memo framed the problem in terms of the damage that U.S. opposition to the ICC was doing to U.S.-European relations, and he proposed that the United States back down and allow the Security Council to refer Darfur to the ICC.[13] "Our position was to oppose anything related to the ICC, but I was thinking, 'Do we really want to raise, yet again, our objection to the ICC—even on a situation we have called genocide?' "[14] Danforth recalls. But Danforth was on his way out. With no one lined up to replace him, Rice took over decision making on the issue, and she tasked Pierre Prosper, the ambassador-at-large for war crimes, with finding an alternative to the ICC.

Prosper met in New York with Security Council representatives from Tanzania, Benin, and the United Kingdom to try to sell them on an alternative: an ad-hoc "Sudan tribunal" administered by the AU and UN and using the infrastructure of the International Criminal Tribunal for Rwanda in Tanzania.[15] The proposal was to remain confidential until support had been secured. As an internal document circulated from Prosper's War Crimes Office explained, "We do not want to be confronted with a decision on whether to veto an ICC resolution in the Security Council."[16]

But Prosper was not the only one doing diplomatic groundwork. Around the same time, the French representative to the UN, Jean-Marc de la Sablière, was holding his own informal meetings with those he hoped would be allies in France's push to get Darfur referred to the ICC. The numbers were on his side. In the 15-member Security Council it takes nine affirmative votes to get a resolution through, and de la Sablière calculated he had them in the nine members of the council who had joined the ICC. De la Sablière's only concern was that the United States would block the majority with its veto.

Prosper played to the Security Council representatives from Tanzania and Benin as Africans, asking, "Is this the message that we want to send to the African continent, that whenever there's a problem...justice has to be exported to The Hague? We say no."[17] By contrast, de la Sablière played to their identity as members of the ICC. His approach seemed to be winning: "The Ambassadors for Tanzania and Benin are very active and engaged—despite huge amount of pressure from U.S.," de la Sablière wrote in his notes after a February 2005 meeting with the nine ICC members on the Security

Council.[18] This "ICC-9," as U.S. cables began referring to the group, was to remain in constant communication as the negotiations progressed.

AT THE END OF JANUARY, the Commission of Inquiry released its 176-page report. The report concluded that war crimes and crimes against humanity that "may be no less serious or heinous than genocide"[19] had occurred in Darfur. The next day, global headlines condensed the detailed report into a single message: "Sudan's Darfur crimes not genocide."[20] The commission concluded that while the underlying physical acts (*actus reus*) required for genocide, as well as the existence of protected groups targeted by those acts, "may be deduced" from what they found in Darfur, "the crucial element of genocidal intent appears to be missing, at least as far as the central government authorities are concerned."[21] In the coming years, policymakers and politicians the world over would use the commission's failure to find genocide as a vindication of their claim that the United States had ulterior motives in labeling Darfur genocide.

John Ralston, a straight-talking Australian with decades of experience in criminal investigations, led the commission's on-the-ground investigation. Ralston recalls that while he personally argued the case to the commissioners that it was genocide, he accepted that reasonable people could disagree. "I don't think there was ever any question that the *actus reus* existed. It was just a question of whether you could attribute genocidal intent. You could certainly attribute intent to local leaders, and in my view also to government leaders— but I could also accept that people had different views on this."[22]

As expected, the commission made the "strong recommendation" that the UN Security Council refer Darfur to the ICC for possible prosecutions.[23]

JUSTICE FOR DARFURIS

A childhood spent playing outdoors in el-Fasher had left Omer Ismail with a persistent craving for being in the fresh air. Even throughout the biting cold of an East Coast winter, he would spend some time each morning sitting outside to read the newspaper, much to the chagrin of his U.S. born-and-bred kids. "Daddy—why are you sitting *out there?*" they would ask incredulously. It was one such morning when he read about the possibility of Darfur being referred to the ICC. His heart leapt. "Darfuris can have their day in court!" For Ismail, seeing al-Bashir's regime brought to justice was a deeply personal issue.

After finishing high school in Darfur, Ismail was one of the few among his classmates to be accepted into the University of Khartoum. As a student there he met many of those who would eventually lead the 1989 coup. "The university encompasses a small elite of the Sudanese people. In a span of ten years you came across almost everyone who is a potential leader in the future—for better or for worse," Ismail explains.

The year before the coup, Ismail began working as a logistician for the French medical organization Médecins Sans Frontières (MSF) on the massive humanitarian operation that was being run in southern Sudan. At the time of the coup, he was responsible for securing the permits for medical relief planes to travel into southern Sudan. As with the bureaucratic system established for aid workers to travel to Darfur in later years, getting permission for doctors and medical supplies to enter the south of the country was a painfully slow process, designed to obstruct rather than facilitate the flow of aid to those in need. After 42 days of effort, culminating in a meeting with the Sudanese military joint chief of staff, Ismail finally secured the permits for an MSF plane to travel into southern Sudan with a physician and medical supplies.

In December 1989, after successfully completing its mission in southern Sudan, the MSF plane headed back to Khartoum. The plane was shot down shortly after takeoff, killing all of the aid workers onboard.[24] For Ismail, the destruction of the plane that he had personally secured the permission for marked a turning point. "A government that shoots the relief plane and doctors who come to help their people is a government that will not tolerate any sort of opposition," he thought, and he began speaking out against the government to the journalists covering the story.

A week later, the badly charred bodies of the relief workers began their journey back to France. A Red Cross plane flew the corpses to Khartoum airport, where Ismail and his boss were waiting to collect them for a funeral service in Khartoum before putting them on a flight to Paris. Together they carried the body bags, one by one, off the plane and into their truck on the tarmac. Once the corpses were loaded, Ismail got into his vehicle and followed behind the truck. A few minutes later the truck in front of him burst into flames; one of the corpses, booby-trapped, had exploded.[25]

Believing that the explosions were a warning to him, Ismail went into hiding. "I had friends in the military and security. They told me to go underground," he says. Their concern was not frivolous. In the six months since the coup, al-Bashir's regime had erected a ruthless internal security service that showed no tolerance for dissident voices. A special branch of the security services operated so-called ghost houses—unmarked locations where anyone suspected of opposition to the regime was taken and tortured; cigarette burns, electric shocks, rape, and mock executions were standard fare.[26] "The last four or five days before I got out they were looking for me. It wasn't only that they didn't approve of the work in the south, but [also that] I had been talking to the foreign press about the plane," explains Ismail. "If I had been found—God knows what would have happened." In January 1990 he made it out of Sudan and was granted refugee status in the United States.

"There is one thing I regret in my trip," Ismail tells me, before clarifying. "It's funny, I still call it my trip [to America] although it's been 20 years." He pauses, letting the notion of 20 years sink in. "There are not many things I regret. This country gave me many things—my wife, my beautiful children. But I regret I did not grow up with my brothers and sisters, or them with me. I don't know their aspirations, thoughts, and fears.... I didn't know their children born there and they didn't know my children born here. I wasn't there when my brothers fell in love and married their wives and when my sisters fell in love and married their husbands," he said, that poetic lilt back in his voice, though this time with the enduring sadness that comes from losing something you never had.

DIPLOMATIC WRANGLING

The U.S. State Department and Prosper in particular spent February 2005 aggressively trying to stop the Darfur situation going to the ICC. Prosper's office circulated a concept paper about the Sudan tribunal proposal. Reading it, one has the sense the drafter was tasked with making the argument that black is white.

The concept paper's section on funding states, "Any court that takes on Sudan war crimes would require an expansion of its staff and budget. The ICC, for example, has a limited presence in Africa, and this staff is occupied with the Uganda and Congo investigations. The Rwandan tribunal in contrast, has extensive infrastructure on the ground...."[27] In reality, the ICC already had funding (none of it from the United States) set aside for a third major investigation and the capacity to hire additional staff. By contrast, the proposed Sudan tribunal would have to start raising funds from scratch. The estimated cost of the tribunal was $30 million for the first six to eight months and then up to $100 million annually; the United States proposed that this funding come from the assessed contributions scheme, to which every member of the UN contributes. As Senate Foreign Relations Subcommittee member Senator Patrick Leahey asked upon hearing of the proposal, "Given the fact that the United Kingdom, France and virtually every member of the European Union has ratified the Rome Treaty...what is the likelihood of obtaining funding for a new court from assessed contributions?"[28] Nevertheless, the paper closes with the absurdity that there would not be "a significant difference in cost" between the ICC and the Sudan tribunal, and that in fact the latter "may be less costly."

Throughout February, the State Department issued démarches on the Sudan tribunal idea to its embassies across Africa. Its démarche to the U.S.

embassy in Senegal, the first country to have joined the ICC, contained a talking point to convince the Senegalese to support the Sudan tribunal over the ICC for use "at Post's discretion." It stated, "So far the only referrals to the ICC have related to activities in Africa."[29] The suggestion of bias by the ICC against Africa was something that would return to haunt the U.S. government as its approach to the ICC's role in Darfur shifted in the years ahead.

The French worked their diplomatic channels in favor of the ICC as hard as the Americans worked against it. As one of the lawyers at the French mission to the UN explains, the French believed it would be difficult for the United States to veto a proposal on justice for a situation that they had labeled genocide. But both France and the United Kingdom believed they could only get the United States to abstain from vetoing an ICC referral if they convinced them the ICC was the only game in town. "Many people thought the U.S. would veto anything on the ICC.... So you had countries in the position of saying no to a new Sudan tribunal while fearing an ICC veto. They felt like they were taking an enormous risk and that the result would be impunity."[30] The one argument that seemed to convince those who wavered was that they had a responsibility as signatories to the Rome Statute to support the ICC, and that a Security Council decision to deal with accountability for Darfur outside of the ICC would seriously undermine the stature of the new court they had fought so hard to bring to life.[31]

On February 14, 2005, the United States circulated a draft resolution on Sudan to the UN Security Council. The eight-page resolution had three components. It called for a peacekeeping force in southern Sudan to assist with implementing the Comprehensive Peace Agreement (CPA), for travel bans and assets freezes on those who violated the April 2004 cease-fire agreement in Darfur, and for accountability for crimes committed in Darfur—without reference to the ICC.[32]

A week after the draft circulated, Rice brought on Robert Zoellick as her deputy. Fifty-one-year-old Zoellick had a reputation as one of the best negotiators of his generation. Described as brilliant by some and arrogant by others, Zoellick came directly from his role as the U.S. trade representative. Formally speaking, it was a demotion. Rice asked Zoellick to take the lead on the Darfur file; he was known for giving 200 percent to whatever he took on. True to form, Zoellick immersed himself in the literature on Sudan. He was particularly impressed with the analysis he read by Harvard scholar Alex de Waal and asked his staff to gather more materials by de Waal to distribute to reporters who traveled with him to Sudan.

Fearing that the State Department was on course to back itself into vetoing even those provisions of the February 14 draft with which it agreed, Zoellick suggested that while the issue of accountability remained at an impasse, the

United States split its draft resolution into three discrete parts.[33] The long-term effect was to solidify what had already been the instinct of the Security Council members—to put the issues related to the CPA and those related to Darfur in separate silos. In the short term it gave the United States breathing room on the ICC question while ensuring the issues they cared about, like the deployment of peacekeepers to the south, continued to progress. It also gave time for those for and against the ICC to make their voices heard.

ADVOCATES FOCUSED ELSEWHERE

The growing constituency of Darfur advocates was surprisingly disengaged on the justice question. Although the Save Darfur Coalition had been in existence for eight months at this point, neither the coalition as a whole nor its organizational members were particularly outspoken about getting Darfur referred to the ICC. Given that the ICC seemed to signal a new commitment to prosecute those responsible for genocide, the crime that brought most regular citizens into the Darfur issue, one would have expected these new advocates to lobby hard for the ICC. But in many cases they had a limited understanding of this new, decidedly foreign court that was so controversial at home, and they were too engaged with building up their own organizations—raising funds, hiring staff, and working out how to operate—to learn more.

The Save Darfur Coalition spent February gathering support for their first major campaign, called "100 Hours of Conscience." The four-day campaign was due to begin on March 17, 2005, with a minute of silence across college campuses, and, taking their cue from the Senator Paul Simon story, this would be followed by a letter-writing campaign to members of congress. Adding to the coalition's reticence to put resources into supporting an ICC referral was the fact that the ICC was a divisive issue within the Jewish community. Like the United States, the Israeli government was opposed to the ICC, and many, although not all,[34] of the Jewish groups within the coalition, were uncomfortable taking any position indicating support for the court.[35] David Rubenstein remembers it was the fear of a lack of consensus that led the Save Darfur Coalition not to take any position on the ICC; instead, they called for accountability in generic terms, much as the U.S. government had been doing.

Even those Save Darfur Coalition members who had traditionally taken a pro-ICC approach were not focused on the referral. Human Rights First was a typical case; its then-president, Michael Posner, decided that convincing the United States not to veto an ICC referral was such a long shot, it was not worth putting the resources into.[36]

Sam Bell also remembers being ambivalent about the prospect of a referral. He, Mark Hanis, and Andrew Sniderman were focused on what they saw as the main issue: civilian protection. They planned to launch a "100 Days of Action" campaign for Darfur on April 6, 2005, the eleventh anniversary of the Rwandan genocide, hoping to raise $1 million for AMIS. The idea was that by funding peacekeepers, American citizens would demonstrate their desire to protect Darfuris and shame the U.S. government into increasing its own funding of AMIS.

Buoyed by early encouragement from Gayle Smith at the Democratic think-tank, the Center for American Progress, John Prendergast, a senior adviser at the International Crisis Group, and Samantha Power, author of "*A Problem from Hell*," the students pushed forward with building their organization. As Sniderman recalls, "We replied to every single e-mail, called as many people as we could—big fish, small fish, and everything in between."[37] During the first week of March, Sniderman was house-sitting for one of his professors. Among the e-mails he received that week was one from a woman named Pam Omidyar: "We are very interested in your work and want to see how we can help let more people know about it. Would it be possible to speak today?..."

Sniderman jotted down Omidyar's phone number on a list of other work calls and headed out to walk his professor's dog, requisite plastic bag in one hand, phone in the other. "The call goes like any other introductory call. I spend a lot of time explaining what it is that we do, trying to build her interest. Meanwhile, she has a crying child on her hip, and I'm walking this yappy dog," recalls Sniderman. "Finally, she asks what she can do to help. By this time, I've sold the organization to strangers so many times, I'm acting like a robot on auto-pilot. I am literally picking up dog shit as I go through the usual list—'Well, we can still use volunteers to organize letter-writing events and small fund raisers, we have trouble paying some of our interns basic living expenses...'" Omidyar paused before gently saying something along the lines of, "I want to help. I have a foundation. I think I can do more."

After the call, Sniderman went back to the house and Googled Omidyar's name. Had he checked earlier, he would have known she ran a major philanthropic organization and was married to the billionaire founder of eBay. Through Omidyar's organization, Humanity United, the young activists would receive thousands and then millions of dollars of support in the coming years.

With a grant of $44,000 from Humanity United, the Swarthmore students hired 22 staff. "Everyone was an intern with a little stipend, a totally flat structure," recalls Bell. While most of them worked out of the basement office at Swarthmore College, Bell took four of the interns to set up a base in Washington, D.C. "We had this tiny little office with no windows, five people in this tiny room. It was really tough," he remembers. "We hadn't made any decisions on process or decision making. There were a lot of hurt feelings.

It was a learning experience." As for most of the new Darfur advocates, putting the time into developing their organization was a higher priority for the Swarthmore students than supporting a court that their government was so staunchly opposed to.

SHIFTING POSITIONS

Within congress, the representatives who had pushed so hard for the Darfur genocide resolutions were, much like the Save Darfur Coalition, in a bind over the ICC. Conscious that they were at their most effective when speaking with one voice and aware that the question of the ICC could divide them along partisan lines, Sudan's congressional champions mostly decided to avoid making any comment on the ICC.[38] But their silence stood in stark contrast to the virulent anti-ICC rhetoric that the Europeans were used to seeing come out of the U.S. congress. De la Sablière recalls that it was after meeting with Republican congress members who told him they would not oppose the ICC when it came to Sudan that he started to think, "Yes, we really can do this."[39]

As these traditional opponents of the ICC started to reveal their relative neutrality on a Darfur referral, it became clear to Rice that this was not a battle worth straining fragile U.S.-European relations over. "We wanted to get an armistice with the Europeans over the ICC issue. It was a destructive dispute with no endpoint to it," explains one of Rice's closest advisers, Philip Zelikow.[40] But just as the United States began to back down from its anti-ICC stance, African countries began to waver. Under pressure from the United States, they had started to buy into Prosper's argument that the ICC was about exporting justice from Africa to Europe. As this became apparent, a coalition of African advocates intervened.

A group of human rights advocates from African organizations had gathered on the sidelines of an African Commission meeting in Pretoria, South Africa, just after Powell's genocide testimony. The African human rights community was concerned that non-Western voices were not being heard on Darfur.[41] Dismas Nkunda, a Ugandan journalist who had covered the 1994 genocide in Rwanda, raised the possibility of forming a coalition of African-based NGOs, a Darfur Consortium, to advocate on Darfur. Following the release of the UN Commission of Inquiry report, the Darfur Consortium launched a campaign in Cairo to press the Security Council to refer Darfur to the ICC.

Upon hearing that African countries were moving toward Prosper's Sudan tribunal idea, Nkunda wrote to the AU chair, Nigerian president Olusegun Obasanjo, arguing, "Africa helped create the ICC, African countries have the greatest number of ratifications. . . . The ICC is an African court." Obasanjo called Nkunda back and said he agreed.[42] Nkunda flew to New York to begin intensive lobbying of Security Council members. At a time when the United States was trying to sell the Sudan tribunal as an "African solution," it was powerful signal to have Nkunda advocating at the UN for the ICC.[43]

HARD BARGAINING

On March 24, 2005, the first of the severed resolutions from the original U.S. draft was put to a vote. UN Security Council Resolution 1590 was passed, authorizing a UN Mission in Sudan (UNMIS) of 10,000 military personnel in southern Sudan to support the implementation of the CPA.[44] France's strategy had been to use the deployment of troops to the south, which they knew the United States was committed to, as a bargaining chip. By allowing the U.S. delegation to get the deployment they really wanted before dealing with the issue of the ICC, de la Sablière had lost his leverage. He called Paris and got permission to present a resolution on the ICC as soon as possible.

Rice called her counterpart in Paris to try and get a delay but was told it was de la Sablière's call to make. "I said I would agree not to [put it on the] table the next day if they got me a draft by 9:30 a.m. that showed they were really serious about negotiating. If not, I would [propose] our draft at 10 a.m.," recalls de la Sablière. It was not an empty threat. Paris had agreed, and with the ICC-9 all willing to vote in favor, it would take a veto to stop it going forward—something the United Kingdom and France still believed the United States wanted to avoid.

The next afternoon was tense. As promised, the United States sent a draft to de la Sablière, although not the kind he was hoping for. A fax of the draft came through at the French Mission while the ICC-9 was meeting. Its sweeping exemptions in relation to those who were not members of the ICC would have excluded not just Americans from jurisdiction of the court but every Sudanese national as well. Moreover, despite the fact that the referral would be coming from the UN Security Council, the U.S. draft specified that the ICC's investigation of Darfur would have to be funded entirely by the countries that had joined the ICC, with no financial support from the UN. De la Sablière told the U.S. delegate that he would not forward the draft to Paris for approval.[45]

The United States maintained its position on funding, but by that evening it had adjusted the language on who would be exempted from the ICC's jurisdiction, proposing wording that the Security Council had previously agreed to in an August 2003 resolution concerning peacekeeping in Liberia. That resolution exempted peacekeeping officials from countries that had not joined the ICC from the court's jurisdiction.[46] At the time, France abstained from the resolution, not because they didn't agree with the deployment of peacekeepers to Liberia, but because they felt the jurisdiction language undermined the cause of international justice. Now the United States was asking for this very same language on the Darfur referral. France was in a diplomatic bind. When the UN Security Council members met the following day, de la Sablière asked for a 24-hour delay on the vote.

One of the unofficial rules of the diplomatic game at the Security Council is that once particular wording has been adopted, it is "agreed language" that the council will pass again in the future. De la Sablière knew that the jurisdiction language fell into this privileged category and that even his ICC-9 would have to support it. The French decided they would vote for the resolution, but they couldn't sponsor it; de la Sablière asked the United Kingdom representative, Emyr Jones Parry, to sponsor the resolution on the condition that there would be no changes to the text. As the United Kingdom had no prior record of refusing exclusive jurisdiction language, its delegate stepped up.[47]

At 9:30 p.m. on March 31, the UN Security Council members gathered for an informal meeting. Jones Parry told the president of the council that he had a piece of paper in his hand, but that he was not going to present it. However, he said, "If the President were informally to invite me to share it with the other council members, and if the Chair were to ascertain if there are nine votes in favor and no veto, then I would, for the UK, be prepared to sponsor it."[48] With some sense of a guarantee of its passage, Jones Parry presented the resolution.

Prosper recalls that even once the British took over the resolution, the final decision went right down to the wire.[49] In the space of two-and-a-half hours that evening, the U.S. representative had called Jones Parry three times to argue the case for an amendment recognizing that not all council members were part of the ICC and variously invoking the secretary of state and the White House. Jones Parry would not budge.

Sitting at the UN Security Council, Blackberry in hand under the table, a senior U.S. official recalls awaiting instructions on which way to vote, even as the meeting was finally underway. At 10:35 p.m. on March 31, 2005, UN Security Council Resolution 1593, referring Darfur to the ICC, was passed with 11 votes for, none against, and 4 abstentions—Algeria, Brazil, China, and the United States.[50]

At a press briefing the next morning, the Under-Secretary of State Nicholas Burns provided an insightful summary of the abstention decision: "I think that what the Secretary has been able to achieve here is indicative of the improved working relations that we have under her tenure with Europe in general and with other members of the Security Council. I think you all know she's been to Europe twice since she became Secretary of State."[51]

CHECKING OFF JUSTICE

The decision to refer Darfur to the ICC was to have far greater repercussions than anyone in the U.S. government realized at the time. As one U.S. official explained to me, "We were quite relieved when it went to the ICC. It meant we had set accountability off on a track of its own."[52] The referral was seen as an end, rather than as a beginning. "I think they just did it to get the issue off their backs," reflects the head of UN peacekeeping. "You know—let's do something. Let's send the justice cavalry in."[53]

With the "justice box" checked, the United States went straight back to its core policy priorities on Sudan. The very next month, the CIA flew the head of Sudanese intelligence, Salah Gosh, on a private jet to its headquarters in Langley, Virginia. Sudan might be under scrutiny from the ICC, but that didn't stop the CIA from cozying up to their officials to try and extract counterterrorism information.[54]

Rather than a heroic story of Darfur advocates pushing the U.S. government to do something that was against its stated interests,[55] the referral of Darfur to the ICC should be memorialized as an example of effective and coordinated negotiating by European diplomats. On the surface it seemed the odds were heavily stacked against the United States abstaining. As the French and British understood, however, the international political costs to the Bush administration, whose human rights credentials were already under attack, would be enormous if they were seen to support impunity in a situation that they, and they alone, had called genocide.

Many within the U.S. administration also felt that the costs of a veto were too high for U.S.-European relations to bear. But rather than opt immediately for an abstention, the State Department put masses of energy into keeping the ICC off the agenda. The skill of the French and the British was to unify with other countries on the Security Council to ensure not only that the ICC was on the agenda, but that it was the only accountability option that made it into a resolution. Getting a diverse set of countries to support this approach seems to have been possible because of the responsibility those countries felt, as members of the ICC, to support the court. Only through their unity were they able to force the United States into a choice between abstaining from an ICC referral or impunity.

The United States gained a significant amount of political capital both internationally and among Darfur advocates for letting the Darfur issue go to the ICC. In this, they got more credit than they deserved. As the Europeans understood, Powell's genocide determination effectively constrained the Americans from vetoing the referral; legally and politically the first state in history to invoke the Genocide Convention could hardly veto a resolution designed to punish the perpetrators. Moreover, with the jurisdiction clause, the United States did not have to give up any policy objection to the ICC; it simply had to hold its nose on its in-principle objection to the court. In addition, the only alternative it had proposed—a Sudan tribunal—would have cost the United States millions of dollars. Instead, they got the cost-free option of the ICC.

Contrary to conventional wisdom, the growing Darfur movement was not a significant part of this decision. Although some Darfur advocates voiced their support, the most influential advocates were those based in Africa. Stateside, it was the silence of the court's traditional opponents in congress that was the most important signal. Had Secretary Rice felt less in need of building relations with Europe, then the domestic politics might have been more significant. But at such a challenging time in trans-Atlantic relations, and with a host of other issues lined up for Rice to do battle with the Europeans over, the ICC ended up being a low-cost way for the United States to gain some diplomatic capital.

CHAPTER 6

WHO WILL PROVIDE PROTECTION?

Throughout 2003, when Darfuris were so in need of protection, the State Department persisted in viewing Darfur as a crisis to be addressed in primarily humanitarian terms, lest it disrupt the north-south peace negotiations. But by 2005, with the signing of the north-south peace agreement out of the way, those most concerned about Darfur in the White House had shifted their focus to the question of who would protect Darfuris. It was Powell's genocide determination, and the shadow of Rwanda, looming large.

"You have different policies for different problems," says one of President Bush's senior advisers. "This was the mistake of Rwanda. People looked at it as a civil war, and so the policy to deal with a civil war is a peace agreement.... This was not the case in Darfur. By the U.S. saying it is genocide, it was a flipping of the policy priorities. If it's genocide, you prioritize security over politics."[1] Although it is true that different problems require different policies, this approach assumes all genocides are the same problem with respect to why they are undertaken and how they can be brought to an end. The assumption is a questionable one,[2] and the roots of its uncertainty stretch back decades to an unresolved debate among those who actually drafted the Genocide Convention.[3]

Their debate was over how to define genocide with respect to motive and intent. To put this in more accessible terms: Someone can be charged with murder for intending to kill a person (and actually doing so), even though their motive for the killing was to claim the victim's life insurance. Killing was the means to another end, but the crime is still murder. While everyone agrees that for genocide to be committed, the intent of the perpetrator must be to destroy the group, views differ on whether or not the perpetrator must be motivated solely by the desire to destroy the group or if other motives may be in play.[4] Put differently, if the perpetrator's motive was a desire to defeat an insurgency, is the crime still genocide?

One set of the drafters of the Genocide Convention (the "single intent/ motive" group) believed that for a crime to be labeled genocide, motive and intent had to be the same, namely, to destroy the group. Others (the "mixed intent/motive" group) argued that as long as the intent was to destroy the group, the crime was genocide regardless of the motive. In the end, neither group won the debate; the issue remained unresolved.[5]

Today, those who have different views on how genocides end are rarely aware of these early origins of their disagreement. Those who believe genocide can only end with the overthrow of the perpetrator (or the completion of the group's destruction) tend to be those who use "essentialist" genocides like the Holocaust or Rwanda as their schema for what genocide looks like, a position that resonates with the single intent/motive approach. Given the association with these most well-known genocides, this is the view the general public tends to take as well. Others, myself included, who are open to believing that there are several ways that genocide can end generally have a larger range of scenarios in mind, including "instrumentalist" genocides such as those in southern Sudan and Guatemala, which fit with the mixed intent/ motive approach.[6] This seemingly obscure legal debate has serious policy implications.

If you believe that a regime may be conducting genocide as a means to an end, such as destroying the group to defeat an insurgency, then the possibility exists that the regime can be pressured to stop destroying the group if the regime can be convinced either that there is an alternative means to reach its end goal or that the cost of continuing to pursue genocide outweighs the value of its end goal. If, however, the end goal is the destruction of the group and nothing else, then you lose hope of convincing the regime to stop. In the latter case, once genocide begins, the perpetrator will likely continue to destroy others until he is removed from power (or until he actually succeeds in destroying the group). This is what leads to the view that if it is genocide, you must prioritize security over politics. There is no point engaging in politics—incentives and pressures—if the perpetrators cannot be convinced to change their behavior. Unless you overthrow the genocidal regime, the only option you have is to try to protect the group until someone else overthrows the regime. Outside of government, this view that protection should be prioritized over politics was prevalent among Darfur advocates.

AT THE END OF summer 2005, Sam Bell, Mark Hanis, and two others who had just graduated college with them pooled their resources to rent a rundown apartment in Washington, D.C., taking turns who got to sleep on the couch and who got the floor. Although they were developing their organizational model to incorporate the broader goal of building a permanent constituency against genocide—calling themselves the Genocide Intervention Network, or GI-Net for short—they retained the objective of fund-raising for AMIS peacekeepers.

GI-Net's idea of direct support to AMIS was controversial, and the Save Darfur Coalition would not sign on to support their fund-raising. In part, this was a fear of the unknown. The idea was new and untested. Private funding for a military operation also raised the dreaded specter of mercenaries. The first person to take GI-Net's idea of funding AMIS seriously was Gayle Smith. Smith had two decades experience in Africa and had been the senior director of African Affairs in Clinton's National Security Council. After a steady stream of rejections to their proposal, Smith provided the first positive response. "Let's make this happen!" she had e-mailed them when they were still students on the Swarthmore campus.[7]

Since then, they had raised $300,000 to support AMIS. But they soon realized that fund-raising had been the easy part. Smith had initially assured them that she could organize to put the funds to good use. But as months rolled by and the money was still sitting in their U.S. account, the GI-Net team started to worry. After numerous overseas phone conversations, leading precisely nowhere, they decided the only way to make progress was through a face-to-face meeting.

Starting to make his way up the five-story walk-up that was the AU headquarters in Addis Ababa, Sam Bell began to get a fuller appreciation of the logistical challenges the AU was facing. "Before I left, I had gone to a meeting with [Robert] Zoellick on the seventh floor of the State Department. It was knock-your-socks-off protocol. Visiting the AU headquarters was the exact opposite. Their people were sitting on lawn furniture. There was nowhere to wait. It just felt like chaos."

Bell was told that the quickest way to dispense the money was to work through one of the AU's implementing partners, who in turn suggested the funds be used to buy computers for every displaced camp to record incidents of sexual assault. Bell recalls, "We didn't want to *record* assaults; we wanted to *stop* them." However, GI-Net needed to give away the money they had raised somehow, and so in the end a compromise was reached. They funded African Humanitarian Action to support patrols that would protect displaced women as they left the camps to collect firewood, a time when they were at the greatest risk of being raped.

After that, GI-Net gave up on the idea of working directly with the AU. "Part of it was totally understandable. They had 12 guys trying to coordinate a 7,000-person mission. They were maxed out. We had $300K to offer, and it was a billion dollar project. So maybe it was the right call for them," says Bell.

AMIS FAILING

"The AU is not up to the task. People will continue to die." This was the message in the first cable that former U.S. Lt. Col. Ronald Capps recalls sending from Darfur back to Washington. After retiring from active duty in October 2004, Capps had been sent by the State Department to Darfur to work with AMIS. "I had just come from Iraq. This was so much bigger, and there were only 800 of them [AMIS troops],"[8] Capps explains.

The AU also realized that the number of troops they had first deployed was insufficient to deal with the situation.[9] At the AU's Peace and Security meeting on October 20, 2004, they had authorized an increase in the number of military personnel to 2,314.[10] By April 2005 they had upped the authorization to 7,731 troops.[11] In practice however, AMIS would not reach this number for another year, and even then, an even distribution of troops only equated to one soldier per 25 square miles. It was the equivalent of having one police officer for all of Manhattan.

If there was anyone who knew about the consequences of underresourced peacekeeping, it was the AMIS deputy force commander, Rwandan general Jean Bosco Kazura. He had been in the Tutsi-led rebel force that had entered Rwanda in 1994 to finally stop the killing of their people as the rest of the world stood by. When I met Kazura after he returned from Darfur, I asked what his AMIS troops had needed but did not have. He rephrased: "The question should be, what did we have?" Kazura's mission in Darfur was an exercise in frustration, made all the more intense by his personal background. Recalling one of the many Janjaweed attacks, Kazura said, "It took us seven hours to get there. By the time we arrived all we could do was help them to bury 20 dead bodies." Nevertheless, he and his troops continued to try and do what they could. "I got us to go with the APCs [armored personnel carriers] from Fasher to Shangil Tobay, so we could at least show the population that we were around. When we arrived, they were very happy...but all I could think was, if we are actually attacked, I don't know what we will do."[12]

Throughout 2005 advocates persisted in arguing that AMIS would be capable of protecting civilians if only they had more resources. During the August congressional recess, GI-Net ran a "Genocide Hits Home" campaign, which encouraged constituents to visit their representatives in their home districts and demand they help AMIS protect more people.[13] For a Day of Action for Darfur in September 2005, the Save Darfur Coalition provided citizen activists with a PowerPoint presentation to use in their local communities. The attached script stated that for AMIS to be effective they needed "a stronger civilian protection mandate, a major increase in the number of troops on the ground, and a much larger logistical and monetary contribution from the UN, the EU, and NATO."[14]

The external pressure from advocates to boost the size of AMIS influenced discussions inside government, although not without some unintended consequences. As one midlevel State Department official describes it, "It turned into a game about numbers—how many troops can we deploy? What gets lost is the nuance—like if we don't have the ten right people in headquarters the whole thing will fall apart."[15] But for those under political pressure, airlifting in an additional 400 AMIS troops, with pictures to show for it,[16] was a better way to manage advocacy demands than coming out with a statement that they were working to improve AMIS management techniques. "Those of us working closest to the AU realized that you could expand ten times over and they still wouldn't have the capacity," the same official recalls. "You can't run a peacekeeping operation on voluntary contributions and have your partners do all the logistics for you. We knew we couldn't solve it with more money or more personnel. But the politicos all pushed for an expansion of AMIS throughout 2005."[17]

By late 2005 it was clear that the merits of their early deployment notwithstanding, AMIS could not protect civilians. Indeed, they were increasingly unable to protect themselves. In September an AMIS patrol went to investigate an attack carried out in Hafara, North Darfur[18]; ten civilians had been killed by Janjaweed militias, and as word spread about the attack, more than 4,000 frightened people fled the area.[19] But on their way to investigate, the patrol fell prey to Janjaweed, and three of them were shot.[20] If AMIS forces could not even keep themselves safe, how could they protect others? And if AMIS was not going to protect civilians, who would?

RULING OUT U.S. FORCE

"We looked at U.S. military options," Bush's National Security Adviser Stephen Hadley tells me, before quickly moving to explain how unenthusiastic the Pentagon was about the idea.[21] As Assistant Secretary for African Affairs Jendayi Frazer remembers it, "[Officials at the Department of] Defense weren't keen, so they would come up with these ridiculous estimates like 'you need 120,000 troops to succeed.' Then of course they would say, 'Well, we don't have that because of Iraq.'"[22]

The possibility of deploying a small number of U.S. troops was also ruled out with the argument, made by Defense Secretary Donald Rumsfeld, that if even a handful of "our boys" got into harm's way, a larger number would then be needed to go in and rescue them.[23] It was the same argument that Clinton administration officials had used to justify not sending U.S. troops into Rwanda during the 1994 genocide. But this time Defense officials didn't have to intimate that an African conflict was not worth risking American lives over. Instead, Iraq was used to explain that U.S capacity would simply be unavailable should the need arise. In fact, almost everyone I interviewed on this placed the obstacles generated by U.S. military capacity being stretched in Iraq and Afghanistan at the forefront of their responses.

There were only two people who told me outright that capacity was not the real issue. One was a senior Defense Department official, who patiently explained the Pentagon's contingency planning process in which military planners routinely sketch out estimates of what would be required if the president directed them to deploy in a particular setting. Consistent with this routine, planners inside the Pentagon had assessed what would be required to address the situation in Darfur.

In the summer of 2004 the State Department asked the Pentagon for an estimate of what it would take to secure the displaced camps inside Darfur. Based on the 40 main camps in existence at the time, and assuming they were to provide round-the-clock mobile security, the Pentagon estimated that they would need 35,000 U.S. troops. But this was the estimate for a consensual deployment. With many in al-Bashir's regime suspecting that what the U.S. congress really wanted was regime change in Sudan, there was no way that Khartoum would authorize a U.S. deployment. And the calculation for a nonconsensual deployment was very different.

The Pentagon estimated that there were about 30,000 Sudanese Army troops in Darfur, not including the Janjaweed. Standard planning assumptions factor in that a 3:1 ratio of intervening to opposing forces is needed at the start of a nonconsensual deployment for it to have a chance of success. "You may be able to lower that number later, but you have to show your strength to start," the Defense official explained. On this basis, the total figure required would be near the 120,000 troop estimate that Frazer found so preposterous. However, U.S. commitments in Iraq and Afghanistan would not have served as an absolute bar on moving ahead with a Darfur deployment if that is what the president had instructed the military to do. "It would have meant taking resources from elsewhere. So for us, institutionally, it was a relief [not to be asked to deploy to Darfur], a weight off the nation in terms of sweat and blood. But we were ready to take that step if that is the step we were told to take."[24]

The other person who believed that capacity was not the real issue was John Bolton, who was the U.S. ambassador to the UN at the time: "We had the capacity. The issue was that we had a war in two Islamic countries and how many dead Americans can you have at any given time?"[25] As evident in banners reading "Out of Iraq and Into Darfur" displayed on the fringes of some advocacy events, there are those who would argue that if

American soldiers were to be risking their lives anywhere, better in Darfur than Iraq. In practice, however, no member of the Save Darfur Coalition actually called for the deployment of U.S. troops. In some cases, this was because they accepted the conventional wisdom that the United States did not have the capacity, absorbing the superficial constraints of the situation even more readily than those inside government. But in other cases, the decision not to call for U.S. boots on the ground arose from an assessment of efficacy. "The argument against sending in U.S. troops was summed up for me in three words," says David Rubenstein: "And then what?"

It was a question the military themselves were asking. As Hadley explains it, the military opposed a Darfur deployment "not because they weren't sympathetic and not because they wouldn't have done it if the president had ordered it, but because it looked like a mission without an end."

The argument about capacity masked one of two nonexclusive possibilities: either the protection of Darfuris was not enough of a U.S. priority to take the risks involved in redeploying resources from elsewhere and/or those responsible did not think that the deployment of U.S. troops would be effective. According to Hadley, the president's decision not to order a U.S. deployment was made on the basis of efficacy. "President Bush was hearing from our allies in the region that if the U.S. deployed it would be a lightning rod for al-Qaeda...they didn't like the idea of another U.S. intervention in another Muslim country." As the National Security Council's director of strategic planning recalls it, "While the president wanted to do more, he knew that there wasn't a viable and sustainable military option."[26]

The positions of those who felt that a U.S. deployment would inflame rather than calm the situation and those who thought that more American lives should not be sacrificed in another Muslim country led to the same outcome. A U.S. deployment was never seriously mapped out. "There was a resistance to even do planning for fear that if you planned you might be asked to execute the plan," explains one of the president's policy advisors.[27] "President Bush very reluctantly decided not to have the U.S. go in," says Hadley. Bush's next idea was to have NATO intervene.

RULING OUT NATO

Fellow staffers took to calling Michael Gerson "the conscience of the White House." Mostly they meant it in a good way. When others started calling him "the Sudan desk officer," they were not being quite so charitable. As Bush's first-term speechwriter, who coined the infamous phrase "axis of evil," Gerson was known for having a particularly close relationship with the president. Like Bush, he was a deeply committed evangelical Christian, and they shared a common worldview. But when Bush's second term approached,

Gerson had thoughts of resigning. "I wasn't getting to focus on any issues I cared about," he recalls. Rather than lose him, Bush instructed Gerson to find a new head of speechwriting and to move into the chief-of-staff's office. When Gerson drew up a wish list of issues he wanted to work on, Darfur was on it. Gerson began what he calls "stoking the interest" the president had on Darfur. "I had the ability to put things in his inbox. So I would send him articles...a few harsh ones, attacking his policy." And as Gerson recalls it, Bush would get upset.

One of the articles that particularly distressed the president was ostensibly a book review. The review, written by Nicholas Kristof and entitled *Genocide in Slow Motion*, accused Bush of having only a passing interest in Darfur.[28] After reading the article, the president called Gerson into the Oval Office. "I just want you to know what I'm doing on this," he told Gerson, before explaining that he wanted NATO to take a lead role in Darfur.[29] NATO had been airlifting AMIS troops into Darfur since July 2005.[30] But rattled by Kristof's public shaming, Bush's desire to "do something" led him to see if NATO could do more.

A couple of weeks later, Bush let this aspiration for Darfur policy come through publicly without having first told the rest of his staff, let alone secured any institutional support. Speaking to a town hall meeting in Florida, he told his audience that a UN force was needed, "[B]ut it's going to require a—I think a NATO stewardship, planning, facilitating, organizing, probably double the number of peacekeepers that are there now, in order to start bringing some sense of security."[31]

The press covering the event operated on a not-unreasonable belief that if the president of the United States spoke publicly about NATO taking a lead role in Darfur, he was signaling an "American commitment" to the approach.[32] They were not the only ones. One of the Save Darfur staff, Alex Meixner, remembers the day vividly. "Someone came running into my office—'So are we done? Can we pop the corks now?'" It was a naive reaction but, as Meixner observed, out of the entire staff only he and Rubenstein were older than 23 at the time.[33]

Members of the Bush administration were considerably less enthused. Defense Secretary Donald Rumsfeld called John Bolton to his office. "We all kept hearing things from the White House—really from Mike Gerson—about what the president cared about and would do," says Bolton. "Rumsfeld called me in just to assure me that whatever little voice of morality there was in the White House, the president's feet at least were on the ground."[34]

"Was Darfur a serious U.S. national interest?" I asked Bolton. "No," he answered, "but that doesn't mean it's not important. It just means that the UN is the appropriate venue through which to deal with it."[35] In theory he is right. The UN should be able to take up operations that serve the common good but are not enough of an interest for any single country to take the lead on. Bolton, however, has also made a career out of decrying the UN's ability do anything well.

After his off-the-cuff comments in Florida, Bush got on the phone to the head of NATO, but they had absolutely no interest in expanding their involvement.[36] Darfur had the misfortune of falling in the midst of growing tensions between the EU defense forces and NATO over their respective areas of engagement.[37] The result was a bureaucratic stalemate, and given the already tense relationship that the Bush administration had with the Europeans over Iraq, the United States didn't have the political capital to push through the impasse. "Only when it became clear that NATO was not a live option did we realize you were left with the UN," recalls Gerson.

THE BOTTOM LINE

As 2005 progressed, the countries that funded AMIS (United States, United Kingdom, Norway, Netherlands, France, and Canada) had grown tired of footing the bill for an operation that was increasingly seen as a failure.[38] An assessment scheduled for December 2005 to define the challenges faced by AMIS served as the perfect vehicle for the donor countries to signal that AMIS' time was up. The report's passive bureaucratic language belied the political sensitivity of its recommendation that, due to the "increasingly complex" requirements put upon AMIS, "consideration be given to how an international presence can be sustained in Darfur in 2006 and beyond... cognizant of the uncertainty of sustaining funding based on a system of voluntary contribution."[39] In plain English, the verdict was that AMIS was out of its depth, and its funders could not, or would not, guarantee its financial future. They were looking to share the burden through the UN peacekeeping budget's assessed contributions scheme, which all members of the UN pay into.

While the words "United Nations" are nowhere to be found in the report's conclusion, it was clear to an informed reader that the UN is where salvation was being sought. With the recommendation on UN financing for regional organizations never adopted, the UN was unable to provide funds to AMIS through the UN's assessed contributions scheme. As a result, sharing the financial burden across all UN members necessitated a move to a UN deployment.[40]

At the AU Peace and Security Council meeting in January 2006, AU chair, then the president of Mali, Alpha Konare, expressed the AU's support, "in principle, to a transition from AMIS to a UN operation."[41] During the meeting, Konare articulated the driving factor behind the announcement. At an operating cost of $17 million per month, "the funds received so far... are almost exhausted. At present, no commitment has been made by partners for the funding of the mission beyond March 2006."[42]

Unknown to advocates and journalists at the time, Konare's agreement to the transition was not voluntary. The week before the meeting, those funding AMIS, the United States key among them, had informed Konare that there would be no funding beyond March unless AMIS began handing over the peacekeeping operation to the UN.[43] The funders' strong-arm tactics had been successful to the extent that they had secured an AU statement supporting a transition. But an agreement obtained this way was open to sabotage.

The next month, Konare went to Khartoum to meet with President al-Bashir.[44] Frustrated that the AU was being pushed into a UN transition when, in his view, AMIS would be perfectly capable if they were just given the resources they needed, Konare told al-Bashir his hand had been forced.[45] Al-Bashir described his understanding of the situation after meeting with Konare: "Donors insisted that the AU should agree to transfer the AMIS mandate in Darfur to the UN, as well as endorse the participation of troops from outside the African continent in the operation. They said that such arrangements were the only way to convince public opinion in their respective countries of the feasibility of financing peacekeeping operations in Darfur. This was how donors pressured Konare to accept the transition...."[46]

Konare's reluctance to accept a transition didn't reflect the position of the AMIS commander General Kazura. He felt that the primary issue was to improve the capacity of the forces on the ground, and that whether that was under the banner of AMIS or the UN was irrelevant: "Think about it from the perspective of a peasant in west Darfur," said Kazura. "Do you think he cares whether it is AU or UN? No—all he cares about is whether they are capable of protection."[47]

But for Konare, Darfur remained the test case for the nascent AU to prove itself. With Konare's position clear, al-Bashir knew that he had room to maneuver. Less than a week after their meeting, he called a special session of the Sudanese Parliament, which decided that Sudan would "refuse all attempts to transfer the African Union forces' mission in Darfur to forces from the United Nations...."[48] By the end of February 2006 al-Bashir had ratcheted up the rhetoric further, stating that Darfur would be a "graveyard" for any UN forces coming into the area.[49]

UN ON THE AGENDA

It was against this backdrop in early 2006 that the U.S. government and advocates alike began putting their utmost into getting the UN deployed to Darfur. The Save Darfur Coalition launched a Million Voices campaign, involving the collation of uniformly worded postcards from citizen advocates across the country. The postcards urged President Bush to support "a stronger multinational force to protect the civilians of Darfur." Just as with the AMIS assessment report, the words "United Nations" were not specified, but there was broad consensus that this was the multinational force that advocates were asking for.

The Million Voices campaign was really the first example of the Save Darfur Coalition organizing a sizable push on the executive branch of the U.S. government. Since each congressperson responds to a circumscribed district, with a modicum of organization it is relatively easy to pull together enough constituents in a given district to influence that district's representative. But the executive branch, the most critical part of government on a foreign policy issue like Darfur, represents the entire country, and so the impact of a constituency is diluted. The postcards were a way around this problem. People of all ages wrote to the president. "I wake up every morning, go to school, and come home to a warm house and warm food...all the while these families in Darfur are being torn apart," wrote a teenager in Ohio. "I may not know everything about Sudan and the genocide, but I know people need our help," wrote a schoolteacher from Maine.[50]

The postcard campaign was led by Gloria White-Hammond. By the middle of 2005 leaders within the Save Darfur Coalition started to realize they had alienated southern Sudan advocates and began to seek their inclusion. Save Darfur cofounder Ruth Messinger had heard about "this inspirational pastor" from Boston and decided that White-Hammond was exactly the kind of person Save Darfur needed. "She had connections to all the communities that we didn't," recalls Messinger.[51]

Messinger invited White-Hammond to a Save Darfur planning meeting in Washington, D.C., and literally as they were walking into the meeting room told her that she intended to nominate her to chair the upcoming campaign. White-Hammond looked around at a room of people she didn't know and panicked. She wrote Messinger a note on the back of a slip of paper saying she wasn't sure she could do it. But by the end of the meeting her nomination had been accepted.

After the meeting, White-Hammond stipulated two conditions that would have to be met for her to come on board. "Number one was to acknowledge that the south had faced their own genocide, which meant we could involve southerners and the Christian Right.... Number two was that we refrain from 'Bush-bashing.'" With those conditions agreed, she joined the Save Darfur Coalition as national chairperson of the Million Voices campaign.

Integral to the campaign were nationwide rallies planned for April 30, 2006, with the biggest event planned for Washington. Having taken six months leave from her medical clinic to work on the campaign, White-Hammond spent a couple of days a week at the Save Darfur office in Washington working to build numbers for the rally. "It was frustrating because it was white men doing this. In many ways I felt marginalized," she says, reflecting on her initial encounters with the coalition. "They didn't know me, so they assumed I didn't have much to say. It was very interesting being a black woman in this space."

White-Hammond knew that as much as Save Darfur worked to bus groups in from around the country for the rally, the bulk of the crowd would come from the local D.C. area, which, as she puts it, "is chocolate city, and they ain't gonna be reading the ads in the *Washington Post*." She wanted to get an ad in a black church bulletin, but it would cost $1,000. "When I asked Dave [Rubenstein] he said, 'A thousand dollars sounds like a lot.' I said, 'You know what? I'll go and get my own money.'" White-Hammond called Pam Omidyar, who had reached out to her earlier in the year, and explained the issue, securing significantly more than she needed to place the ad.

THERE IS A WIDESPREAD belief that the growing Darfur advocacy movement led the charge for getting UN troops on the ground in Darfur. But advocates actually put considerable time and energy into boosting the resources of AMIS before finally shifting their focus toward the UN in early 2006. For advocates, the shift to the UN was driven by reports that AMIS was not only unable to protect Darfuris but was increasingly unable to protect itself. The growing advocacy outcry for a transition to the UN suited the financial concerns that the United States and other Western governments had about continuing to fund a failing AMIS force. The need for a UN transition also conformed with the view of AMIS peacekeepers, if not their political leadership, that they were out of their depth. The net result was that the first quarter of 2006 saw an alignment of those inside and outside the U.S. government, albeit motivated by somewhat different interests, to get the UN to deploy to Darfur. But none of these actors was really prepared for what it would take to move a UN deployment from idea to implementation. Much like handing off justice to the ICC, delegating protection to the UN was another form of outsourcing. In neither case did most of the Americans involved appreciate that they would not be able to divorce their own action, or inaction, from the success or failure of these international institutions.

CHAPTER 7

WHO WILL PUSH FOR PEACE?

S am Bell was with his mom and sister, heading down the crowded esca-
lators of the D.C. Metro system, when he first heard voices chanting
"Save Darfur!" It seemed as though Washington's entire public trans-
port system was overrun with people decked out in green wristbands. But
what struck Bell is that he didn't know the people who were chanting. "That
was big. At a lot of the smaller events, I would know many if not most of the
dozens or hundreds of people who would show up," he recalls.

Resurfacing from the underground Metro system in the bright sun of a
late April morning, Bell felt a bit surreal when he saw tens of thousands of
people streaming onto the Washington Mall. As the glistening white dome
of the Capitol came into sight, his mind flashed back to a planning call in
December 2005, when it was just a couple of people on the phone talking
about trying to organize a rally. Here, just a few months later, thousands
gathered on the mall. The crowds were replicated in 29 different locations
across the country.[1]

As Bell and his family took up positions in the crowd, David Rubenstein
appeared onstage. Wearing a sweat-soaked SAVE DARFUR t-shirt, looking both
exhausted and elated in the extreme, he thanked those who had helped pull
together the massive turnout. What followed was a high-profile lineup of
religious leaders, politicians, human rights advocates, and celebrities.

The selection of speakers had been controversial. U.S.-based members of
the Darfur Consortium received complaints from Darfuris in the diaspora
that they weren't being included.[2] Gloria White-Hammond had also been
frustrated at the lack of outreach to Darfuris, let alone southern Sudanese.
"It was very much the white American way," she says. "The idea you would
start a movement to 'save' anybody, and then not have the movement led by
those people. How presumptuous. Imagine a civil rights movement without

African Americans in leadership, or a women's movement without women." She remembers watching a group of southern Sudanese enter the Mall and "just feeling so gratified to see so many of them there after they had been feeling alienated." She ran to join them, walking alongside the group as they took their place in the crowd.

Omer Ismail arrived backstage with his wife and children shortly before Barack Obama, a man very few then imagined would soon be responsible for U.S. policy on Darfur, was scheduled to speak. When Ismail and his family were introduced to then-Senator Obama, Ismail's nine-year-old daughter, Laila, piped up: "If I could vote, I would vote for you to be president!" Senator Obama smiled, saying he hadn't decided yet if he would run. Obama went onstage to give a characteristically stirring speech. "Silence, acquiescence, paralysis in the face of genocide is wrong," he told the crowd.

The day was memorable for Ismail in many ways. After years of struggling to make what was happening in Darfur salient to a U.S. audience, the sight of thousands of ordinary Americans turning up to show their support for Darfur was validating. "People like us can be believable, and people can see we are like them, and we have families to protect."

Ismail walked onto the stage alongside GI-Net's original supporter, Gayle Smith, as well as *A Problem from Hell*" author, Samantha Power, and the International Crisis Group's senior adviser, John Prendergast. Ismail hadn't been assigned a speaking role but says that standing up there, he felt a sense of solidarity with the massive crowd he looked at. "Everyone was coming together to say no to these crimes.... I felt that day that the whole world was standing by our side, and the Darfur problem had reached the eyes and ears of the whole world."

White-Hammond eventually headed backstage as well. She had been assigned to speak toward the end of the program and had asked a couple of Sudanese children to join her onstage. Though she was nervous, she recalls that "I was at least trying to be cool for them." Reaching the microphone, she made the kind of electrifying speech that only those with years at the pulpit can carry off, calling for peace and justice to reign throughout all of Sudan. All she remembers, though, is that after the stress of trying to ensure people actually turned out for the rally, she looked at the size of the crowd and thought, "Oh My God—it really worked."

Standing in the midst of the crowd, Bell was also feeling awed by the size of the turnout that he had helped to create. "I had some moments when I cringed because speakers were off message or got something wrong. But overall I was just really proud that this thing we had said—that Americans really care—was actually true," he says. "There are plenty of times when you are saying the words but maybe there's a seed of doubt in your mind. Do people actually care about this? The image of those folks on the Mall proved to me that from here on out enough Americans do give a shit in general and will give a shit for a particular cause."

MEANWHILE IN ABUJA

For three years, Sudanese officials had been meeting with Darfuri rebel leaders in the Nigerian capital of Abuja, going through the motions of trying to assemble a peace deal even as Darfur continued to burn. Sponsored by the African Union and Arab League, the talks had led nowhere: The rebel leaders had diminishing control over their people on the ground, and the Sudanese government had zero interest in genuine compromise. Indeed, Hussien Adam, the local Sudanese government official who had worked so hard to get international aid flowing to the displaced, resigned soon after the talks began, concluding that Khartoum had no real interest in peace or dialogue. "They feared the unification of Darfuris against them—all Darfuris for all Darfur."[3]

Meanwhile, key groups that might have helped bring about stability were purposely excluded: The AU's lead mediator in the peace process, Salim Ahmed Salim, remembers that Arab Darfuris asked to join the negotiations but the mediation team refused them, accepting the claim of the Sudanese government and the rebel groups that this would "racialize" the conflict.[4] It is a decision Salim came to regret: "The Arabs said to us—we are part of the problem and so we have to be part of the solution. They were right."[5]

So for months on end, the rebel leaders enjoyed the perks of endless peace talks—hotel rooms and free meals—without ever being required to say yes to anything. But for a brief two months, that whole dynamic changed, as the U.S. government displayed genuine interest in the nitty gritty details of peace negotiations for Darfur. Pressured by advocates screaming "Save Darfur!" at rallies in Washington and prodded by a president who wanted to "do something" about Darfur, the U.S. government entered the negotiations in a serious way, hopeful that its intervention might pave the way, finally, to the introduction of peacekeeping troops that everybody believed would provide the protection ordinary Darfuris so desperately needed.

Driving the U.S. train was Robert Zoellick, the talented diplomat who had given up a cabinet post to serve as Secretary Rice's deputy and was looking for a foreign policy success for the struggling administration. The day after the big Washington rally, the U.S. State Department announced it was sending Zoellick to Abuja to secure a peace deal for Darfur.

Sending America's top negotiator to broker a peace agreement for a remote region of Africa was not what one would expect in the ordinary course of events. The timing of the announcement, the day after the rallies, generated the conclusion that Zoellick was being sent in response to the advocacy outcry.[6] (Although as Sam Bell remembers, "We were all on the lawn calling for peacekeepers. [A peace agreement] was not at all the policy we were talking about.") But another factor was equally if not more important: Zoellick and other U.S. officials had become increasingly convinced that bringing the peace talks to a successful close might prove the ticket to getting out of the Darfur morass.

By 2006, U.S. officials were firmly convinced that only a robust UN force, not the troubled African Union contingent, could provide adequate civilian protection in Darfur. And for months, UN officials had been telling U.S. officials that the only way they could get UN peacekeepers into Darfur was if they first secured a peace agreement. This was long-time UN theology. Since the end of the Cold War, UN peacekeepers had been increasingly pushed into gray areas where the line between "peacekeeping" and "peace enforcement" becomes blurred. Traditional peacekeeping is designed for a situation in which the parties to the conflict have reached a peace agreement and request that the UN deploy to assist them in maintaining that agreement. By contrast, what UN officials call "peace enforcement" is more akin to what most people think of as a combat situation. UN Security Council members have invariably authorized a peacekeeping operation when what is actually needed is someone to step in and stop the fighting. The cost is paid by civilians on the ground when, as in both Rwanda in 1994 and the Bosnian enclave of Srebrenica in 1995, underresourced peacekeepers are left to represent the international community as bystanders to genocide.[7]

Peacekeeping, as opposed to peace enforcement, requires that there is actually a peace to keep. And in early 2006, there was no peace agreement in sight for Darfur. So the UN Department of Peacekeeping Operations (DPKO) staff had been telling anyone who would listen that they could not deploy peacekeepers unless a peace agreement was in place. The assistant secretary-general of DPKO, Hedi Annabi, kept going to the experts meeting at the Security Council and saying the same thing over and over again until, as one DPKO staffer put it, "the Security Council looked around and said, 'Okay, so who is in charge of a peace agreement? No one? Well, someone go and get one.'"[8] That "someone" was Zoellick.

WASHINGTON TAKES AN INTEREST

Sometimes an image captures a moment in a way that compresses a complex story into a single message. So it was with the January 2005 photo of Vice President Taha and soon-to-be Vice President Garang: beaming smiles on their faces, shaking hands, and holding copies of the signed text of the CPA. Hailed as bringing an end to two decades of war, Taha was anointed the Sudanese government's peacemaker. U.S. State Department officials involved in the CPA negotiations referred to Taha with words like "practical," "reasonable," and "dependable." In the eyes of the U.S. government, Taha was their guy; Taha could deliver.

Taha's rise as a U.S. State Department favorite occurred, not coincidentally, in roughly equal proportion to his demise as a powerful member of the NCP. By the time the CPA was signed, the prevailing view in Khartoum was that Taha had given southern Sudan too many concessions; what the United States viewed as "reasonable," Sudanese hardliners saw as "weak." Al-Bashir had handed the Darfur file to Taha—but this time he wasn't trusted to conduct negotiations alone. He was given joint control with Majzoub al-Khalifa, a staunch Islamist and ruthless negotiator who promised not to give so much away. U.S. State Department officials were notified of this shift in the balance of power by Zoellick's expert of choice, Alex de Waal.

Alex de Waal is now a lecturer at Harvard. But in the 1980s, he was a 20-something Oxford doctoral student of Darfur. Fluent in Arabic, he had a decades-long history with the region that made him an anomaly among the outsiders scrambling to become overnight experts on Darfur. As U.S. media, advocacy, and government energy focused on getting a transition from AMIS to the UN, de Waal was living out of a suitcase in Abuja's less-than-stellar Chida Hotel, assisting the AU with its negotiations.

Each morning de Waal would take breakfast in the hotel's dining room, which had become a prime venue for the sort of informal exchanges of information necessary to oil any long negotiation process. On one such morning in late January 2006, he ate with a member of the Sudanese government delegation, strategically placed in the president's office. This man rarely provided any information directly relevant to the day's negotiations, but, as de Waal recalls, whenever he did provide specific information, it always turned out to be accurate. During the meal that morning, de Waal learned that Vice President Taha no longer had control of the Darfur file.[9]

Later that day, de Waal notified the Americans that their favorite negotiator was no longer in charge. Zoellick e-mailed back, asking how sure de Waal was. "I told him that [the source] was well-placed, spoke directly with Bashir, and had always been reliable in the past."[10] De Waal's monthly report to senior officials at the UN and AU (which also reached the British foreign office and the U.S. State Department including Zoellick himself) summarized Taha's ousting in black and white: "Bashir is now handling Darfur directly with Majzoub al-Khalifa."[11]

Notwithstanding this information, Zoellick retained his faith in Taha, meeting him in Brussels in March 2006 to raise the issue of a transition from AMIS to the UN, which was still the U.S. government's "first priority" on Darfur.[12] After the meeting, Zoellick was upbeat: "I noticed that Vice President Taha said...the government didn't necessarily object to a UN mission. They were trying to relate it to the Abuja peace process."[13] Zoellick says that, although Taha made no "specific promise" to him that if a Darfur peace agreement was forthcoming Sudan would accept UN troops, Taha's position was "forward-leaning."[14] Jendayi Frazer, who was the assistant secretary for African Affairs at the State Department, is more direct: "Taha told Zoellick on the phone that if we got a peace agreement then we could have UN forces in Darfur. I know because I was listening to the conversation."[15]

The truth is that the Sudanese government had no intention of living up to this representation. Every statement out of Khartoum showed opposition to a UN force. What then accounted for Khartoum's interest in getting a peace agreement signed? It seems that key NCP members believed that a Darfur peace agreement was their ticket to normalization of relations with the United States.[16] As President al-Bashir recalls it, the former U.S. envoy, John Danforth, promised to have "the sanctions on Sudan lifted and relations between the two countries normalized immediately following the signing of the Comprehensive Peace Agreement."[17] But once the CPA was signed, Bush had maintained the sanctions, saying that normalization could not occur while atrocities were being committed in Darfur.[18] Zoellick says that when he took over the Darfur file he did not promise normalization, but told the Sudanese that "the path to improved or better [...] relations with the United States would depend on peace in Darfur."[19] Al-Bashir meanwhile claims Zoellick promised the Sudanese that by signing a peace agreement on Darfur his government would finally get the normalization with the United States that he had expected for signing the CPA.[20] "Sudanese attach great importance to normalization with the U.S. And it opens the doors to everything else—the World Bank, the IMF," the AU's lead mediator, Salim Ahmed Salim, told me. "Khartoum is often very very difficult—but they are not stupid."[21]

Perhaps only clear in hindsight, a rare confluence of interests existed in early 2006 between the U.S. and Sudanese governments to reach a peace agreement for Darfur. But the two governments were motivated by different factors, and in neither case was the peace agreement seen as an end in itself. It was a recipe for failure and disappointment on both sides: Khartoum had no interest in a strong civilian protection force in Darfur, and U.S. advocates would not stand by and let Washington normalize relations with a genocidal regime. More importantly, railroading the rebels into an agreement simply in order to get a signed piece of paper was unlikely to provide the foundations of a sustainable peace.

At least one person in the U.S. government saw the reality clearly. Ron Capps, the former U.S. lieutenant colonel who was then entering the sixth month of his second rotation in Darfur for the State Department, was worried about the reports he was getting from Abuja. He believed that by pressuring the parties to reach an agreement, U.S. policy was heading in the wrong direction. But he was struggling to have his views heard, so he decided to draft a dissent channel letter. Created by the U.S. State Department in 1971 in the context of the Vietnam War, the dissent channel's purpose is to allow U.S. foreign service officers to express their dissenting views on substantive matters of foreign policy to those at the top of the policymaking process after all other avenues had been exhausted.[22]

Out of courtesy, Capps let the U.S. chargé d'affaires in Sudan, Galluci's successor, Cameron Hume, know that he was writing a dissent channel cable. As Capps recalls it, "Cameron said, 'Great, I support the dissent channel but here's what you should know: A total of seven people will ever see it.'" Hume then proposed the alternatives of "jointly writing something neither of us are happy with" or for Capps to write it on his own, but for Hume to add a paragraph at the beginning and send it through the front channel, ensuring it would receive a wider audience. Capps chose the latter. "Cameron wrote something that basically said, please pay attention to this. He listed the reasons why I knew what I was talking about and said, 'I benefit from his counsel even if I don't endorse his conclusions,' which I thought was a nice way of saying that he agreed with me but couldn't say so," says Capps.[23]

The predictions contained in Capps' memo, which he says went "to everyone—Secretary of State, Policy, African Affairs, Sudan Programs...,"[24] show an eerie prescience. Capps observed that "under enormous pressure from the international community," the parties in Abuja were getting close to some sort of agreement, but that such an agreement would not help stop the violence in Darfur. The reasons for his skepticism included the splintering of the rebel groups, that Darfur's Arabs were not represented in the negotiations, and that the conflict was already spreading across the border into Chad. "United Nations planners have said privately that their worst-case scenario is one where a force arrives to keep a peace that neither party to the conflict supports or wants enforced. Unfortunately, this is also the most likely scenario."[25]

The cable was sent on April 28. That same day, Darfur advocates, who had very little awareness that there even was a negotiation process underway in Abuja, were presenting their views on U.S. policy directly to President Bush.

APRIL 2006 WAS A heady time for the advocates. As Alex Meixner, Save Darfur's U.S. policy coordinator, remembers, "Our political stock was on the rise."[26] The Million Voices campaign was generating postcards from citizens across the country, and the nationwide rallies planned for the end of April were attracting widespread attention. In the buildup to the rallies, Michael Gerson called one of the leaders within the Christian evangelical community, a long-time southern Sudan advocate named Faith McDonnell, to ask who should be invited to a pre-rally meeting with President Bush. On April 28, two days before the rallies, White-Hammond, Rubenstein, and six other advocates, including Simon Deng, a former slave from southern Sudan, and Rabbi David Saperstein, a Jewish community leader, arrived at the White House.

Gerson talked them through the rehearsal that is always done before a meeting with the president; Stephen Hadley, Jendayi Frazer, as well as the National Security Council's director of African Affairs and the presidential aide responsible for liaising with the evangelical community were also in the room. "So this is about Darfur, right?" asked Saperstein, reflecting the tension within the assembled group between those who were southern Sudan advocates and those who were Darfur advocates. They were told that it was about Darfur, but it could be about whatever they wanted. Saperstein proposed that David Rubenstein present the opening remarks. "Since it's about Darfur then Dave should lead off" Saperstein suggested, as White-Hammond quietly whispered to Simon Deng, "Don't worry, we'll make sure we get you on the agenda."

Rubenstein began figuring out how best to make his opening. He had the coalition's talking points prepared but didn't want to just read them out. "I was thinking how to start in a way that would get the president's attention." The rehearsal coordinator pointed to a wooden box on a table in the center of the room. In the middle of the box was a gold coin, and the coordinator instructed the group, "Whatever you do, don't touch that coin. If the president feels like he's in trouble he presses it and the room fills with Secret Service." Rubenstein looked at the coin and decided he would tell the president: If you're in trouble, you have a button on the table you can push and people will come to help. The people of Darfur have been pushing the button for three years, and still no one has come.

With the rehearsal complete, President Bush entered the room and sat down behind his desk. Talking with his glasses in his mouth, the president told the group how earlier in the day he had met with refugees from North Korea and had wept when he heard their stories. He told them that he believed in an Almighty, and that a gift of the Almighty is freedom: "freedom from disease, freedom from despair, and freedom from genocide." He talked of his firm belief that force was necessary in Darfur: "There have to be consequences for murder and rape, which means you have to have a presence on the ground that can use force." He referred to AMIS as a "stand-by-and-watch-it-happen" force that could not protect anyone. However, he also explained the decision he had come to: A unilateral U.S. deployment in Darfur would do more harm than good. Bush then raised the possibility of appointing a special envoy to work on Darfur, but also explained the challenges of State Department sensitivities, stealing a glance at Jendayi Frazer for confirmation.

"He doesn't want to upset people who work for him who think they are doing a good job," Rubenstein wrote in his notes.

The floor was then opened to the advocates. "Mr. President, you have a button on the table—" Rubenstein began. "I push that button when I need coffee," the president interjected, thwarting Rubenstein's opening. He nevertheless managed to deliver the coalition's talking points, which largely echoed the president's remarks. He emphasized the need for a protection force and for a special envoy. (A peace agreement was not on his list of talking points.)

White-Hammond read the message on the Million Voices postcards she had been helping collect. Bush asked if it was calling for an end to genocide by unilateral intervention, and White-Hammond replied that it was not. "Surprised, not pleasantly surprised, that Darfur advocates were not calling for an invasion," Rubenstein wrote in his notes. Scheduled for 20 minutes, the meeting lasted an hour. Simon Deng, sitting immediately to the president's left, had plenty of time to talk about the issues for southern Sudanese. "Likes Simon Deng," Rubenstein noted.

After the meeting Bush told the media, "I just had an extraordinary conversation with fellow citizens from different faiths. They agree with thousands of our citizens—hundreds of thousands of our citizens—that genocide in Sudan is unacceptable.... For those of you who are going out to march for justice, you represent the best of our country."[27]

Back in Darfur, Ron Capps received no official response to his memo.[28]

A TOUGH NEGOTIATION

Zoellick is a shrewd negotiator who has had success bringing disparate factions together, especially in trade negotiations. But the Darfur account was to prove beyond his capacity, with complexity layered on complexity thwarting even the best of intentions.

One complication was intra-rebel discord. By June 2004, the secretary general of the Sudan Liberation Army, an ethnic Zaghawa by the name of Minni Minawi, was plotting to take over the leadership of the SLA from its current Fur president, Abdel Wahid.[29] Militarily untrained but ruthless and ambitious, Minawi exploited the fears of his fellow kinsmen to begin a war among the rebels.

A minority in the Darfur region, the Zaghawa are fearful of being dominated by the Fur, who are the majority. Although both have a common enemy in the central government, there is a history of mistrust between the two groups,[30] and—for some at least—this fear was all that was needed to lead them into attack. In one of the first intra-rebel attacks in June 2004, Zaghawa rebels loyal to Minawi raped 28 Fur women and killed 22 Fur civilians.[31] The Fur-Zaghawa conflict escalated. Then in October 2005, Minawi called a SLA leadership conference in the North Darfur town of Haskanita. SLA president Abdel Wahid, his supporters, and even some of Minawi's own commanders refused to attend, and in their absence Minawi was "elected" president of the SLA. From now on there would be at least two SLA groups—SLA Minni Minawi and SLA Abdel Wahid.

There was also an international dimension affecting the negotiations. In early December 2005 Sudanese officials met with Chadian militia leader Mahamat Nour.[32] Nour had been recruited by Sudan's security services back in 1998 and had been working for the Sudanese government in West Darfur since 2003 as a Janjaweed coordinator. But by December 2005, the Sudanese government felt he could be more useful in destabilizing the areas of eastern Chad that Darfuri rebel groups used as safe havens.[33]

Chad's president, Idriss Deby, is a Zaghawa who came to power in a 1990 coup, thanks to the support both of his fellow Zaghawa in Darfur and to the man who had recently mounted his own coup in Sudan, Omar al-Bashir.[34] Throughout the 1990s, al-Bashir had in Deby a grateful neighbor on Sudan's western border. But the conflict in Darfur placed Deby in an impossible position. When, in the interests of his relationship with al-Bashir, he sent the Chadian army to fight Darfuri rebels, his predominantly Zaghawa troops refused to enter battle against their ethnic kinsmen. Khartoum soon grew suspicious that Deby's affiliation with the Zaghawa—the group to which both Minni Minawi and JEM leader Khalil Ibrahim belonged—was preventing Deby from being the stalwart ally against the Darfuri rebels that the Sudanese government hoped he would be.[35]

Just a week after Nour met with the Sudanese officials, he formed a Chadian rebel coalition against Deby, at which point Deby abandoned his attempt to remain neutral. By the start of 2006 the Chadian president was supporting his Zaghawa kinsmen in JEM as a counterweight to Khartoum's support of the Chadian rebels. "Read my lips," the AU's lead mediator told me, "unless normalization occurs between Chad and Sudan, there will be no peace in Darfur."[36]

Thus the seventh round of talks began inauspiciously at the end of 2005. Twenty-one long months after negotiations had first opened in Abuja, there still was no peace agreement in sight. But where most participants saw insurmountable obstacles, the top U.S. negotiator saw an improbable opportunity to push an agreement through.

Despite the fact that al-Bashir had recently said that Darfur would become a graveyard for any UN forces trying to deploy there, and despite the fact that they had been informed that Taha no longer had the power to deliver promises on Darfur, Zoellick and other officials in the U.S. State Department were willing to push forward when Taha said, or even just implied, that the Sudanese government would allow UN troops into Darfur if a peace agreement was signed.

RAISING THE PRESSURE

In April 2006 Zoellick went to Paris, where he quizzed Salim on the status of the negotiations in Abuja. Salim was an experienced diplomat, but Zoellick was frustrated with the slow speed of the negotiations and pushed Salim to present the parties with the proposals he had. Salim was dubious that this would be a useful approach: "I knew some of the things in there [those proposals] would be unacceptable to the [rebel] movements."[37]

In mid-April, Nour's Sudanese-sponsored rebel coalition attempted to overthrow Chad's President Deby. As Deby's support for the Darfuri rebels had grown, it had become clear to Khartoum that they could not win militarily as long as the rebels continued receiving support from Chad. But if Deby could be overthrown, this calculation would change; without Deby's support, the Darfuri rebels would be weakened militarily and Khartoum's negotiating hand would be strengthened.

Nour launched his attack from Darfur, taking just a week to move with his troops west from the border to reach the Chadian capital on April 13, 2006.[38] Speaking by phone to a Sudanese reporter, Nour laughed as he explained, "We are assuring the people of Chad that towns are falling from the hands of the regime into the hands of the revolutionary men like ripe fruits fall from trees during its season."[39] But his optimism was short-lived. Knowing what the loss of Deby would mean for them, JEM rebels came to the embattled president's rescue.[40] With the attempt to overthrow Deby unsuccessful, Khartoum was forced to make the best it could of the negotiations in Abuja.

On April 25, Salim presented the parties with an 87-page document. It omitted two of the rebel movements' core demands—a vice presidency for Darfuris (as the southerners were awarded with the CPA) and the restoration of Darfur to a single region (undoing the three-way division imposed by al-Bashir in 1994).[41] Majzoub al-Khalifa, on behalf of the Sudanese government, reacted so positively to the proposal that he even organized the Sudanese press to snap a photo of him holding it. The reaction of the rebel movements was exactly the opposite.[42] Nevertheless, the United States still hoped an agreement was possible.

THE EVENING AFTER THE April 30 "Save Darfur" rallies, as Zoellick flew to Abuja, Bush, who retained his faith in Taha as the man who delivered the CPA, called al-Bashir directly to ask him to send Taha back to the peace talks.[43] Taha had left Abuja after Nour's failed attempt to overthrow President Deby. But al-Bashir already had an agreement his government was happy to sign, and the only possible thing left to negotiate were changes to the text that would mollify the rebels. The request for Taha's return was never granted, and Majzoub al-Khalifa remained the Sudanese government's representative.

Zoellick and his British counterpart, Hilary Benn, spent their first day in Abuja trying to understand what it would take to get the rebels to sign and pushing the government to accept changes to a document they had already agreed to. It was an uphill battle, and Zoellick persisted through the evening once all the parties had retired back to the Chida Hotel.

Zoellick was in the middle of pressing al-Khalifa to concede to the amendments when the Chida Hotel's ever-unreliable electricity connection failed and the diplomats were plunged into darkness. His aides reached for their Blackberrys while Zoellick, unfazed, continued "browbeating the hell out of Majzoub" by the light of his staffers' phones.[44] As the clock passed midnight, there was still no indication al-Khalifa would agree.

Alex de Waal's diary the next day records the outcome of these efforts as being "too close to call."[45] That night he drafted a "failure statement" for the AU mediation team to read out in the event that no agreement was reached. Meanwhile, Zoellick, unable to sleep, concluded the only option left was to present the parties with a binary choice. Just as he had done when he was the U.S. trade representative leading complex negotiations among as many as 148 different states, he would give the rebels and the government a document that he felt fairly reflected all the concerns and demand that they accept or reject it as is.[46]

The next morning de Waal drafted a "success statement." Later that day, Zoellick got Minawi to agree with the changes that had been made to the text.[47] Things seemed to be looking up. That evening, with what the mediation team termed the "obituary" and "wedding announcement" in hand, everyone moved into Aguda House on Obasanjo's presidential grounds for what would be a 36-hour marathon to pressure the parties into a deal.

After a 20-minute speech it became clear that Minawi would refuse to sign until further amendments were made to the power- and wealth-sharing parts of the agreement. Zoellick, who had secured Minawi's approval of the document just 12 hours earlier, was outraged. "Have no doubt where I stand," he told Minawi, "I am a good friend and I am a fearsome enemy."[48] Next Abdel Wahid was summoned, and he also expressed reluctance to accept the take-it-or-leave-it document. Zoellick stood up and handed him a letter, signed by President Bush, saying, "I assure you that the United States will strongly support the implementation of the Darfur Peace Accord. I will insist on holding accountable those who are not supporting the implementation of the Accord."[49] Nonetheless, Abdel Wahid asked for more time. Next Khalil Ibrahim came in and rejected the document on behalf of JEM. De Waal scribbled in his notebook, "Khalil walks off into oblivion." It was now

3:15 a.m. Minawi returned and was also presented with a personal letter from Bush assuring him of the U.S. commitment to the implementation of the agreement.

This painful back-and-forth continued until the mediation broke just before 5 a.m., only to resume again four hours later. At 9:20 a.m. on Friday, May 5, Minawi finally accepted the agreement; Obasanjo had to prompt the weary observers to applaud. Neither Abdel Wahid's faction of the SLA nor the JEM would sign.

As soon as Zoellick's team got back from Abuja, David Rubenstein received an upbeat phone call from one of Zoellick's staffers, Chris Padilla, to tell him all about the agreement. "Zoellick must have thought he was doing something good for us," surmises Rubenstein.[50] Yet Zoellick says that on the plane back to Washington his overall feeling was of uncertainty. "It was a question mark. Abdel Wahid had missed an opportunity. If he had signed, I think we would have had a good shot of pressing to get a UN force in." Zoellick believed that with security and a peace accord, there was a real chance of making progress.[51]

The next week, Zoellick stood beside Condoleezza Rice in the Roosevelt Room as President Bush told the press, "With the peace agreement signed on Friday, Darfur has a chance to begin anew."[52] Hearing this from his desk at GI-Net, Sam Bell was skeptical. The advocacy movement had never been engaged with the Abuja process in the first place, so it was not surprising that, as Bell puts it, "[The peace agreement] didn't change our calculations much."

Back at the AMIS headquarters in Addis Ababa the mood was more optimistic—if only due to a belief that this surely meant the UN would take over from their embattled operation. "My overall feeling was of jubilation. Getting it signed was our main goal.... We were getting exhausted," recalls Geoffrey Mugumya, who headed the AU's Peace and Security division at the time.[53] At the UN, the special representative for Sudan, Jan Pronk, was unconvinced. "I never understood the preference for an agreement that was flawed. If you were going to get one party to sign, it should have been the other one. Abdel Wahid had the popular support."[54] A Darfuri refugee with whom I subsequently spoke in Cairo echoed Pronk's view, remembering that upon hearing Minawi was the only rebel to sign the Darfur Peace Agreement he told his friends, "This will lead nowhere. Minni Minawi is not a leader. He cannot even advocate for his own cause."[55]

I met Minawi some three years after he signed the agreement. Entering his Khartoum residence, a modern villa hidden behind salmon-colored concrete walls, the first thing I noticed was the Sudanese government number plates on his shiny new black Mercedes Benz, one of the perks of his role of special assistant to the president after he signed the peace agreement. A diplomat once described Minawi to me as "a man with the charisma of an oyster." At the time I assumed the characterization to be overly harsh, but after meeting Minawi, it was hard to disagree.

Minawi finished up one pack of Benson & Hedges as I made my introductions, and an assistant was on hand to provide him with a new pack so his chain-smoking could continue without interruption. Also without interruption was his persistent flicking between channels on his satellite television as he stared blankly toward the screen while dismissing in a solid monotone any notion that his challenge for the SLA leadership at the Haskanita conference had been controversial. "Haskanita was a very fair conference. The representative of the U.S. oversaw it." But Minawi did not sugar-coat his experience of having been brought into the government. "I can see the president anytime I want. But he doesn't trust me—and after three years here, I don't trust him."[56] The power-sharing provisions of the agreement that bought Minawi a government title and a cushy Khartoum residence amounted to no representation for Darfuris at all. But real representation for Darfuris was not what any of those around the table at Abuja had been focused on in any case.

UN DEPLOYMENT

With a "peace agreement" in its pocket, the United States now moved to collect the dividends. Just three days after the Darfur Peace Agreement was signed, the United States circulated a draft UN Security Council resolution to lay the groundwork for a transition from AMIS to the UN peacekeepers. The next day Secretary Rice attended a meeting with the Security Council, hastily convened by the U.S. delegation.[57] She urged council members to support the U.S. resolution, which stated that "in view of the signing of the Darfur Peace Agreement, concrete steps should be taken to effect the transition from AMIS to a United Nations operation."[58] The resolution passed unanimously. China, Russia, and Qatar each made very clear statements after their votes, however, to specify that their willingness to support the resolution did not mean they would support a nonconsensual UN deployment.

The problem was that Khartoum had no intention of consenting to the deployment of UN troops in Darfur, and, incredibly, the final text of the Darfur Peace Agreement had made no mention of a role for UN peacekeepers. The net result was that Taha's assurances notwithstanding, there was nothing to bind the Sudanese government to accepting a UN force now that the peace agreement was signed.

"Zoellick was told not to worry about including the provision for a UN force in the DPA...it was promised by the Sudanese government, regardless of it being in the text,"[59] explains a State Department official. Frazer concurs, recalling that Khartoum said it would make the change from AMIS to the UN later, once a Security Council resolution on deployment had been authorized.[60]

In 2009 Lam Akol, Sudan's foreign minister in 2006, told me what he claims was the Sudanese government's official line throughout the negotiations. He says they pointed out that the UN peacekeeping force in the south only came after the signing of the CPA, and then said, "*If* a peace agreement negotiated in Abuja *provides* for such a force, then that is what will happen." He looked at me with a sly smile and said, "Unfortunately for them, when the Abuja agreement came, it stressed that it was the *AU* there. A *UN* force is nowhere in the document."[61]

"The Sudanese government was opposed to the UN,"[62] Salim tells me, explaining his reason for not asking that the UN be put into the agreement. Pronk says he felt strongly that the UN needed to be specified, "but the U.S. and U.K. said no—it will complicate matters."[63] In short, the need to rapidly get "an agreement" was prioritized over the time-consuming task of getting the kind of agreement, from all parties to the conflict, that UN peacekeepers would really have needed to mount a peacekeeping, as opposed to peace enforcement, operation.

Despite President Bush's personal letter to Minawi, the U.S. government ended up taking no interest in the implementation of the agreement that Zoellick had pulled out all the stops for. "You should have seen Zoellick," says Salim, reflecting on the final hours of the negotiations with a degree of awe. "When you hear Zoellick speaking you feel that things will be done...but the sad thing was that the threats turned out not to be credible."[64] A month after the Darfur Peace Agreement was concluded, Zoellick left the U.S. government. The agreement had been very much his show, and when he left, there was no one committed to following through. Four months after the agreement was signed, Pronk told the UN Security Council it was "nearly dead."[65] But its moribund status did not mean it had no impact—it had an effect, just not the one intended.

The lack of consensus over the agreement within the different rebel movements catalyzed a destructive process of endless fracturing. "When they signed the Darfur Peace Agreement there were three factions. By the time I arrived, there were more than ten,"[66] explains Colonel Ephrem Rurangua, a Rwandan who became deputy force commander in Darfur at the beginning of 2007. The fracturing made it virtually impossible for any peacekeeping contingent to build the relations needed to facilitate operations.

As Rurangua describes it, his officers would build a relationship with one rebel commander only to be held hostage by a new rebel faction the next day and would have to go through the process of explaining to this new faction that AMIS was a neutral force, not working for the government. Eventually his troops began refusing to go on patrol. "They weren't being paid, and they were being asked to patrol areas under the command of different factions who could attack them—and they didn't have the means to defend themselves."[67]

Even more debilitating was the impact on subsequent attempts at peace negotiations. With the rebels having no unified movement, let alone negotiating position, Khartoum had increasing credibility to argue that it was impossible to enter into talks with them.

WHEN PRESIDENT BUSH STOOD before journalists to tell them that his deputy secretary of state had secured a peace agreement for Darfur, he probably believed he would be applauded by the advocacy movement. Indeed, this was the reaction of some advocates at a time when simply getting the U.S. government to "do something" on Darfur counted as success. But as the months ahead would show, the rushed peace agreement between the government and just one rebel faction, without the consent of either side for the deployment of UN peacekeepers to oversee the agreement's implementation, actually made the situation worse.

Michael Gerson unwittingly summed up the central flaw in the U.S. approach to the peace negotiations, revealing that the primary goal was never to negotiate a sustainable peace but to just to get a piece of paper that could be used to push the UN to deploy. Gerson said: "The Darfur peace agreement was important for one reason—it paved the way to a UN mandated force. Without the agreement I don't think that could have happened. The UN do not see themselves as peace enforcers—this at least gave the illusion of a peace to keep."[68]

CHAPTER 8

THE LIMITATIONS OF THE RWANDA MODEL

Three years after the eruption of the conflict in Darfur, with 18 months of citizen-driven organizing under its belt, the Darfur movement had demonstrated its relevance in the U.S. political arena. The way they had done it came with certain costs. However, the mass movement approach had been remarkably successful in lobbying congress, and the nationwide rallies had shown that a large number of people were both aware of and willing to be active on Darfur. In short, the movement had succeeded in building the outcry they had been told was missing, and needed, for Rwanda; they had generated a substantial measure of political will within the U.S. system.

THE REALM OF DOMESTIC POLITICS

In the year before the rallies, what had initially been ad-hoc collaborative efforts among Darfur advocacy groups and a Quaker organization called the Friends Committee on National Legislation became increasingly formalized. A Friends Committee staff member began sending out regular e-mails on Darfur-related legislation as it progressed through the various committees of the House and Senate.[1] The information allowed the Save Darfur Coalition, GI-Net, and others to coordinate their lobbying and support the efforts of the congressional champions on Sudan. One example was a collaborative effort on funding the transition from AMIS to the UN. President Bush initially requested $69.8 million from congress for both the UN deployment in southern Sudan and the transition to a UN deployment in Darfur. Advocacy leaders, who had by now developed strong working relationships with key congressional staffers, pushed to get the funding increased. In the House Appropriations Committee, Congressman Frank Wolf increased the amount by $60 million, and Senator Robert Menendez supported this approach in the senate. The Friends Committee helped organize a sign-on letter campaign for citizen advocates.[2] The final appropriation included $129.8M for UN peacekeeping operations in Sudan, almost double the original request.[3]

Government officials who had been working on African issues for years without ever seeing such attention to their countries of concern were impressed, if a little jealous. "On other African issues, if you had just a fraction of the attention and funds that Darfur got, you really could have achieved a lot," one African Affairs staffer told me, not without some frustration. A Sudan program officer remembers, "We would meet with Save Darfur and tell them what amount of money was needed, then they would go over to Appropriations and come back with *more!*"[4]

By ensuring that members of congress received strong support from their constituents for appropriating funding for Darfur, the mass movement had played a critical role in getting almost a billion dollars worth of humanitarian aid to Darfur by September 2006, as well as getting the United States to foot the $280 million bill for the construction of the bases for the AMIS operation.[5]

The advocacy community's sophistication at organizing domestically progressed in leaps and bounds. GI-Net established two tools to help constituents lobby their members of congress. To reduce the barriers to regular citizens calling their representatives, GI-Net established a toll-free number, 1-800-GENOCIDE. When citizens called the number, they were given talking points about the key legislation pending on Darfur and were put through to their representative's office to deliver the message. GI-Net also graded every member of congress from A+ to F on how they had responded to Darfur. Once this information was published, citizens represented by low-scoring politicians began using the scorecards to pressure them into action. In some cases citizens used the scorecards in face-to-face meetings with representatives, while others published articles in their local papers to publicly shame low-scoring representatives from the area. Meanwhile, members of congress with high scores found themselves receiving calls of support from their constituents, calls that for the first time built a positive political incentive to respond to foreign atrocities. These representatives strengthened the accountability system further by publicizing their high scores on their websites and press releases, thus distinguishing themselves from those without such scores to promote.

As citizens made greater use of the scorecards, the GI-Net office found itself receiving phone calls from members of congress themselves—not only their staff—asking what actions they would need to take to get a score upgrade. Out of the 167 representatives who scored an F in August 2006, 166 took action, like voting for legislation to fund aid for Darfur, to improve their scores in the following 18 months.[6] Sam Bell remembers one congressional staffer telling him that her boss "complains at least once a week about the fact that he was given a C+ and yells about finding a way to raise his grade because every time he goes back to his district he gets harassed by high schoolers who've checked out the [GI-Net] website." It was a sea change from the complete absence of constituent interest expressed to congress during the Rwandan genocide just over a decade earlier, when Representative Patricia Shroeder had memorably observed that she received more calls from her constituents about Rwanda's endangered gorilla population than she did about the Rwandan people.[7]

No longer was there any question about whether a significant number of Americans could be moved to care about Darfur. Nor was there any doubt that when congress was their target, the Darfur movement could affect the policy process. But how successful was the movement in influencing the branch of government most responsible for foreign policy—the administration?

One of the main campaigns to influence the Bush administration revolved around getting a special envoy appointed, to have someone inside government whose focus was completely dedicated to Sudan. Citizen activists took every opportunity to call for a special envoy, and they got the congressional champions on their side. On July 5, 2006, Congressmen Michael Capuano, Donald Payne, Tom Tancredo, and Frank Wolf wrote President Bush a joint letter requesting that he immediately appoint a special envoy for Sudan.[8] The Save Darfur Coalition supplemented their voices by taking out major ads in various newspapers, which in turn prompted journalists to raise the issue at one of the daily press briefings with the State Department.[9] In contrast to a policy question like whether to refer the situation to the ICC, the call for a special envoy was one on which it was easy to gain consensus across a diverse constituency of advocates. Moreover, the appointment of an envoy was solely within the U.S. government's power to deliver.

Three months later, a relatively short time in the context of the U.S. government's sprawling bureaucracy, advocates got what they were after. In September 2006 Bush appointed former USAID head Andrew Natsios— who began drawing attention to Darfur back in 2003—to the role of special envoy.[10] Advocates were triumphant. "It's clear the pressure you, and hundreds of thousands of Darfur activists just like you, have applied is having an impact," David Rubenstein e-mailed Save Darfur's constituents.[11]

When pressuring congress, advocates could reach their representatives' offices directly. Reaching the president usually required indirect messengers. For the most part advocates relied on the media as their means of communication. It was not by chance that Michael Gerson could always find a steady stream of articles to draw the president's attention to. In 2005 GI-Net and the Center for American Progress had launched an online petition to boost media coverage of Darfur. Entitled "Be a Witness," the petition noted that "in June 2005 CNN, FOX News, NBC/MSNBC, ABC, and CBS ran 50 times as many stories about Michael Jackson and 12 times as many stories about Tom Cruise as they did about the genocide in Darfur." While targeted at the television networks, its impact spread to the print media after Nicholas Kristof featured the campaign in one of his columns.[12] The Save Darfur Coalition then began calling on citizen activists to write letters to the editor and op-eds in their community newspapers to further build interest in Darfur, an approach they sustained in the years ahead.

Two particularly striking observations about the media coverage on Darfur emerge. First, it went from being painfully absent during the first 14 months of the crisis when most of the direct killing was carried out[13] to headline news around the tenth anniversary of the Rwandan genocide. Second, from the time of this April 2004 coverage, media interest was not only sustained but actually grew; by 2007–2008, Darfur attracted 48 percent more coverage in the U.S. print media than it had in 2004–2005.[14]

The media coverage that the April 30 rallies attracted had catapulted Save Darfur into the spotlight and given them brand-name recognition. In August 2006 one of the staff at Save Darfur got a call from a man saying he represented an anonymous donor who wanted to give several million dollars for the organization to spend the following month. The staffer referred the call on, flagging the likelihood that it was a hoax. It wasn't. But the donation came with a condition: The money could only be spent on paid advertising. As Save Darfur staff recall it, their initial reaction was one of gratitude, and they quickly solicited an advertising agency to come up with designs.

I asked Rubenstein if he saw any dilemma accepting money from an anonymous source with that kind of condition attached. He said he believed that the intentions of the donor/s were irrelevant since everything the money was spent on was "entirely consistent with our mission and strategy." Save Darfur's U.S. policy coordinator, Alex Meixner, says he thought the insistence on advertising was odd, "like perhaps someone was attempting a sociological/ political-science experiment," but stressed that he didn't think the content of their messaging was being affected, just the volume.[15] However, the volume alone sent its own message; between October 2006 and September 2007, Save Darfur spent $33.8 million, more than two-thirds of its total budget, on paid advertising.[16] Anyone who didn't know about the conditional donation had no option but to assume this allocation of resources reflected Save Darfur priorities. Suddenly Save Darfur ads were cropping up across the country—on billboards in subway stations and at prime time on major television networks. "Just a year and a half before, we were all alone in thinking about this. There was no momentum.... Now we had ads on NBC," recalls Sam Bell.

By October 2006 the Darfur advocates, again working in coordination with the Friends Committee and the congressional champions, succeeded in getting congress to pass legislation ensuring that U.S. sanctions remained on the Sudanese government until a demanding set of conditions were satis-fied.[17] In the words of one State Department official, "Darfur would have to be as peaceful as Nebraska for those conditions to be met."[18]

The Sudanese foreign minister at the time, Lam Akol, believes that it was because of the mass movement that the U.S. government reneged on its offer to remove sanctions on Sudan after the Darfur Peace Agreement was signed. Indeed, he says that in a meeting with Jendayi Frazer at the Waldorf Astoria hotel in New York, she told him that the U.S. government was "convinced, she used the word, convinced" that Sudan was not a state sponsor of terror, but that U.S. public opinion prevented the administration from removing them from the sanctioned list.[19] I asked Frazer if this was true. "It's hard for me to know whether I said that exactly," she began, "but it was very clear that Sudan should not be on the State Sponsors of Terror list, and I probably did say that it would be difficult to remove them because of congressional opinion."[20]

Working through congress and the media, in addition to developing new pressure points of their own, Darfur advocates had managed to get the U.S. government not only to devote financial and staffing resources to Darfur, but also to constrain the terms of its economic and diplomatic relationship with Sudan; this was no small accomplishment for a new domestic constituency. It is impossible to say for certain if there had been no Darfur movement whether the more traditional, elite-model approach to advocacy could have achieved the same results. The new mass movement depended heavily on the field reporting and analysis from the likes of Amnesty, Human Rights Watch, and the International Crisis Group, so any impact the movement had must factor in their reliance on the work of more traditional actors. But certainly the mass movement's influence on the U.S. policy process for Darfur was greater than the impact traditional human rights advocacy efforts alone were having on U.S. policy toward other African crises at the time. Yet, impressive as these efforts had been, the mass movement approach came with its own costs.

TELLING THE RIGHT STORY

If you want to build a mass movement you must, by definition, attract people who are not already specialists in the issue you are advocating. When your issue is complex, like Darfur, you have to simplify the issue to make it acces-sible to people who have no background knowledge. "Our role was to protect innocent Darfuri civilians, and we painted the picture to do that in the simplest strokes that we thought had integrity," explains Rubenstein. "The emergency in Darfur presents the starkest challenge to the world since the Rwanda geno-cide in 1994" was the message that greeted those who went to the Save Darfur website in January 2005. In April 2005 Save Darfur added: "[R]ebels in Darfur, seeking an end to the region's chronic economic and political marginalization, also took up arms to protect their communities against a 20-year campaign by government-backed militias recruited among groups of Arab extraction in Darfur and Chad."[21] Eighteen months later, the same information was still on the website, with nothing additional to indicate that crimes against civilians were also being committed by rebel groups.[22] State Department specialists observed this with frustration. "Advocates made it all sound so easy, simplifying the rebels as lily white,"[23] recalls Robert Zoellick's special assistant.

For those who believed that building a mass constituency of regular citizens was the way to build political will, there was no good alternative to simplification at the beginning. But 18 months into their organizing, it was reasonable to expect the movement's leaders to have started educating their constituents on the way that the conflict was changing over time. No longer was the crisis dominated by government-sponsored massacres. Instead, the Sudanese government was foremost among several actors obstructing Darfur's displaced population from getting the resources they needed to survive. The rebels too were contributing to the problem.

In the aftermath of the Darfur Peace Agreement, signed only by Minni Minawi, with the previous rebel structures now in tatters, there was space for new, often self-appointed, rebel leaders to request their place at the negotiating table—a table invariably located in a capital city outside Sudan, with hotel accommodations and a generous daily allowance attached. In jostling for position, a premium was placed on obtaining the goods associated with rebel leadership—guns, vehicles, and Thurayas (the bulky satellite phones that are the only form of telecommunication sure to work across vast swathes of Darfur's desert).

Vehicles and Thurayas were items that the humanitarian community had in abundance, and carjackings of aid workers by aspiring rebels became commonplace. Standard signage on humanitarians' white Land Cruisers the world over is a sticker with a picture of a gun and a prohibitive red strike through it. The idea is to advertise to everyone that humanitarians are not party to the conflict and have no guns onboard. But in the context of Darfur, it sent a different message. "We might as well have a sign in Arabic that says 'Steal me, please! We can't protect ourselves anyway!" vented one aid worker after the twelfth carjacking of the month in South Darfur state.[24] Despite the wry humor, the impact on aid workers was serious. But it was civilians who paid the biggest price. As insecurity increased, the areas into which aid operations could reach decreased, worsening access beyond the obstacles the Sudanese government, through informal bureaucratic means, was continuing to put in place. The month of July 2006 saw almost half a million Darfuris without access to food aid.[25] The UN secretary-general reported that in August 2006 humanitarian access was the lowest it had been since 2004, before the government restrictions on the entry of humanitarian organizations into Darfur had been formally suspended.[26]

Mortality estimates for Darfur are controversial. The remoteness of the region combined with the Sudanese government's aggressive efforts to prevent outside investigators entering the area mean researchers have largely relied on extrapolating from a sample of displaced camps or from the accounts of survivors who made it across the border to Chad.[27] Nonetheless, a 2010 study in the respected medical journal *The Lancet* shows that beyond the specific numbers involved, the main cause of death in Darfur clearly changed over the course of the conflict, with a sharp decline in direct killings from 2005 onward but an increase in disease-related mortality among those living in crowded displacement camps. In the 18-month period from July 2006 to September 2007 an estimated 5,300 people were killed through violence, as compared to an estimated 33,000 in just 6 months from September 2003 to March 2004.[28] However, the total number of "excess deaths" (those above what one would expect in the ordinary course of events) from July 2006 to September 2007 was an estimated 98,187 people; these deaths were due to nonviolent causes mostly resulting from the reduction in humanitarian operations.[29] At the close of 2006, Darfur was a deadly place to be but not for the same reasons as during the massacres of 2003-2004.

This shift in the primary cause of death from government-sponsored massacres to disease-related fatalities could be gleaned by an attentive reader from the Save Darfur website.[30] But for members of the public who came into the Darfur movement through stories of the 2003-2004 massacres, it would take explicit direction to get them to update their narrative of the conflict; simply posting some information in the textual segments of Save Darfur's site was insufficient.

The failure of citizen advocates to embrace the evolving contours of the crisis made the movement vulnerable to criticism and pushed it toward policy demands that did not always address the situation on the ground. The policy to deal with a multisided, cross-border conflict was not the same as the policy needed to address a crisis dominated by one-sided massacres. In an advisory memo to the deputy secretary of state before his upcoming trip to Sudan in April 2007, Andrew Natsios wrote: "The media, beltway, think tanks, congress, and advocacy groups believe that 'the slaughter continues' on a genocidal scale, a belief which is driving us towards policies which may not get us where we need to go to 'save' Darfur. The field data does not support the image...."[31]

Of course, policymakers had the option—indeed, the responsibility—of filtering any unhelpful demands out of the policy process. But as the Darfur movement gained political strength, there were at least some government officials who, when faced with an advocacy demand that was not aligned with what was needed on the ground, were more motivated to say what advocates wanted to hear than to do what Darfuris needed. Natsios warned the deputy secretary of state that trying to correct advocates' misperceptions of the conflict would be "politically dangerous given the emotions around the issue and funding [*sic*] raising imperatives of the advocacy groups which rely on apocalyptic language."[32]

In Natsios' view, the time-lag between changes on the ground and changes in the Darfur movement's framing of the conflict was attributable to cynical motives. But inside the movement other factors were at play. Not only was there the basic challenge of getting a new message out to a constituency of regular citizens who were squeezing in their voluntary advocacy efforts around the demands of work and family. There were also factors related to what might be called the culture of the Darfur advocacy community.

FIXATING ON A WORD

Born against the backdrop of the narrative of failure in Rwanda, the new Darfur movement found lessons in the 1994 genocide that became articles of faith. One was not to view the violence through the prism of civil war because to do so risked mistakenly drawing moral equivalence between the parties. As Rubenstein puts it, "the rebels weren't a sovereign government bombing innocent civilian populations based on ethnic background." Fear of appearing to draw equivalence loomed large and contributed to the movement's reluctance to highlight rebel crimes. The other article of faith was to never shy away from using the word genocide.

The questioning by Senator Menendez of testimony Natsios gave before the Senate Foreign Relations Committee in early 2007 was an example of the sensitivities around the word.

MENENDEZ: So would you tell the committee what is the situation in Darfur? Is it a genocide?
NATSIOS: In Darfur, Senator, right now there is very little fighting in Darfur.
MENENDEZ: That does not mean...
NATSIOS: Senator, could I finish?
MENENDEZ: The question is, do you consider...
NATSIOS: Senator...
MENENDEZ: Answer my question. I have a limited amount of time, Ambassador. If I ask you to be specific and answer my question.
NATSIOS: I'm answering your question.
MENENDEZ: Do you—you can't answer if you haven't heard it. Do you consider the ongoing situation in Darfur a genocide, yes or no?
NATSIOS: What you just...
MENENDEZ: Yes or no.
NATSIOS: Senator, please. What you just read did not take place in Darfur...
MENENDEZ: I didn't...
NATSIOS: There is very little...
MENENDEZ: I'm asking you yes or no.

NATSIOS: There is very little violence in Darfur right now.

MENENDEZ: What do you not understand?

NATSIOS: Senator, I just answered your question.

MENENDEZ: Is the circumstances in Darfur today a continuing genocide, yes or no?[33]

As with all congressional activity on Darfur, it was not just advocates who were watching. The regime in Khartoum had also followed the hearing closely. Afterward, Natsios received a phone call. "[They] told me, the fact that you held out for that long makes us think you are genuine. You say the same thing there that you say to us."[34]

While many of the administration officials I interviewed highlighted the fact that Khartoum follows congressional proceedings as their justification for being cautious with their public remarks, most overlooked the possibility that advocates were just as aware of the way congressional dynamics were absorbed in Khartoum. Natsios believed that by pushing back against the use of the g-word during congressional questioning, he was building trust with Khartoum; advocates believed that when congress pushed administration officials hard, it signaled to Khartoum that the American public would not let them get away with the softer line that they feared U.S. officials visiting Khartoum might convey in private. The seemingly parochial act of getting a congressional committee to call a member of the administration to testify was in fact one of the clearest ways for U.S.-based advocates to communicate their position directly to the Sudanese government.

By the time Natsios gave his testimony in 2007, the period of coordinated government and Janjaweed assaults that had killed so many in 2003 and 2004 had largely stopped. But the conditions under which Darfuris forced to flee from their homes now lived were precarious at best. No longer able to tend their farms and frequently unable to sustain what little livestock managed to survive the attacks, the Darfuri population in the displaced camps found themselves in the unfamiliar position of dependency.

"Life here is like night and day with my life before," explained a Darfuri mother of six in one of the Chadian refugee camps, which were generally better than those inside Darfur. "At home we had our freedom, but here we are in a camp, like a prison. You have no freedom to collect grass or firewood. With grass we could build our shelter, but we cannot go out," she explained, referring to the threat of death for men and rape for women that lay beyond the perimeters of the camps in Chad and Darfur, where marauding militia preyed on those who left the camp confines. "[Also] we prefer the food we had before. What we needed, we farmed. Whatever we needed, we could get for ourselves."[35]

The humanitarian operation—the largest in the world in spite of the vast areas of Darfur it could not reach—ensured that the majority of the displaced survived. But it was a life in limbo. Although there were comparatively few major attacks, the general breakdown of law and order and the impact of the recent devastation ensured that no one felt safe. The insecurity that prevailed across the region meant that the displaced could not return to what did—or mostly did not—remain of their homes. The result was a stranded population of two million primarily non-Arabs who, while not currently under attack *en masse*, knew themselves to be defenseless should those who had forced them to flee in the first place decide to attack again. And even if they could have returned to their former homes, there was no option of returning to their former lives. Darfur had been irrevocably changed. Entire villages no longer existed. And the social fabric that secured the interdependency required to survive in the remotest areas of Darfur had been torn apart.

Public disputes, like that of Natsios and Menendez, turned this multilayered reality into a debate over whether or not to describe the situation using one particular word, genocide. This would have been problematic enough if there was consensus among those engaging in the debate over what they meant when they said genocide. But there wasn't.

When the general public invokes the word genocide, it seems they are trying to describe a brutal situation involving mass killing of a particular people. They have the Holocaust and, to a lesser extent, Rwanda in mind. Most people have never read, and never will read, the 1948 Genocide Convention; and most people do not focus on the legal details of the definition of the word.

When lawyers use the word genocide, they use it to describe a situation that meets the elements listed in the 1948 Genocide Convention. They know that a massive amount of killing of a particular people does not automatically equate to genocide. In fact, the outright act of killing is much less important in legal circles than it is to the general public. Lawyers know that genocide can be conducted through means other than direct killing, such as imposing conditions of life that are intended to destroy the group or forcibly transferring children from the group. And while the intent must be to destroy a substantial number of the particular group, when killing is the means employed, this number does not need to approach anything like the number killed in the Holocaust or Rwanda in order to constitute genocide.[36] Lawyers focus on whether the people killed are members of a particular "national, ethnical, racial, or religious" group and whether the stringent requirement of so-called special intent is met, that is, was the perpetrators' purpose to destroy the particular group "in whole or in part, as such"? This attention to special intent shifts the focus from the mass killings that the public looks for to the minds of those responsible for the destruction.

On Darfur, two kinds of debates swirled about genocide, reflecting these two different understandings of what it meant. The first debate, which began in 2004-2005, focused on the legal conception of the word. Both the U.S. State

Department and the UN Commission of Inquiry found acts that can constitute genocide were committed against Darfur's non-Arab groups. However,
they reached different conclusions on whether or not to call the situation
genocide because they had different views on the question of special intent.
While the State Department felt that the facts on the ground showed that
the purpose of the Sudanese government and the Janjaweed was to destroy
at least part of the Fur, Massaleit, and Zaghawa, the UN Commission was
not convinced.[37] It was this disagreement over the existence of special intent
that led to the genocide debate between the U.S. government and most other
governments. The second debate was more like the one between Natsios and
Menendez: It focused on the features more salient in the public's conception
of the word. It was a debate that began in 2006 as more reports came in that
the number of deaths due to direct killing had dropped.

Some of the leaders in the Darfur advocacy movement were aware of the
two different issues at play when the word genocide came up. "[By 2007] I
felt a little uncomfortable using the term [ongoing genocide] because I think
people hear it and think that the situation on the ground is the same as it
was," Sam Bell explained. Having read the Genocide Convention, however,
he maintained that Darfur was an ongoing genocide, even with the drop in
the rate of direct killings, because the perpetrators continued to meet the
special intent requirement. Jerry Fowler, one of the Save Darfur cofounders,
also identified the disconnect between the public perception of genocide and
the focus of legal scholars. "I feel pretty confident that when people think
about genocide, they're not thinking about the issues that come into the
debate [over special intent]."[38]

With so much confusion, public feuds over the use of the word genocide
continued with predictable regularity. It was a debate that Omer Ismail hated
hearing. "For people inside who suffered it, the people who died, died. But
for the people who live, who carry the scars every day, discussing whether it
is genocide or not genocide is just more hurting to them," he says. "You cannot quantify what people have been through into a word and then dissect that
word to the point where it all just comes down to semantics. It is the ultimate
insult."

There was more at stake, however, than simply describing the situation;
the label applied would affect both the intensity of the response to the crisis
and the kinds of responses that received consideration. There was a widespread belief that a situation labeled genocide would attract more government
resources (both attention and money) than a situation that was not labeled
genocide. Part of this belief was historical, layered upon an understanding
of the U.S. government's Rwanda policy in 1994. While Powell's claim that
calling Darfur genocide did not necessitate additional action had challenged
the Clinton administration's position, the amount of congressional funding

that Sudan attracted (second only to Iraq and Afghanistan) relative to a comparably dire situation in the Democratic Republic of the Congo over the same time period suggests that a link between the genocide label and government resources prevailed.[39]

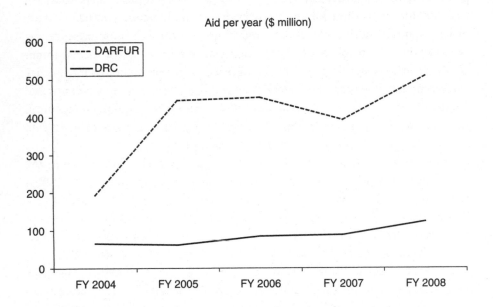

Aid per year ($ million)

One could argue that advocacy attention rather than the genocide label per se was what generated greater resources for Darfur. But the two factors cannot be so readily disentangled; a situation labeled genocide may also attract more advocacy attention than one not so labeled. As Rubenstein recalls it, "The Jewish community really was moved to respond by the term 'genocide,' and that was an enormous part of the effectiveness of the Save Darfur movement."

In addition, there were the different policy implications that flowed from the way the situation was defined. Different views of where the Darfur conflict lay on the spectrum between multisided civil war and one-sided mass killing had a profound impact on what policy options were seen to be appropriate. Viewing the conflict as a largely one-sided massacre is what drove advocates to focus on security rather than aid, punishment rather than negotiation. As long as the situation was labeled genocide, many people inside and outside the government would continue to believe that security must be prioritized over politics.

But regardless of the label, by late 2006, what the people of Darfur needed was a commitment by all parties to a cease-fire and a resumption of negotiations. This is not to say that the deployment of a protection force did not remain a vital need—it did. But the reality was that the AMIS force was unable to protect civilians from outright violence. A political agreement among all the parties to the conflict, including disparate rebels groups and Darfuri Arabs, to end major fighting and facilitate humanitarian access was the primary piece of a solution, followed by a force that could help protect civilians against anyone who violated the agreement. Peacekeepers were unable to do their job without the political pieces also being put into place—something that the hastily concluded Darfur Peace Agreement had failed to do. The prioritization of security over politics failed to recognize the interdependency of the two. But unlike the appointment of a special envoy or the appropriation of funds, creating the political environment needed for peacekeepers to act effectively was not solely within the U.S. government's power to deliver, which made it a much harder goal for advocates to pursue.

LIMITATIONS OF THE MASS MOVEMENT'S REACH

"Everything we learnt from Bosnia tells us that this won't work," the newest recruit to the UN's Department of Peacekeeping Operations (DPKO) caught herself saying out loud.[40] While the official document containing prerequisites for a successful UN peacekeeping deployment were still being drafted, every DPKO employee knew in substance what they consisted of. And none of them was to be found in Darfur.[41] "Everyone in DPKO was skeptical, very skeptical, about the chance of succeeding," recalls another member of DPKO's Darfur team. "We started planning [for a UN deployment to Darfur], but it's because we were being pressured to plan. We knew that the Sudanese government didn't see the value in it."[42]

Former French diplomat Jean-Marie Guéhenno was the head of DPKO when Darfur was put onto the department's agenda. I met with him at his Manhattan home shortly after his 2008 retirement from the UN. Guéhenno's manner is serious but warm, and he was keen to convey the broader context in which peacekeepers were being asked to operate. "There are two ways that peacekeeping could go now," he told me. "Either it retreats and only takes on traditional tasks where you have a peace agreement and it's between states. Or it follows the present trend, and gets involved in situations where there are spoilers…. If you want to act in gray areas, you need a more proactive force…as for Darfur, it is not even a gray area—it's a black area. I am not sure the government wants an effective peacekeeping force."[43]

The consent of the host government is one of the fundamental requirements of a peacekeeping operation. "I made the point many times to U.S. interlocutors. If you have a state and you don't have their consent, then it's an invasion, what most people call war," recalls Guéhenno. But here again the set of assumptions about what does and does not follow from a situation of genocide affected U.S. thinking. As Jendayi Frazer put it, "We don't need consent when they're conducting genocide."[44]

Morally speaking, Frazer is right. When atrocities are underway, the protection of civilians should trump sovereignty. And under the Responsibility to Protect (R2P), if all other options had been exhausted and a UN deployment without the consent of the Sudanese government was expected to succeed in protecting civilians, then that is what should happen. But, as was already clear, R2P was still just a theory when a strong state like Sudan was concerned. If Sudan did not consent, then, as Guéhenno had repeatedly explained to Frazer and other U.S. officials, you could not deploy a "peacekeeping mission" as the phrase is generally defined.

Any mission to protect civilians using outside forces without the consent of the Sudanese government would not only be tantamount to invasion in rhetorical and legal terms, it would bring with it logistical and military complications rising near the level of practical impossibility. No country, not even the United States, was willing to fight a real war with real costs in terms of lives lost in order to protect Darfuris. And until any country was willing to do that, the theoretical debates could continue ad infinitum. The reality was that Sudanese consent was a necessity.

It was a fundamental point that many U.S. officials were either unwilling or unable to absorb. One of the most striking consistencies across the interviews I did at the State Department was the genuine surprise officials expressed at what one staffer described as "the intransigence of Bashir."[45] The possibility that their demands would be met by the word "no" was never seriously factored into the calculations of many U.S. bureaucrats. But al-Bashir could afford such intransigence. Following the U.S. invasion of Iraq, it was easy enough for him to convince members of the Arab League that any Western pressure over Darfur was the prelude to another U.S. invasion in a Muslim country. In addition, al-Bashir knew he could count on support from his key economic ally, China.

The relationship between China and Sudan started down its current path in the late 1990s. Persistent and egregious human rights violations in the north-south war led activists in the United States and Canada to pressure Western oil companies to withdraw from Sudan. China was ready and waiting to fill the gap.

In 1993 China became a net importer of oil.[46] In 1999 it imported 1 percent of its oil from Sudan. By 2006 that figure had risen to 7 percent, and China had become Sudan's largest oil buyer; by 2010 it accounted for two-thirds of Sudan's oil exports.[47] The International Energy Agency predicts that by 2030 China will be importing the same amount of oil each year as the United States, currently the world's largest oil consumer.[48] While in the oil trade China is an importer, when it comes to an equally important commodity to the Sudanese government—weapons—the relationship runs in the opposite direction. According to figures provided by Khartoum to UN Comtrade, China was the largest exporter of small arms and other weaponry to Sudan over the period of 2003 to 2008.[49] And the economic relationship between China and Sudan is not based on trade alone.

As Western donors increasingly tied their development assistance to improvements in human rights and good governance, China's official policy of "noninterference" with the countries they invest in provided Khartoum with an attractive alternative. In 2005 China's direct foreign investment in Sudan was $352 million,[50] making it Sudan's largest foreign investor. Beijing's fingerprints are on a host of infrastructure projects, partly arising out of the 40 percent holding that the Chinese state-owned oil company, the China National Petroleum Corporation, has in Sudan's oil consortium, but also related to the development of the Merowe dam, the largest hydropower project in Africa.[51] Of course, China is not the only country with significant economic ties to Sudan. Malaysia, India, and the Gulf states also invest massively in Sudan. But China is Sudan's only close economic ally that is also a permanent member of the Security Council, and as such holds a veto on any resolution before the council.[52]

In 2004 China had threatened to veto the very first UN Security Council resolution on Darfur, which contained a provision to monitor Khartoum's compliance with the council's demand that they disarm the Janjaweed. Capitulating to the threat of a veto, the council removed the monitoring mechanism.[53] As the crisis in Darfur continued, insiders on the Security Council started to refer to China as Khartoum's "heat shield"—ensuring that other countries' attempts to apply pressures to Sudan would ultimately be deflected by the threat of China's veto. This heat shield function was to prove critical as drafting began on what would eventually become Resolution 1706, authorizing the deployment of UN peacekeepers to Darfur. "It was all about [accommodating] China," recalls one of the officials involved in the drafting process.[54] While it may have been "all about China" in the hallways of the United Nations, the advocacy community was yet to set China in their sights. So it fell to the wordsmiths at the UN Security Council to find a way to get a resolution on a UN deployment approved.

Conscious of China's position that it would not support any resolution on the deployment of UN peacekeepers without the consent of the Sudanese government, Britain tried some "creative lawyering," drafting language that would give a nod to consent without actually requiring it. The U.S. representative to the UN, John Bolton, was adamant that the mere word "consent" should not be included. He instructed one of his staff to go through a thesaurus to try and find an alternative. "In the end he got me going in there pushing for 'invites the acquiescence!'" recalls the staffer.[55]

Not all of those working on the resolution thought that China would actually go ahead with its threatened veto if nonconsensual language were presented, but no one wanted there to be any abstentions. This stems from a culture among Security Council members that values consensus decision making; passing a resolution without abstentions from the five permanent members marks a gold standard. In the legal sense, this is ludicrous. Under the UN Charter, a resolution that passes with abstentions has the same value as a resolution that passes without abstentions. But as a political matter, there is a certain logic to it. If the resolution is likely to face difficulties in the implementation phase, then it is helpful to be able to say that the resolution represents a unified position. Given China's relationship with Sudan, it was reasonable to believe that a weaker resolution that China voted for would ultimately be worth more than a stronger resolution that China abstained on. In practice, neither would be achieved.

The Americans and the British presented their peacekeeping resolution for a vote on August 31, 2006. The resolution, numbered 1706, stated that the UN Mission in Sudan should be strengthened by "up to 17,300 military personnel and by an appropriate civilian component including up to 3,300 civilian police personnel and up to 16 Formed Police Units"[56] in order to take on a mission in Darfur. The force's mandate included the protection of "civilians under threat of physical violence." Issued under Chapter VII—the strongest part of the UN Charter, which allows the Security Council to use force to maintain or restore international peace and security and is binding on members of the UN—the resolution nevertheless "invites the consent" of the Sudanese government to the deployment.

The resolution passed but not unanimously. Sudan's Arab League ally Qatar abstained, and at the very last minute Russia, under pressure from Qatar, reversed its position and decided to abstain as well. Despite the hours of creative lawyering that had gone into the consent language, China also abstained.

The Sudanese president wasted no time responding to the council's "invitation." "The Sudanese people will not consent to any resolution that will violate its sovereignty" was the way he phrased it.[57] It was a position that came as something of a rude awakening to advocates who had imagined that the resolution's passage per se would equal success. As Bell remembers, their thinking had been, "If the Security Council authorizes it, then we've overcome the big barrier. What are they going to do? Not accept the peacekeepers?!" As Khartoum was taking every opportunity to convey, that is exactly what it was going to do.

Khartoum had been clear from the beginning that it would not consent to a UN deployment in Darfur, and no country wanted to contribute troops to a nonconsensual deployment. It was against this backdrop that Western countries in particular told the UN to "do something," as if this made the problem someone else's responsibility. "If the Sudanese government does not approve this peacekeeping force quickly, the United Nations must act...the credibility of the United Nations is at stake," President Bush told the UN General Assembly in September 2006.[58] But since the individual countries that make up the UN were unwilling or unable to get an effective force deployed, the UN as just the collective of those countries could hardly be expected to achieve a different outcome.

WHEN THEY BEGAN their advocacy efforts in late 2004, the new Darfur activists imagined a UN Security Council resolution like 1706 would ensure that Darfuris received the protection that Rwandans never had. But now Darfur advocates started to realize that this "success" did not automatically translate into protection for Darfuris.

By the end of 2006, Darfur advocates had achieved remarkable progress on policy demands that the U.S. government could deliver on its own. Still, unilateral U.S. action could not deliver justice, protection, and peace to Darfur. And while established channels existed through which regular American citizens could pressure their own government, there were no such channels when it came to other countries and organizations.

PART III

REVISITING ASSUMPTIONS

CHAPTER 9

SEARCHING FOR A NEW WAY FORWARD

By the end of 2006 advocates had succeeded in getting many of the things they had been asking for: a UN Security Council resolution authorizing the deployment of peacekeepers, a special envoy, and domestic legislation to ensure that U.S. sanctions remained on the Sudanese government. But advocates were beginning to realize that achieving these goals, challenging as they had been, were mere prerequisites to even beginning to push for change on the ground.

Sam Bell remembers late 2006 as a time when advocates started focusing on implementation. "It was something of a revelation that just because the international community wants to do something, that doesn't mean it will happen." It also marked a broader shift in thinking for Bell and his colleagues. The "Dallaire model" that had been so prominent in their original theory was based on the international community intervening directly: "To be very basic about it, a Bangladeshi stands between a Janjaweed and a Darfuri civilian," explains Bell. It was the kind of thinking that arose from a belief that a genocidal regime cannot be pressured into changing its behavior but can only have behavioral change imposed upon it by force. GI-Net now began to revisit this assumption and started to consider working indirectly to impose costs that would pressure Khartoum to change.

AIMING FOR THE BACK POCKET

The team at GI-Net began looking for ways to increase economic pressure on the Sudanese government. But with the exception of capital market sanctions that would prohibit companies doing business with Sudan from raising capital in the U.S. financial markets, and which Sudan Campaign advocates had previously tried, and failed, to get political support for, the U.S. government had already maximized the economic sanctions that it alone could apply.

President Clinton had put wide-ranging sanctions on Sudan back in 1997,[1] and the legislation that advocates had pushed congress to pass in late 2006 ensured these sanctions would stay in place. U.S. government officials I interviewed reported frustration with this, arguing that they would have had more leverage to get behavioral change from Khartoum if either there were fewer sanctions already in place so that they could use the threat of increased sanctions to pressure Khartoum or they had the flexibility to offer the reward of lifting some sanctions if Khartoum took certain actions.[2]

With limited options left for pressuring Khartoum economically through the U.S. government, GI-Net started ramping up its involvement in the divestment campaign that had begun on college campuses two years earlier. I had been involved in organizing the first Darfur divestment campaign back on the Harvard campus in 2004, and it had seemed like a good idea for two reasons. First, it was an easy way to engage people. The theory behind a divestment campaign is straightforward and lends itself to the sort of two-minute story that can be readily digested by people with no background in finance. The goal of the divestment campaign was to have investors withdraw capital from companies whose business ventures in Sudan increase Sudanese government revenue that Sudan might use to expand its military budget. As stock prices fall and uncertainty and controversy rise, the hope is that companies are forced into a choice: stop doing business with Sudan or lose investors and share value.

Second, once people engaged with the idea, they could take concrete actions at a local level to move divestment from theory to reality. This notion of giving people something to actually *do* is an obvious yet often overlooked ingredient in building a mass movement. Asking people to write a check for humanitarian relief or join a Facebook page to support peacekeepers does not turn them into activists. To be an activist one must actually act.

By April of the following year, our campaign had succeeded, with the Harvard Corporation divesting its PetroChina shares.[3] Of course, in real terms the $4.4 million Harvard divested was inconsequential relative to the size of PetroChina. But to focus on this missed the significance of the decision. What it showed was that it was possible to get a university to divest for Darfur. By the end of 2006, 26 universities had divested, and another 15 campuses had initiated campaigns.[4]

As those of us first involved in getting our universities to divest began to graduate, a core group set their sights on larger goals. The group, eventually named the Sudan Divestment Task Force, drafted model legislation to get state legislatures around the country to divest. With their shared student roots, GI-Net and the task force went into formal partnership.

The task force was successful in convincing many states to divest.[5] In September 2006 California became the fifth state to do so, which meant that finally divestment was beginning to reach a scale that mattered.[6] (If California had been a country in 2006, its economy would have been the eighth largest in the world, larger than the economies of all the states in sub-Saharan Africa combined.[7]) In one of the clearest metrics of the Sudanese government actually feeling pressured by a U.S.-based advocacy campaign, Khartoum spent close to a million dollars on an eight-page advertising spread in the *New York Times* encouraging investment in companies doing business in Sudan, a country with a "peaceful, prosperous and democratic future."[8]

INCREASING THE SPECIFICITY OF POLICY DEMANDS

Other leaders in the advocacy movement were also pinning their hopes on what new ventures might achieve. In early 2007 John Prendergast and Gayle Smith cofounded an advocacy group called the Enough Project to focus on atrocity crimes in Africa, in partnership with their respective employers, the International Crisis Group and the Center for American Progress. They launched with a plain-English policy paper written by Prendergast entitled "The Answer to Darfur," which set out a comprehensive list of aggressive policy recommendations.

The first inklings of the organization went back to the summer of 2005 with a conference organized by Humanity United. "We convened experts to help us think about how an effective advocacy movement might function," explains Pam Omidyar. "One thing that became clear was that the movement needed to move away from a message of 'do something' to asking policymakers to 'do something specific.' As part of that, we devised a three-pronged approach—one that integrated field-based research, grass-roots advocacy, and experts in the policy community all working in concert...."[9] After the conference, Prendergast, Smith, and Samantha Power began discussing an organizational model that would take the analytical skills of International Crisis Group reporting and marry their policy recommendations to actions for a mass movement to follow through on. Humanity United granted $7.98 million to the development of the project over the coming five years.[10]

The discussion of how to take International Crisis Group analysis and repackage it for a significantly wider audience took place over the course of 2006, and the resulting Enough Project launched in 2007. An intentionally populist endeavor, the organization drew the involvement of celebrities such as *Hotel Rwanda* star Don Cheadle and NBA basketball star Tracy McGrady. While the emphasis on policy specifics was new, the Enough Project was mostly a natural extension of the logic involved in the origins of the Darfur movement. The working assumption was that the U.S. government was unlikely to act spontaneously to stop atrocities committed against Africans, but that if the government did decide to act, it could make a difference. Omer

Ismail joined the Enough Project, hopeful of what change the new venture might be able to bring.

David Rubenstein's approach to citizen advocacy involved getting American voters to urge their government to "do something." In his view, "the closer we could get to a bumper sticker, the better we'd do as an organization." He believed it was the role of activists to get the issue on the agenda, but trusted policymakers to then play their part. Enough's approach was more skeptical. "For too long there's been an idea that there are these smart policy people in Washington who understand these complicated hard places," said Enough's director, John Norris, explaining why activists needed to move beyond holding rallies and writing letters to engage in the policy specifics.[11] Exactly where they would get the information from which to develop those policy specifics became a challenge when, less than a year after launching, the International Crisis Group and its team of field researchers decided to withdraw from the project.[12] The Enough Project subsequently established its own team of field-based researchers, although Enough's mass movement advocacy led Khartoum to restrict its access, making on-the-ground research a challenge.

TRYING TO GO GLOBAL

Sam Bell recalls that by late 2006 there was a sense of success in having established the American advocacy base, but it was accompanied by a sinking realization that such success would not be worth as much if it wasn't global. The idea that advocacy efforts needed to expand beyond U.S. borders was intermittently present early on. The day after Powell made his genocide determination, Rubenstein scheduled a conference call to discuss reaching potential allies overseas. After the call, an e-mail was drafted asking coalition members to reach out to their international contacts.[13] However, the e-mail was never sent, and the movement occupied itself with mobilizing those closer to home. The need to build a U.S. base of support was always seen as the priority because there was a high degree of consensus that if Washington wanted to, it could "save Darfur."

I asked Rubenstein why the need for support outside the United States was left on the back burner for so long. "I think it is important to note that a key priority of Save Darfur Coalition was that President Bush speak out internationally on the issue," he replied defensively. But Rubenstein says he subsequently realized, "Bush had burned so many of his bridges in terms of credibility he couldn't do it." There was an extent to which this was true. In both Europe and the Arab world, any statements that Bush made about Darfur were generally viewed as hypocritical against the backdrop of Iraq, and the particular travesties of Abu Ghraib and Guantanamo. U.S. "soft power" (the ability to influence others through noncoercive measures[14]) was at an all-time low, and Bush simply talking about Darfur would not convince other countries to spend their resources on the crisis. Yet talking publicly about Darfur was not the president's only option. He could have used the leverage of economic and diplomatic incentives and pressures that the United States still had in its bilateral relations with countries who had influence over Khartoum, such as China and Egypt. But there were always other priorities more aligned to traditional national interests than Darfur to attend to in these relationships.

"The U.S. could have done more to pressure China," acknowledges one of the staff in the National Security Council's Strategic Planning section. Darfur was often included in the president's talking points, but it never made it to the top tier. "The U.S.-China relationship was so overburdened that there was limited bandwidth...you had North Korea, China's domestic rights violations, revaluation of the currency."[15]

And there was an additional reason for the United States to hesitate. "We were somewhat self-deterred from charging down that trail...because of what could happen if it succeeded," explains Peter Feaver, director of Strategic Planning on the National Security Council.[16] The fear was that if the United States succeeded in getting Sudan's allies to threaten their relationship with Khartoum over Darfur, Khartoum might retaliate, harming other interests it knew the United States cared about. "On counterterrorism cooperation and on the south, Khartoum had gone a long way towards meeting our demands," says Feaver. "So there was a fear that steps we might take to pressure them on Darfur would hurt the Government of National Unity and that they might create problems in the south."[17] Al-Bashir's regime had effectively held Darfur hostage to other U.S. interests in Sudan, and, without ever admitting it, the U.S. government capitulated.

With the U.S. government unwilling to seriously pressure international actors, it was left to advocates to come up with alternative ways to get their message beyond U.S. borders. One opportunity that soon arose was the January 2007 African Union Summit. The summit is the once yearly gathering of all the AU member states, and protocol has it that the host state gets to chair the meeting. The year before, Sudan had hosted the meeting, but it had not gone as planned; Darfur had cast a stain on Khartoum's credibility. Under pressure from African nations, Khartoum had withdrawn its bid for the AU chair, conditional upon being given it the following year.[18]

As the 2007 AU Summit approached, U.S. advocacy groups swung into action, bombarding Assistant Secretary of State Jendayi Frazer with faxes and e-mails urging her to do everything in her power to ensure that al-Bashir did not chair the AU. I happened to be at the State Department's Sudan Programs Group conducting interviews the day after the advocacy campaign was launched, and the staff complained to me that Frazer was spending her time calling technicians to work out how to deal with the multitude of advocacy e-mails; "as soon as she hits delete and block spam another screen [full of e-mails] appears."[19] Frazer received the message loud and clear, and at the summit she spoke out against Sudan. When the chair was ultimately given to Ghana, Darfur advocacy groups sent congratulatory e-mails out to their constituents who had been responsible for clogging Frazer's inbox.

Talking to those who were at the AU at the time, though, it's not clear that the victory was the advocates' to claim. Dismas Nkunda from the Darfur Consortium remembers speaking to the AU staff who told him that none of the African countries wanted al-Bashir to chair the AU. Advocacy organizations with contacts at the AU received the same message. But given the relative ease of a quick-hit advocacy campaign on the issue, the consensus was that there was no harm in getting their constituents involved as it would create an easy victory, which seems to be exactly what it did.[20]

The other way to reach beyond U.S. borders was to foster citizen advocates in other countries to pressure their own governments on Darfur. This was an approach that the Darfur movement had already begun to try, although the initial motivation was not only about getting foreign citizens engaged but also about making the movement less vulnerable to charges of Zionism.

"If we return to the last demonstrations in the United States, and the groups that organized the demonstrations, we find they are all Jewish organizations," the Sudanese president had told reporters shortly after the April 2006 rallies.[21] After reading the coverage, a frustrated David Rubenstein e-mailed fellow staff: "How are we going to convince everyone we are not a Zionist conspiracy?!" One of his employees looked at the e-mail and laughed out loud; it was written by someone with the surname Rubenstein and addressed to Loeb and Shapiro.

Save Darfur was not a Zionist conspiracy. While some advocates say it "didn't hurt" that Darfur provided a counternarrative to Arab victimization in the Israel-Palestine context, Jewish organizations were drawn to Darfur because of the resonance the genocide label had and because of the connection that had been made to Rwanda, which spoke to a particular guilt among some segments of the Jewish community about not having acted to stop the 1994 genocide.[22] The result was that Jewish organizations had been among the first in the United States to advocate on Darfur. They were far from being the only organizations involved in the April 2006 rallies, as al-Bashir claimed. But as a former journalist turned professional human rights advocate, Jill Savitt, remembers thinking, the more general observation about the preponderance of Jewish organizations in the coalition "had the trouble of being true."[23]

Savitt, in her early 40s, has the aura of a star college student, hyperarticulate and self-assured. In the late spring of 2006 she was the communications director at Human Rights First. Knowing that Save Darfur was planning another rally, Savitt began to talk with her colleagues about how to ensure this rally looked more globally inclusive and less predominantly Jewish. She discussed the problem with co-workers who had the strongest international connections, and she reached out to those who were now part of the African-based Darfur Consortium.

Two months later, Savitt held a conference call about the rally planned for September 2006; 25 different countries were represented on the call. I asked her what was requested of them. "Get someone lighting a candle, in a public space," Savitt replied. "We said, 'Ten people, a candle, and a photographer. Hold it in the park, your backyard, your office, it doesn't matter!' ... It was about saying 'this many groups and therefore this many countries.' "[24] Rubenstein was enthusiastic about globalizing the movement's reach, and Save Darfur began issuing grants to international organizations to enable them to take part. Grant-making to partners in both Africa and the Arab world would account for almost $1.2 million of the Save Darfur Coalition's spending in the subsequent three years.[25]

The first Global Day for Darfur took place outside the UN building in New York. Photos of demonstrators around the world were projected on a massive screen. "Ten people and a candle" gave the visual impression of a movement with a global face. Such a rapid, if largely superficial, result could not have been accomplished if U.S-based advocates had needed to look for global connections from scratch. The preexisting relationships that could be leveraged through Human Rights First and the Darfur Consortium, along with funding from Save Darfur, were what made the first Global Day possible.

The movement organized another four Global Days for Darfur, although not without some challenges. Through the Darfur Consortium, Dismas Nkunda took the lead on organizing an event in Tanzania for the second Global Day. Tanzania had just decided to send a contingent of female police officers to Darfur as part of the AMIS deployment, and Nkunda saw the event as a way to both spotlight the situation for Darfuri women and applaud the Tanzanian government's decision to contribute personnel. Having obtained all the relevant permissions, he was surprised when the Tanzanian police commissioner called him one week before the event and told him he had to cancel. "But Mr. Commissioner, we are in the final stages of planning," Nkunda protested.[26] The commissioner told him that when they gave permission for the event, they had overlooked that it was taking place on Tanzanian Independence Day; the government had invited a host of African leaders, including President al-Bashir, to join their celebrations.

Nkunda saw the dilemma. Allowing Darfur demonstrations to go forward would be a diplomatic faux pas on a scale that could lead Sudan to reject the deployment of the Tanzanian female police. But when Nkunda called one of the Global Day coordinators in New York, he was told the event must go ahead as planned. "They even started drafting a press release saying that the Tanzanian government was refusing to allow the Global Day to go forward because the Sudanese president was coming," remembers Nkunda, incredulously. Eventually the U.S.-based organizers backed down; the Tanzanian event was successfully held a couple of days after the rest of the Global Days, and the Tanzanian female police officers got to Darfur.

For the third Global Day, Save Darfur asked partner organizations around the globe to obtain a giant hourglass to feature at their events. Symbolizing that time was running out, the uniformity of the hourglass symbol across the geographically diverse event locations was intended to unite the Global Day participants, much as the postcards had unified activists across the United States in the Million Voices campaign. "Our partners were, like, 'What?! You want me to get what? Where am I gonna get that?'"[27] recalls a U.S.-based coordinator for the Darfur Consortium. While a massive hourglass filled with "blood" was on display at the London event, there was simply no way to source such a thing for events across Africa, where advocates were mystified as to why so much time and money should be spent on something so impractical.

By the middle of 2007 enthusiasm for the Global Days had worn off. Advocates in Africa and the Arab world felt that rallies were simply not having an impact, and that they would rather see Save Darfur spending its money on sending a couple of prominent Sudanese who they could take to their capitals to meet with a handful of key people. When asked to organize another rally, they would say, "Yeah, that works for you in America—people get impressed when you turn out thousands of people in the street, but in Kampala that's not going to shift the dynamic."[28]

THE HYBRID OPTION

In the aftermath of Sudan's refusal to accept UN peacekeepers, it was not just advocates who were looking for a new approach. At the UN, alternatives were also desperately being sought. Kofi Annan had been head of UN peacekeeping during the department's failure either to preempt or to respond effectively to genocide in both Rwanda and Srebrenica. In another organization it may have been a career-ender, but Annan had been made secretary-general and spearheaded an effort to take the organization through a set of self-flagellating lessons-learned. However by late 2006 it was clear that Darfur was not going to provide Annan with an example of these lessons being put into practice. So in November, just before the end of his term as secretary-general, Annan made a final effort to salvage something of a positive legacy.

I met with Annan after he left the UN. Sitting in his eco-friendly office in Geneva, he told me he knew that Western troops would not be deployed to

Darfur "because of the environment in the aftermath of Iraq and perceptions in the Islamic world, which Bashir presented very well."[29] Sudan had sent several members of the UN Security Council a letter saying that the mere offer of troops, by any country, to the proposed UN force would be viewed as the prelude to an act of invasion.[30] Still, Annan had felt very strongly that AMIS should not be stranded in Darfur without additional support. "The Security Council and the international community were very happy to say African peacekeepers could go in, when everybody knew they did not have the capacity or resources," says Annan. "I felt it was a copout."

Annan called Bush's new envoy, Andrew Natsios. "We've got a problem," he said. The problem was that Resolution 1706, authorizing the deployment of UN peacekeepers into Darfur, had still not received the consent of the Sudanese government, and now the Security Council was placed in a diplomatically embarrassing situation; unable to enforce a resolution that, legally speaking, should have been binding, their legitimacy was in question. Over the course of a 45-minute conversation Annan outlined his idea for what was soon to become known as "the hybrid." The idea was for the UN and the AU to conduct a joint operation in Darfur, with the AU continuing to provide the bulk of the troops, but with some UN troops also deployed, and with the UN providing the resources as well as leading on organizational and command issues. Natsios wasn't too keen on the idea, but says, "We couldn't say to the UN 'fix it' and then not agree to support them."[31]

Annan called a meeting at the AU headquarters in Addis Ababa. Representatives from more than 30 countries, as well as the AU, Arab League, and UN descended on the Ethiopian capital. Annan's clarity that a hybrid solution was the only way forward was apparent in the way he chaired the meeting; attempts at dissent were ignored as Annan pushed the proposal through. "In many ways it was almost comical," recalls Natsios. "Lam Akol [the Sudanese foreign minister] would raise objections and Kofi would say 'thank you for approving.'" Annan did not put the proposal to a vote, but at the conclusion of the meeting he declared that in the absence of objections, the proposal had been adopted by consensus. He then went out to the awaiting press pool and announced the agreement. "He rammed it through in a very smooth way," recalls Natsios, with more than a tinge of admiration in his voice.[32] But when I asked Lam Akol about Annan's role in the hybrid proposal, he literally laughed out loud. "It wasn't him—it was us!"[33]

I met Akol, who hails from southern Sudan, at his Khartoum residence in August 2009. At the time he was under round-the-clock police guard following threats on his life by SPLM members after he split from them to form a new political party. His living room was furnished with eight paisley upholstered couches and crocheted coaster mats on glass coffee tables. On the far wall from where we sat there was a photograph of Akol beside old photographs of his mother and father. While Akol smiles confidently into the camera, his parents frown mistrustingly into the lens. Hanging above us were photographs from more recent times with Akol in various poses as Sudan's foreign minister: Akol at the UN, Akol along with the officers of Sudan's Higher Security Academy, and Akol at the May 2006 Sino-Africa Cooperation Summit in Beijing. The NCP had used Akol's appointment as foreign minister in the Government of National Unity to show that the ruling regime in Khartoum had become more inclusive. But most southerners viewed Akol as an NCP lackey rather than as a "true" southerner.

According to Akol, the proposal for a hybrid was developed within the Sudanese Ministry of Foreign Affairs after the UN Security Council passed Resolution 1706 authorizing UN peacekeepers. "It was we in the Sudan who developed the idea of a hybrid force," Akol claimed. "Our idea was not to replace the AMIS force but to consolidate them by changing their caps from green to blue. Our thinking was that the AMIS troops are very good but since they rely on the UN for logistics and upkeep, we must find a role for the UN."[34] Akol's characterization of the AMIS troops as "very good" was the height of cynicism. As AMIS deputy force commander, General Kazura, put it, "The Sudanese government were very happy to have us there because they were sure we couldn't do anything. For us to be there was very nice for them."[35] Undertrained, underresourced, and operating in the knowledge that the Sudanese government could expel them at any time, AMIS was unlikely to ever act against the government in Darfur. Yet, having AMIS on the ground enabled Khartoum to say that they were allowing the international community to provide protection.

According to Akol's account, his ministry shopped the proposal for a hybrid operation to Sudanese allies before the meeting in Addis Ababa, securing their support in advance. He then discussed the idea of a hybrid with Annan on the morning of the meeting. Akol says that his meeting with Annan, scheduled for 30 minutes, lasted two hours. "After our meeting Kofi Annan prepared a draft proposal on the basis of our discussion, and so now the credit for the idea goes to him!" said Akol.[36]

The idea that Annan convened a conference with more than 30 international representatives, yet only developed the proposal to present to them on the morning they met is implausible. Annan himself says that his meeting with Lam Akol that morning did only last for 30 minutes and that his office had developed the hybrid proposal well in advance of the conference. Natsios agrees, referring to the notion that the hybrid was Lam Akol's idea as "nonsense."[37] But the fact that Akol viewed the hybrid as Sudan's idea is significant and goes some way toward explaining the challenges that would soon face those tasked with implementing it.

The approved hybrid proposal was something akin to a Rorschach test—vague enough for people to see what they wanted. The different descriptions of the proposal in the aftermath of the meeting are telling. The British representative told the press, "We achieved what we wanted out of 1706 but by different means."[38] In describing it this way, he was unlikely to have had in mind that the proposal involved the UN "paying for the AU to do the job," which is how the Sudanese ambassador to the UN put it, adding that the hybrid "takes 1706 to the graveyard."[39]

THE CRACKS BEGIN TO SHOW

AT HOME ONE EVENING, Gloria White-Hammond was in the middle of ironing when the phone rang. It was Pam Omidyar and Humanity United's CEO, Randy Newcomb, calling to encourage her to take a leadership role in the Save Darfur movement. "I didn't really get it," says White-Hammond. "I mean, I couldn't see what they saw that would make them feel like it would be appropriate for me to take a lead role." It was a moment of disconnect. "I felt that Sudanese needed to be in the lead. People talk about speaking for Sudanese people. I've never seen myself speaking for Sudanese people. I never had a sense of any need to speak for anyone other than myself."

White-Hammond successfully steered the conversation to her commitment to ensuring that the voices of Sudanese women were reflected in the advocacy movement. She said that with Humanity United as a "high engagement, high investment partner," My Sister's Keeper was soon able to hire a field coordinator to oversee the construction of the school in Akon.

Throughout this period White-Hammond was also on the Save Darfur board, although as she describes it, board members were little more than "names on a piece of paper." John Prendergast, also on the board at the time, agrees there was effectively was no board.[40] It was a structural flaw that had not been significant when Save Darfur started out as an ad-hoc collection of people who just wanted to do something for Darfur. But with the success of the rallies and the visibility resulting from the paid advertising campaign, Save Darfur was now a nationally recognized, multimillion-dollar enterprise. And it had neither the systems nor staffing in place to handle the transition.

Reflecting on the period some years later, Rubenstein recalls it as a time when "the cracks started to show." As he frames the problem, "There were some very vocal people who thought our policy prescriptions and demands were insufficient—and that theirs were more valid, people who believed their expertise and commitment to the issues were greater than the staff at Save Darfur." Rubenstein's theory of a "bumper sticker organization" was under attack. Conscious of the criticism, Rubenstein added some policy heft to his staff, which had yet to expand beyond a couple of young professionals and a handful of interns. In late 2006 he hired a former U.S. ambassador, as well as a couple of staff with contacts in the Arab League and AU. But the more fundamental problems with the organization's structure were left unaddressed.

In a rare effort at oversight, the board asked for a reconciled budget. "There were millions of dollars coming in. We knew Dave [Rubenstein] wasn't taking off with the money or anything like that, but still...," says White-Hammond. In a staff meeting the day before the accounting was due, Rubenstein delegated the task to a 21-year-old college student who had deferred her fall semester to stay on at Save Darfur after a summer internship there. She told Rubenstein she had no idea how to do it, recalls Alex Meixner, who was present at the meeting. "He said he had faith in her ability. Now that might have been fine for a little start-up. But when you have suddenly added a lot of zeros to your budget...."[41] It was reflective of a broader problem of accountability, not uncommon in organizations that grow as rapidly as Save Darfur did. The effect of the dearth of accountability mechanisms soon bled over into Save Darfur's efforts to act more substantially at the policy level.

At the time, New Mexico's governor, Bill Richardson, had thrown his hat in the ring for contention as the Democratic Party candidate for the 2008 presidential elections. Richardson, who had served as ambassador to the UN in the Clinton administration, got in touch with Save Darfur to offer his diplomatic services. The Save Darfur staff followed up on the offer, and by December 2006, Rubenstein had raised half a million dollars, which he spent on securing a private plane to take Richardson to Khartoum. But Richardson canceled after al-Bashir initially refused to schedule a time to meet with him, and what in Rubenstein's words was "enough to keep some NGOs going for a year" was wasted on the plane rental.

A meeting with al-Bashir was finally scheduled shortly after the trip had been canceled, and the Save Darfur staff set out again to organize Richardson's travel plans. As Meixner recalls it, part of the thinking was that commitments al-Bashir had made and failed to keep were now several months old. The staff felt that al-Bashir was winning the spin war in the Arab and African media and that they needed to get a counternarrative into the news cycle. The hope was that Richardson, who had experience negotiating with al-Bashir, could get some kind of cease-fire commitment. "If Bashir did follow through on a new commitment, well, wouldn't that be nice. If he didn't, then we'd use it to draw attention to violating a commitment made three days ago rather than six months ago," was the theory that Rubenstein and the other Save Darfur staff were working on.[42]

Rubenstein says the plan had the full buy-in of the staff and that he "sent a note" to the board about it but no one responded. White-Hammond has no recollection of being consulted in advance, and other board members also expressed shock when they first read the news reports that Richardson was being sponsored by Save Darfur to negotiate with al-Bashir.[43]

Once the trip was underway, the fury of advocates came thick and fast. "Save Darfur shouldn't be negotiating!" Jerry Fowler, the chair of the Committee on Conscience at the United States Holocaust Memorial Museum, screamed down the phone at Rubenstein. "We weren't," Rubenstein protested. But Save Darfur's own press release suggested otherwise. "On Save Darfur Coalition Trip, New Mexico Governor Bill Richardson Gets Commitment for Cease-Fire" was the message that went out to some million people on the Save Darfur list-serve. "It was awkward," recalls Rubenstein, emotion visceral across his face. "Jerry was—and still is—one of my greatest heroes."

Those who had not been involved in planning the trip saw it as having handed al-Bashir a public relations victory. An annual Save Darfur Coalition meeting scheduled for a few days after the Richardson trip brought matters to a head. Eric Reeves had been asked to give a keynote speech. Reeves' indignation, never in short supply, came to the fore, and his anger at Save Darfur was built on by others. "John Prendergast said to Rubenstein, 'I think you simplify things in order to understand them,'" recalls one of the Save Darfur staffers who was at the meeting. "Dave just wasn't equipped to respond. He lost the room."[44]

The cease-fire that Richardson had brokered was violated by Sudanese government aircraft within 48 hours. Meixner recalls that they had e-mails and ads regarding the violation ready to go before the meeting, but once the meeting was over Rubenstein no longer wanted to send them out. "My personal opinion is that it had potential, but due to coalition politics it couldn't be followed through on," says Meixner. "We didn't have the chance to turn it around."[45]

White-Hammond had sat through the meeting, increasingly frustrated with the Save Darfur Coalition. "There was no ownership around it. For whatever reason I felt we were not taking responsibility as board members." After the meeting White-Hammond resigned from the board. "I quit as much because I didn't think Dave was managing the organization well as I didn't feel the board was taking responsibility. I knew we wouldn't run our own organizations like that, so why were we sitting back and allowing this to happen?" Her letter of resignation, sent to Rubenstein on January 20, 2007, expressed her profound disappointment with the coalition, but was at pains to refer to each of the junior Save Darfur staff she had worked with as "a veritable gem—they are brilliant, enduring and precious."[46]

FIRST, DO NO HARM

Rubenstein maintained contact with the representative of Save Darfur's anonymous donor, who continued offering funds for advertising. Rubenstein had initially negotiated that some of the donations could be spent on advertising internationally. Working with the Arab American Institute, Save Darfur produced a television media campaign for the Arab world with the message "Palestine, Iraq, Lebanon, Darfur. We must pray for all of them together."[47] But even with this, there remained millions of dollars for buying up paid advertising in the United States. Rubenstein decided to develop a print media campaign around a promise that Natsios had made some three months earlier.

Like all the special envoys that followed him, Natsios had walked into a job that subjected him to intense scrutiny from journalists and activists alike. As the public face of the administration's Darfur policy, everyone looked to Natsios for answers. So when he held his first State Department press briefing on Sudan and said, "There's a point—January 1st [2007] is [*sic*] either we see a change [in Sudan's obstruction of the new peacekeeping deployment] or we go to plan B," it was no surprise that the journalists in the room jumped all over it. "You say plan B, so are you laying down a January 1 deadline, and then after that you'll bring out the big sticks?" asked one journalist. Natsios' answer was evasive, so the journalist pressed harder. "Our imagination could run wild. What is plan B?" Natsios' answer remained un-illuminating. "Plan B is a different approach," he said.[48]

After the briefing, colleagues at the State Department chastised Natsios for being so loose with his language. There was no Plan B per se. Plan B meant trying whatever hadn't already been tried.[49] (In his subsequent memo to Deputy Secretary of State Negroponte, Natsios warned: "Every word you say will be watched by the advocacy groups and instantly disseminated through the internet."[50])

Consistent with Save Darfur's attempt to strengthen its policy approach, Rubenstein and the staff decided to draft an ad that for the first time included specific policy demands, filling in the gaps left unsaid by Natsios. The full-page ad design pictured a young Darfuri girl staring out at the reader. After the preface calling for Plan B to be implemented came a set of bullet points asking for, among other things, the enforcement of a no-fly zone. A no-fly zone was one of those policy options that kept being raised in half-hearted fits and starts throughout the Darfur crisis. "We knew the objections [to a no-fly zone] but the reason we had it in there was to push the envelope," recalls a Save Darfur staffer. "That should not be conflated with us pushing for a military intervention.... All we were calling for was the enforcement of a preexisting Security Council resolution."[51] While that is technically true—in March

2005 UN Security Council Resolution 1591 demanded that the Sudanese government "immediately cease conducting offensive military flights in and over the Darfur region"—if the United States shot down a Sudanese aircraft in Sudanese airspace it would count, both legally and politically, as an act of war, and Khartoum would respond to it as such. The humanitarian community bristled whenever Darfur advocates raised even the rhetorical suggestion of a no-fly zone, believing that if pressed, the Sudanese would ground all flights, thereby ending the primary means through which humanitarians conducted their operations.[52]

The Save Darfur staff had a period of five days to develop the ad. Both Rubenstein and Meixner say they skimmed over the preface language, drafted by a friend Rubenstein had recently hired, because their focus was on the bullet points that laid out their policy prescriptions. When pushed on the implausibility of allowing any text to go to print in the highest profile American newspapers without first proofing every word, both argue that at this point these kinds of ads had become everyday business for the Save Darfur staff. It was an error that Rubenstein now refers to as "the biggest single mistake of my life."

The preface to the full-page ad that ran in both the *New York Times* and the *Washington Post* on February 14, 2007, read: "Congress, international relief organizations and even many in the President's own Administration agree: the time for talk has ended. Plan A has failed. It's time for President Bush and other world leaders to move to Plan B by...implementing a No-Fly Zone."

By including international relief organizations, Save Darfur had, without consultation, signed humanitarian groups up to a policy prescription that none of them could ever have endorsed and that risked causing the Sudanese government to retaliate against their already endangered operations on the ground. The president of InterAction—the largest coalition of U.S. humanitarian organizations—wrote immediately to Rubenstein noting that their operations were "helping keep close to 2 million people in Darfur alive." He conveyed InterAction's "strongest objection to the wording used" in the ad campaign.[53] In the aftermath, Save Darfur agreed to run all future media by InterAction. "For a lot of activists, particularly those new to international advocacy, it was the first time we really took seriously this possibility that we could do something that really made the situation worse," says Sam Bell.

The next month, before Rubenstein was set to take a two-week vacation, he attended what would turn out to be his last Save Darfur board meeting. At the end of the meeting, most of the board separated off while Rubenstein was taken into a room with two of the other board members. "This is painful for us and for you," he was told. "The board voted to dismiss you."[54]

The plan to get rid of Rubenstein had been brewing for a while, but he says it caught him completely off guard. "I was told I had 48 hours to clear out my office. I asked why I had not been given the opportunity to respond and was told that the board thought it would be cleaner," he says, his voice still shaky at the recollection.

A few days later, the *New York Times* ran an article attributing Rubenstein's removal to the humanitarian organizations' anger over the first run of the Plan B ads.[55] But while that mistake still looms large on Rubenstein's conscience, none of the staff felt it was related to his removal. "It was just about the poor governance of the organization. People had been raising concerns for two years that were never considered by the board," one of the Save Darfur staffers explains.[56] "I think he was well-suited to coalition building...to sitting in a room with people and talking earnestly about Darfur and getting them to join," reflects Meixner. But following the success of the 2006 rallies, Save Darfur had moved beyond that stage. "There was a sense that Save Darfur was 'something.' Before it was a project, but by 2007, it's a gorilla," says Bell, who was on the Save Darfur board at the time. "I think that makes people look a little closer and feel more vulnerable about things going wrong."

THOSE INVOLVED IN STARTING the Save Darfur Coalition never planned for it to be a permanent organization; they never imagined that it would become so prominent, let alone so quickly. And those still involved by 2006 failed to factor in the possibility that accepting conditions set by an anonymous donor over how the majority of their annual budget was spent could distort the Save Darfur Coalition's focus and reputation, even with the content of the donor-driven paid advertising staying under its control.

The need to establish structures of decision making and accountability that would be appropriate to a multimillion-dollar enterprise should have been foreseen years earlier, by both Rubenstein and the Save Darfur board. But they were not alone in underestimating what it would take to get effective action on Darfur. The GI-Net team was initially unaware of the challenges involved in actually delivering the money they raised. And in 2004, the students involved in developing the first chapter of STAND had imagined that their advocacy on Darfur would be a semester-long project only.[57] In hindsight this seems naïve, but had these first advocates been fully aware of the years of work that their commitment to Darfur would entail, they may have been too daunted by the scale of the endeavor to ever begin their campaigns.

The biggest challenge throughout this stage of the movement's development, however, was not structural, but substantive. For the first two years of the advocacy movement's existence there had been an exceptionally high degree of consensus among the movement's leaders about what was required to "save Darfur": They would need to ensure that the media stayed on the issue, that congressional representatives heard from their constituents, that

U.S. leaders spoke out strongly against the violence, and that the United States supported the deployment of peacekeepers through the UN Security Council. The checklist was derived from the lessons learned about all that the U.S. public, congress, and executive failed to do during the Rwandan genocide. When the realization finally hit, for at least some in the movement, that they were trying to tackle a multilateral twenty-first-century challenge with a U.S.-centric twentieth-century script, there was no consensus on the way forward.

CHAPTER 10

MOVING CHINA

Dealing belatedly with the reality that the solution to Darfur would not be found through Washington alone, in 2007 the mass movement began to set its sights on China. The seeds of a campaign focused on China's role had existed for some time. Many of the companies targeted through the divestment campaigns at universities and state legislatures were Chinese corporations. Moreover, with China's abstention from Resolution 1706 at the UN and Khartoum's subsequent refusal to accept the resolution, Beijing's political, as opposed to purely economic, power had finally become clear to those outside government walls. As part of its flurry of efforts to engage internationally at the end of 2006, Save Darfur had even arranged for actor George Clooney to travel to Beijing and meet with the Chinese government on Darfur.[1] But as with many of the advocacy efforts at that time, the approach was piecemeal, and Beijing was not subject to any sustained pressure.

Actress Mia Farrow first visited Darfur as UNICEF's ambassador in 2004 and would travel to neighboring Chad some ten times in the subsequent five years to speak with Darfuri refugees. Throughout the second half of 2006, she had been mulling over how to best pressure China. In June 2006 Farrow had appeared on the NBC news show *Hardball* to talk with host Chris Matthews about a recent visit she had made to Darfur. As she came off the air, Matthews asked her what was stopping the UN Security Council from getting peacekeepers into Darfur. "I said, 'China,'" she recalls. Matthews responded, "China? What the hell has China got to do with it?" Farrow did a double-take. "Chris is a smart guy. I realized if he had no idea about China's relationship with the Sudanese government, then there was a lot of work to be done."[2]

That work was given a kick-start by Farrow's son Ronan, who was studying for his law degree at Yale. He and I had been introduced through Darfur activism, and we had gotten into the habit of calling each other to hammer out improvements to op-eds we were both drafting. In early August 2006 he called to get feedback on a piece about the impact of China's oil contracts on Sudan's military budget. The final version, entitled "China's Crude Conscience," was published in the *Wall Street Journal* on August 8, 2006, and immediately raised the profile of the mutually beneficial alliance between China and Sudan. "Thanks to this relationship," wrote Ronan Farrow, "Sudan has purchased the best protection in the world: a veto-wielding member on the U.N. Security Council willing to ensure that Khartoum's campaign of human destruction in Darfur can continue."

While Ronan was working on his article, Mia Farrow began talking with Eric Reeves, the literature professor who had become such an outspoken advocate. They discussed how to influence the Chinese government. "I knew we had to find a way to pressure Beijing, and I thought we could use the 2008 Olympics to do that, but at that stage I didn't quite know how," she remembers, referring to the fact that Beijing had been named to host the 2008 summer games.

In the late summer of 2006 the Farrows attended a concert by cellist Yo-Yo Ma at the Tanglewood Music Festival in Massachusetts. Steven Spielberg was also in the audience that night. A few months earlier, the media had reported that Spielberg had been named artistic director of the opening and closing ceremonies of the 2008 Beijing Olympics. Back home after the concert, looking at the photos from her recent trip to Darfur, Farrow came across an old photo of Yo-Yo Ma with Spielberg's daughter. She began to wonder if Spielberg could help put her photos from Darfur into a form that could be accessed more broadly. She compiled a set of the photos and an explanation of what was happening in Darfur and sent them off to him along with the photo of his daughter, but didn't hear anything back.

In November 2006 Farrow tried to contact Spielberg again. By now she was thinking more concretely about his role in putting a positive face on the Olympics. She wrote Spielberg a letter outlining the relationship between the Chinese government, the Sudanese government, and the Darfur atrocities, attached her son's *Wall Street Journal* article, and then waited. Again she got no response. "I had this vision of him in an office, within an office, within an office. I imagined his 'people' ensured that maybe only three pieces of mail actually landed on his desk—perhaps one letter from the pope, another from the Dalai Lama—something like that. After trying and getting nowhere, I basically gave up on reaching him," she recalls.

Farrow and Reeves continued their discussions about how to use the Beijing Olympics to pressure the Chinese government into taking a different approach to its relationship with Sudan. Farrow got t-shirts made up saying "Genocide Olympics" and sent one to Reeves. They both wore the shirts when they spoke to a group of STAND student activists at Brown University in January 2007, but it did not have the impact Farrow was hoping for. "No one got it. When I started to try and explain it, there were just too many links to draw."

DREAM FOR DARFUR

At the 2007 Save Darfur annual meeting following the Richardson trip debacle, Eric Reeves delivered a vitriolic tirade that included a call for the advocacy movement to recognize China's influence over Khartoum. When Reeves subsequently stormed out of the meeting, Jill Savitt, the communications director from Human Rights First, followed. "Wait! I want to work on China too!" she told him. As Reeves calmed down, he opened his laptop and sat with Savitt in the lobby of the hotel to share the ideas he had for a "viral" campaign to target China.[3]

Savitt spent February working on a proposal for a Human Rights First campaign to pressure China over its arms flows into Sudan and followed the news reports of Chinese president Hu Jintao's visit to Khartoum. While the media headlines suggested that Beijing's non-interference approach to the human rights policies of its trading partners was shifting by virtue of the fact that Hu mentioned Darfur in his discussions with al-Bashir, the objective outcomes of the visit undercut such claims. During his visit Hu canceled debts of nearly $80 million owed to Beijing by the Sudanese government, in addition to giving Khartoum grants totaling more than $100 million and promising to build al-Bashir a new presidential palace.[4]

In March 2007 Farrow gave another presentation on Darfur, this time to a group of artists and intellectuals in New York. She didn't wear the Genocide Olympics t-shirt, but she was still working on how to make the connection for people between the Beijing Olympics and Darfur. In an off-the-cuff comment, she compared the part Steven Spielberg was playing to help China present a glowing image to the world with the role that Hitler's prized filmmaker, Leni Riefenstahl, played by creating a Nazi propaganda film of the 1936 Olympics in Germany. The gasp from the audience was audible as the comparison came out of her mouth. "The reaction told me that this was the link I had been looking for. When I got home, I called Ronan and we started thrashing out ideas for an article."

Working back and forth they pulled together an op-ed over that weekend. They sent it to the *New York Times* and then the *Washington Post*, both of which rejected the piece, before it was accepted by the *Wall Street Journal*. On March 28, 2007, "The Genocide Olympics" made its debut into colloquial vocabulary as the title of their piece, which soon became a news story of its own.

A story about the Genocide Olympics op-ed that ran prominently in the *New York Times* led Human Rights First to get cold feet about moving forward with the proposal Savitt had been working on. Like many other human rights organizations, Human Rights First had never followed the U.S. government's lead in calling the Darfur situation a genocide. With "Genocide Olympics" becoming almost overnight the phrase associated with campaigning on China and Darfur, the organization worried about being drawn into the label by association.[5]

As Human Rights First backed off, Savitt and Reeves managed to secure $500,000 for the campaign from Humanity United,[6] which was now by far the largest financier of the Darfur advocacy movement. Shortly after, Savitt left Human Rights First to work full time at Dream for Darfur, the new organization that would turn Genocide Olympics from a headline into an 18-month campaign.

"We don't think it is appropriate to link the Olympic Games in Beijing with the Darfur issue," the Chinese Ministry of Foreign Affairs said in a statement the day after the Genocide Olympics op-ed.[7] The advocacy movement had been trying to focus China's attention on Darfur for several months,[8] but nothing had garnered such a direct reaction from Beijing. And, after six months of getting no response from Steven Spielberg, Farrow was gratified to learn that just three days after the piece was published, Spielberg wrote directly to Chinese President Hu, stating, "I add my voice to those who ask that China change its policy toward Sudan and pressure the Sudanese government to bring the genocide in Darfur to an end."[9]

The three months following the publication of the Genocide Olympics op-ed saw a 400 percent increase in the number of English-language newspaper headlines linking China with Darfur, compared to the three months prior.[10] There was also a burst of congressional activity. On April 30, 2007, Senator Joe Biden sent a letter with the signatures of 96 senators to President Hu, calling on China to use its influence over Khartoum to help end violence in Darfur.[11] Ten days later, the chair of the House Committee on Foreign Relations delivered a similar letter to the Chinese government on behalf of 108 members of congress.[12] The next day, Beijing announced the deployment of a military engineering unit to assist AMIS in Darfur[13] and appointed a special envoy to focus on the Darfur crisis.[14] I have never been able to speak directly with officials in Beijing, but it seems implausible that the timing of these measures, the first publicly visible steps that Beijing had taken on Darfur, was merely coincidental to the spike in public pressure.

ON THE WEST SIDE OF Manhattan, Jill Savitt and a colleague made their way past a Falun Gong protest and through a maze of security services to reach the grand premises of a former luxury hotel now home to the consulate of the People's Republic of China. Savitt felt a little disorientated as the unfailingly polite deputy counsel general gave them a tour of the building, complete with revolving ballroom, before beginning a meeting marked by high formality.

Savitt knew that the first question a campaign like Dream for Darfur would be asked by the media was whether they had actually met with Chinese government officials. Securing the meeting with Deputy Counsel General Kuang Weilin was an important step, and one Savitt had been surprised to accomplish so quickly. More surprising though were the contents of the four-inch thick stack of papers that Kuang brought to their meeting: printouts from the Dream for Darfur website, each page marked up in hand-written Chinese documenting what Kuang believed to be errors in the campaign's publications. While Kuang went through each page, Savitt noted the single theme of his comments: The Olympics had nothing to do with Darfur. Savitt responded that as host of the Olympics, China had a responsibility to support peace, to which Kuang reiterated his position that the two were unrelated. And so the discussion continued, back and forth.

They were at an impasse, but Savitt wanted to secure the possibility of further discussions. She pushed Kuang to put his concerns in writing and committed to post what he wrote on the Dream for Darfur website. She also began what would be part of a strategy "to make them fear we were bigger than we really were"[15] by painting a picture of what Dream for Darfur would do in the buildup to the Olympics. "We'd like to keep you informed of our plans," was what Savitt told Kuang before discussing their intention to speak with the Olympics' corporate sponsors and describing the expected media attention that would be given to the symbolic Olympic torch relay they planned to run in America and at former sites of genocide around the world.

During this period, the growing public pressure on China was supplemented by diplomatic pressure on both Beijing and Khartoum from Western powers. U.S. pressure began with the implementation of the long-awaited Plan B—tougher measures to push Khartoum to accept deployment of the hybrid peacekeeping operation.

In contrast to their efforts to influence policymakers outside the United States, Darfur advocates were able to rely on tested methods of domestic lobbying to apply pressure in support of Plan B. By April 2007 InterAction-approved versions of the Plan B ads had gone out, and President Bush was feeling the heat as a speech he was scheduled to give at the U.S. Holocaust Memorial Museum loomed. Bush literally threw the first draft back at his speechwriters. The president was under attack, and the content in the speech would not be enough to fend off his critics. "His reputation on bringing peace to Sudan with the CPA was being destroyed by advocacy groups," recalls Natsios. After seeing yet another of Save Darfur's full-page ads, the president banged his fist on the table and demanded his staff give him more coercive options against Khartoum.[16] Finally in May, Bush announced the imposition of Plan B measures against Sudan for its obstruction of the hybrid deployment.[17]

Natsios says he tried to get capital markets sanctions (barring key foreign companies that did business with the Sudanese government from raising capital in U.S. financial markets) into the Plan B package and that National Security Adviser Stephen Hadley also supported such sanctions.[18] Capital markets sanctions were the one form of additional economic pressure still available to the U.S. government. But conscious of the failure of the Sudan Campaign advocates to get capital markets sanctions imposed on oil companies operating in southern Sudan five years earlier, Darfur advocates generally assumed there was no point trying to get the government to change its mind. Opposition to capital markets sanctions came from high within the administration. "[Vice President] Cheney said it would establish a dangerous precedent and politicize the capital markets...eventually capital markets would simply leave the United States and move elsewhere," explains Natsios.[19] The Treasury was also opposed. As a senior Treasury official explains it, they didn't believe that capital markets sanctions would have the desired effect. "If state-owned Chinese oil companies were barred from accessing U.S. capital, they would not pressure Khartoum in return for renewed access to U.S. capital, but would instead simply raise their capital from the London financial markets."[20] However, as Natsios recalls it, there was not even someone from Treasury present at the Plan B sanctions meeting; their red line on this issue had been so clearly marked that other participants reminded him that this option was going nowhere. Without ever being seriously discussed, capital markets sanctions were dismissed. Instead, 30 companies and four individuals were added to the U.S. Specially Designated Nationals list, which prevents U.S. companies and individuals from doing business with those listed.[21]

These sanctions were nothing new. They basically just extended existing sanctions to more people and companies. What was different was that the Bush administration was now able to track prohibited transactions through financial institutions, something the U.S. government had only gained expertise in since 9/11. Those listed as Specially Designated Nationals were barred from conducting transactions in U.S. dollars, the currency that dominates exchanges in the oil market. Compliance with the sanctions regime improved once the U.S. government determined that all of Sudan's U.S. dollar transactions were conducted through just one bank,[22] which stopped facilitating the Sudanese government's transactions once it learned the U.S. government was capable of tracking the prohibited transactions.[23] Natsios says the administration knew from having used the same approach with Iran that the enforcement of sanctions through the financial system would be effective on Sudan for only about six months, "until they found a work-around."[24] (By

September, Sudan's central bank had converted all of its reserves from dollars into Euros and other currencies.[25])

Bush's Plan B announcement came as pressure was building across the Atlantic on Darfur. Earlier in May, France had elected Nicholas Sarkozy to the French presidency. Sarkozy had been strong on Darfur during his campaign (in part spurred by *Collectif Urgence Darfour*, the most successful mass movement for Darfur outside of the United States, and one that the Save Darfur Coalition had supported[26]). As president, Sarkozy brought Médecins Sans Frontières cofounder and outspoken advocate of humanitarian intervention, Bernard Kouchner in as his foreign minister.[27] When Tony Blair resigned as prime minister of Britain the following month, his successor, Gordon Brown, teamed up with Sarkozy to make a joint public commitment to Darfur.[28]

The United States, the United Kingdom, and France (referred to collectively as the P3, the three permanent Western members on the UN Security Council) began working together to draft a new sanctions resolution. They each communicated a single message to Khartoum: Either Sudan fully accepts the implementation of the hybrid peacekeeping operation when a UN Security Council mission to Africa visits in June or the sanctions resolution will be presented; they conveyed the same message to Beijing.[29]

Finally, on June 17, 2007—almost ten months after Resolution 1706 was passed and some seven months since the hybrid force was first agreed to in Addis Ababa—President al-Bashir communicated his unconditional acceptance of the new peacekeeping operation to the Security Council.[30] Although the P3 were remarkably unified in their threat of new sanctions in the preceding months, Khartoum had seen the threat of sanctions previously without being moved. The distinguishing factor on this occasion was not the threat the P3 were making against Khartoum per se, but rather that their unified approach convinced Beijing that there was a real chance the sanctions resolution would be presented for a vote at the Security Council. With the Genocide Olympics spotlight on them, a sanctions resolution would place Beijing in an impossible position, wanting neither to attract further negative publicity to their international reputation by vetoing nor to damage their relationship with Khartoum by not vetoing. According to a British official who worked on the resolution, the lesson from Khartoum's belated acceptance of the hybrid was that "to move the Sudanese you have to have a credible stick, if for no other reason than that moves China."[31]

The P3 subsequently dropped their draft resolution on sanctions and instead worked on a resolution authorizing the deployment of Annan's hybrid AU-UN force to stand in lieu of the failed Security Council Resolution 1706, which had authorized a UN peacekeeping deployment the previous year. They called the new hybrid operation the United Nations / African Union Mission in Darfur (UNAMID). Resolution 1769 authorized the deployment of 19,555 UNAMID military personnel and several thousand more civilian personnel to Darfur. It was passed unanimously by the Security Council on July 31, 2007.[32] With the exception of some cosmetic changes to ensure that Sudan did not lose face by accepting this peacekeeping resolution after having rejected the previous one, the mandate outlined in the two resolutions was the same. I asked a U.S. official who played a lead role in the negotiations what had changed between China's abstention from the first resolution (1706) and its support for the second (1769). "The Olympics,"[33] she replied without hesitation. When I went to Khartoum and asked President al-Bashir's senior adviser what, if any, role China had played, he said, "China advised us to accept the 1769 resolution."[34]

TORCH RELAY

As the official Olympics torch made its journey along the Silk Route, the Dream for Darfur team began their symbolic relay. In August 2007, they set off from the Chadian side of the Darfur border.[35] In the coming months, genocide survivors joined the relay led by Mia Farrow, as she and Savitt traveled to Rwanda, Armenia, Germany, Bosnia and Herzegovina, and Cambodia.[36]

"The world betrayed you. You owe the world nothing but you understand the suffering, the pain our brothers and sisters in Darfur are enduring as we speak,"[37] Farrow told the crowd gathered in Sarajevo as she joined with the Mothers of Srebrenica, whose children were killed during the 1995 genocide, to light a torch for Darfur. Omer Ismail was also there and traveled to several other sites of the relay to speak as a Darfuri.

"This flame honors those who have been lost and those who suffer; this flame celebrates the courage of those who have survived,"[38] Ismail said, lighting a torch from the eternal flame at the Tsisernakaberd Memorial Complex in Yerevan, Armenia. The torch was passed around the black-clothed crowd, honoring those who survived the genocide against the Armenians during World War I.[39] Among them was a man of 98, who had been six years old when the genocide began. "He was talking about it with such pain, you could see pain in every word," says Ismail. "But he was not angry...I noticed it compared to those of generations later who talk with anger more than pain, because there was no accountability, no redress. The wounds of the genocide healed but the anger at the world remained."

A journey to Cambodia also left a powerful impression on Ismail, especially after meeting 62-year-old Vann Nath, a survivor of Tuol Sleng, the notorious torture chambers referred to by the Khmer Rouge as S-21.[40] An artist, Nath had been kept alive by the Khmer Rouge regime to provide portraits of their leadership, "but the biggest exhibit of all was in his head," says Ismail. "And once he got out, he grabbed the paint and painted and painted.

He painted his way to sanity. With a strong will and some magical love of life, he managed to survive."

In addition to the international relay, Dream for Darfur launched a U.S.-based relay in September 2007. They had just four staff, and for much of the time they were down to three as Savitt traveled with Farrow for the international relay. Their organizational plan was to stay small but to leverage the resources of the permanent Darfur organizations to help promote the domestic relay events. This wasn't just driven by a concern for efficiency; it was also based on a belief that for the Genocide Olympics to "go viral," it was important that the campaign wasn't seen to be owned by any one group.

There was some understandable resistance within organizations that Dream for Darfur reached out to, a reluctance to interrupt their regular activities to devote resources to a relay. As Sam Bell recalls it, "We had some debate. Americans doing a Dream for Darfur relay in Vermont—how does that reach the Chinese government exactly? A *Wall Street Journal* article I get, but wouldn't it be more effective for people in Vermont to lobby Senator Leahy [of the subcommittee] on foreign appropriations?" Yet GI-Net ultimately found itself supporting the relays because of the interest of their constituents. "They would do it anyway," says Bell.

The dynamic Bell describes is one that was a constant tension for the Darfur organizations that were moving beyond the model of elite human rights advocacy and trying to reach the broader public. GI-Net, Save Darfur, and Enough believed in building political will by getting regular citizens concerned about Darfur. But not all citizens have the willingness or ability to understand the intricacies of the international policymaking process, and not all can get articles published in the *Wall Street Journal* or arrange meetings with ambassadors at the UN. There have to be other ways for citizens to express their concern. Lobbying their representatives was one way to do this, but it couldn't be the sole activity for sustaining citizen action on Darfur over multiple years. "There is something to it when our critics talk about playing to the crowd," says Bell, "but it's not like we sit in a room and plan that . . . these people come in with Genocide Olympics and people are really jazzed about it. Our Vermont people really wanna do a torch relay, dammit!"

Regular citizens in communities across the country mobilized around the idea of holding a symbolic torch relay for Darfur. From Salt Lake City to Miami, activists got their local mayors, musicians, and sports stars involved. To speak at the events, they drew on the Sudanese diaspora as well as survivors of genocide in Rwanda and Bosnia now resident in their communities. "He who does not learn from Rwanda is doomed to repeat it in Darfur," read the t-shirt of one of the activists at a relay in Seattle.[41] With a tagline like Genocide Olympics, it wasn't surprising that parallels to Rwanda and the guilt associated with it continued to be a feature of the framework that citizen activists were working within. "You do run the risk of having to play to constituents who are interested but not engaged enough to get the nuance," reflects Bell. But, he says, most constituent activity moves beyond this. "I think most of their energy and time is actually spent educating themselves...forwarding Human Rights Watch reports to their groups with relevant passages highlighted. But, those hours spent educating don't make news. What makes news is a torch relay."

The U.S. relay culminated on Human Rights Day in December 2007 outside the Chinese Embassy in Washington. It was now more than six months since the Genocide Olympics piece criticized Spielberg, but still the media ran articles, in both their news and entertainment coverage, associating him with Darfur.[42] The continued connection was not by chance. The Dream for Darfur team cultivated a number of reporters whom they encouraged to call Spielberg's offices asking if he had decided to quit. They even mocked up an ad calling on him to resign and sent it to *Vanity Fair.* "We had no money for it, but we asked if they had a nonprofit rate, figuring they would have to at least tell him about it," recalls Savitt. The oft-mourned media obsession with celebrities was used by Dream for Darfur to good effect, as Savitt sent each additional article on Spielberg, Farrow, Darfur, and the Olympics back to Kuang at the Chinese Embassy.

A NEW ENVOY

"He certainly seemed like a real bully for the cause. I was impressed," said Gloria White-Hammond, describing her first impressions of Richard Williamson, the man President Bush appointed as his special envoy on Sudan after Andrew Natsios resigned in December 2007.[43] Williamson had been the U.S. ambassador to the UN Commission on Human Rights in April 2004 and had stormed out in protest against a resolution that refused to recognize the ethnic cleansing taking place in Darfur.

"From day one he does outreach. He's been round the block," was Bell's characterization of the new envoy. "The first meeting with advocates he starts off bantering with JP, like they went to school together or something," says Bell, referring to Enough Project cofounder John Prendergast, whose public profile had skyrocketed following a joint book project with Hollywood star Don Cheadle. "I think he knew how that would be perceived by everyone in the room, that it would make people think he was on the right side."

Taking the reins, Williamson established a better relationship with the advocacy community in the first weeks of his tenure than Natsios had at any time he was the envoy. "I've been in 8 different government jobs in the past 30 years, and I've never been on an issue that has had so much public involvement," says Williamson. "Now not all of it is good. I got 100,000 emails from them the week I took the job. That's not helpful; it just pisses you off. But they could be more sophisticated and they had different strengths. You had Jerry Fowler, a herder; John Prendergast, who throws bombs; Mia Farrow, who bleeds. It was effective. They sustained the interest of congress."[44] Moreover, Williamson says that advocates didn't just keep the issue on the agenda. "It was useful that these people were spending time on this issue—they came up with different sources of information," he says, explaining why he would attend meetings they organized at the Democratic think tank Center for American Progress. "I wasn't meeting with them for political reasons—no one in that room was voting for George Bush!" he laughs.

WILLIAMSON WAS NOTHING if not a savvy operator. But like Natsios before him, he was entering a fraught bureaucratic environment whose structure increased the likelihood of tension. The Sudan Programs Group in the State Department, where the bulk of the day-to-day work on Sudan took place, reported to the assistant secretary for African Affairs, a post that Jendayi Frazer had held since 2005. By contrast, the special envoy reported directly to the president. Theoretically this gave the special envoy access that would allow him to raise the profile of Sudan among the long list of competing foreign policy priorities. In practice it was not so straightforward.

Both Natsios and Williamson were envoys on a part-time basis, without their own budgets beyond their salaries and travel expenses. While Natsios held meetings in his Georgetown University office, Williamson was further removed still at his law firm office in Chicago. Overlapping on matters of substance with the Sudan Programs Group and yet not part of their line of reporting, it was not surprising that miscommunication and turf warfare prevailed.

"Sudan Programs Group reporting to Jendayi Frazer is a fatal flaw," Williamson told me, not mincing words as he referred to two of the staff reporting to Frazer as "sycophants who didn't care about Sudan or really anything but keeping Jendayi happy." Williamson says that the situation was so bad he threatened to resign. Natsios had been equally scathing. In response to their criticisms, Frazer is nonchalant. "In D.C., in politics, in policymaking—it's almost like a contact sport. You take hits," she says. "And if you come off the field crying and complaining, you're probably just a loser. You probably just lost a lot.... I know they go round town saying a bunch of stuff about me, but you know, all that's saying is I had influence on the policy. I'm okay with that."[45]

The debilitating interactions Frazer had with both Natsios and Williamson were less about policy substance and more about an entrenched bureaucracy reacting against having a point person on Sudan imposed outside the line of reporting. This was not the scenario advocates had in mind when they pushed for the appointment of a special envoy.

WILLIAMSON MADE HIS FIRST visit to Sudan at the end of February 2008. "After you were announced, we read what you had written and I decided I didn't want to meet with you," al-Bashir told him. "Believe me, I never wanted to meet with you!" Williamson replied, to which al-Bashir hooted with laughter. Williamson was to pursue an aggressive stance toward al-Bashir in both private and public throughout his tenure. "They know they do bad stuff, and they know we know they do bad stuff," Williamson explained, arguing there was nothing to gain by taking anything less than an overtly aggressive approach to the regime. His style stood in stark contrast to the Chinese envoy, Liu Guijin, who happened to be visiting Khartoum at the same time. But Williamson believed that the Chinese were increasingly concerned about the effect that public perception of their relations with Khartoum would have on the upcoming Olympic Games. Williamson had recently met with the Chinese ambassador in the United States: "The second or third question out of the ambassador's mouth was, 'So what's Mia Farrow up to?' They didn't want the embarrassment."

THE SPIELBERG EFFECT

"China hopes that these games will be its post-Tiananmen Square coming out party. But how can Beijing host the Olympic Games at home and underwrite genocide in Darfur?" Mia Farrow asked the crowd gathered in Central Park. It was a freezing February afternoon in New York. Farrow, waiflike, was visibly shivering. The rally marked the successful culmination of a day of coordinated events to pressure China. The Nobel Women's Initiative, a group of six female Nobel Peace Prize laureates, had published an open letter urging China to act for Darfur; Olympic athletes had rallied at Chinese embassies; the Save Darfur Coalition had helped turn out grassroots support.

Dream for Darfur and the Nobel women had contacted Spielberg's office, asking him to join the open letter the laureates were writing but had received no reply. John Prendergast, Samantha Power, and others had met with Spielberg directly over the course of the prior year, presenting the case for China's ability to influence Khartoum.[46] Spielberg had met with the Chinese special envoy to Sudan when he was in New York in September and in November had come out with a public statement addressed to the Chinese government.[47] But since then, the Dream for Darfur team had heard nothing from his office.

After the rally, Savitt, Farrow, and a reporter who was covering their work got together for hamburgers at a local diner. They were quite upbeat about the day's events as Farrow headed home and Savitt and the reporter went back to the office. Shortly after, Savitt's phone rang. It was a journalist: What is your reaction to Steven Spielberg's resignation from the Olympics? he asked. Savitt was stunned.

While the rally had been underway, Spielberg had released a statement of resignation: "I find that my conscience will not allow me to continue business as usual. At this point, my time and energy must be spent not on Olympic ceremonies but on doing all I can to help bring an end to the unspeakable crimes against humanity that continue to be committed in Darfur."[48] The announcement rapidly became a news lead, eclipsing all the other events that Dream for Darfur had organized that day, events that would undoubtedly have generated further media speculation and public pressure on Spielberg to resign. "The timing was very smart on their part," says Savitt, in a tone of begrudging respect. "For him to have pulled out, I will always respect him," says White-Hammond. "And he was clear about it. He wasn't like, 'I need to spend more time with my family.'"

In the 24 hours following Spielberg's resignation, there was an explosion of news articles about Darfur and the Olympics.[49] It was a windfall of free media to the Dream for Darfur campaign, and calls of congratulations rang into their office from activists around the country. But what did it mean for Darfur that a Hollywood director had resigned from an event in Beijing?

As Bell had noted, after Khartoum's rejection of the Security Council resolution on a UN deployment, advocates had moved away from the idea of direct intervention and toward finding indirect targets that could be leveraged to pressure Sudan. But the reality was that outside of targeting the U.S. government, there existed few established channels through which U.S.-based advocates could act. It was hard enough to get China to be responsive to its own citizens' demands about issues inside China; there was no reason for the Chinese government to pay attention to the concerns of U.S. citizens about an issue in Africa.

The Olympics was a unique opportunity: It offered a reason for the Chinese government to care about the opinion of U.S. activists, provided that they posed enough of a threat to China's Olympics image. Spielberg's resignation undoubtedly achieved this intermediate goal of showing the Chinese government that Darfur activists could threaten their image. But in pushing Spielberg, advocates had reached a target who was still multiple steps removed from Darfur. The real measure of success would be whether his resignation and the growing threat it brought to China's Olympics image would lead Beijing to use its leverage over Khartoum on Darfur.

Spielberg's resignation did increase responsiveness from other indirect targets that had also been identified by Dream for Darfur as having the ability to threaten China's image. In November 2007 Dream for Darfur had released scorecards grading the Olympics' corporate sponsors on the extent to which they were using their influence to attract attention to Darfur and requesting that sponsors meet with Mia Farrow to talk about how to improve their scores. The media had covered the release of the scorecards, but none of the sponsors had been in touch. Spielberg's resignation changed this non-responsiveness literally overnight; the next day, nine of the sponsors called to schedule meetings with Farrow and the Dream for Darfur team.[50]

Spielberg's resignation was also followed by responsiveness of a pernicious kind. In late February 2008 the FBI began investigating cyber attacks originating in China on Save Darfur's website, and people to whom Savitt had previously sent e-mails began receiving an e-mail that appeared to be from her address: "There is no link between Darfur and the Olympics. Best Wishes, Jill Savitt."[51] But there were also some positive signs. At a press conference, China's special envoy to Darfur explained, "We have a good relationship with Sudan. We stand in an advantageous position from which to talk to them, so we should use this as leverage. We will persuade them in a direct way to work with the international community and show greater flexibility."[52] While in one sense "just words," the envoy's comments marked a clear shift from China's previous public statements about its role in Darfur.

A few months later, China's shifting position was evident at the UN Security Council. When Costa Rica, with a population of just 4.5 million, rotated onto the Security Council as a nonpermanent member, it signaled it would use its time on the council to support the International Criminal Court. Costa Rica felt that since referring the Darfur case to the ICC in 2005, council members had distanced themselves from the court, and so proposed that the council issue a presidential statement in support of the ICC's work.

Unlike a resolution, a Security Council presidential statement is not binding as a matter of law, but because it can only pass with the consensus of all 15 council members, it sends a strong political message of unity. When the other members heard of Costa Rica's plan, they didn't take it seriously. "No one worries about us. They assumed we would fail, but figured it was just our pet project," recalls a staffer at the Costa Rican mission.[53] Costa Rica has a reputation at the council for supporting international law. "We don't have money, people, or an army. Human rights, the rule of law—it's all we have. Our security strategy is based on the UN working," Costa Rica's political counselor at the UN, Jorge Ballestero, explained to me.[54]

Libya, China, Russia, and South Africa all rejected the draft presidential statement that Costa Rica circulated. Negotiations continued for two weeks with no consensus reached, at which point the Costa Ricans decided, "Well, if you won't play this game, we'll change the game." They told the council they would present it as a resolution instead.

For a resolution to pass, Costa Rica needed only nine votes—as long as none of the permanent members exercised their veto. At that stage they had 11 members, including the United States, on their side for the presidential statement. But once they threatened to present a legally binding resolution, the United States wavered, not wanting to vote for an ICC resolution but not wanting to veto it either. However, it was the Chinese mission that really panicked. They begged Costa Rica not to present the resolution, promising to sign a presidential statement supporting the ICC if Costa Rica agreed not move forward with the resolution. But, as the Costa Ricans told China, the biggest impediment to a presidential statement going through at that point was Libya. "China said, 'Well, we can talk to our friends,'" recalls Ballestero with a twinkle in his eye.

That night, Ballestero made the final revisions to their proposed presidential statement. By now its conclusion read that the council urges the government of Sudan "to cooperate fully with the Court, consistent with resolution 1593 (2005), in order to put an end to impunity for the crimes committed in Darfur." Resolution 1593 was the council's original referral of Darfur to the ICC, a resolution that both China and the United States had abstained from. "I thought, 'If this flies, I'll get drunk'—and I did!" says Ballestero gleefully. "It recognized that there is impunity in Darfur and that the court can help stop it," he said of the statement that all 15 members of the Security Council signed. I asked Ballestero why the Chinese decided to support a presidential statement rather than see a resolution presented. "It's easier to hide behind the shield of consensus than to vote," he said, "and China could not afford, in the face of the Olympics, to have another issue besides Tibet."

CONVENTIONAL WISDOM HAS IT that China is moved by quiet and tactful diplomacy. "On China, advocacy was really unhelpful. China's foreign policy means they will never do anything overtly," says Taiya Smith, who was Robert Zoellick's special assistant in 2006 and went on to become U.S. Treasury Secretary Henry Paulson's lead negotiator in China. In countless interviews I was told versions of the same theory: The traditional name-and-shame tactics of human rights advocacy do not work with China. As Natsios testified before the Senate Foreign Relations Committee in April 2007, "There's been a lot of China-bashing in the West. And I'm not sure, to be very frank with you, right now it's very helpful."[55]

Yet, everyone I spoke with who was directly involved in negotiating with the Chinese on Darfur policy at the UN during this period seemed to believe that the threat of damage to its Olympics image was the one and only effective point of leverage over Beijing. As one U.S. government official put it, "Activists finally 'cracked the code' on moving China."[56] This didn't mean that China moved into line with the activist position, but it did move from obstructing all outside involvement with Darfur back to a position of neutrality. In an admittedly rare instance, the Olympics, when activists in the West could threaten an image China actually cared about, public shaming had worked.

CHAPTER 11

THE ICC IN ACTION

In June 2008 Special Envoy Richard Williamson sat with the U.S. delegation at the UN Security Council listening to the prosecutor of the International Criminal Court, Luis Moreno Ocampo, present a report on his investigations.

Moreno Ocampo had announced his first Darfur case in early 2007, charging a Sudanese government minister, Ahmed Harun, and a Janjaweed militia coordinator, Ali Kushayb, with a cumulative total of 98 counts of crimes against humanity and war crimes.[1] "Exceedingly cautious" was how Eric Reeves described the first case.[2] Most Darfur activists barely responded at all, largely due to a lack of familiarity with Harun and Kushayb. "I definitely didn't know who those folks were until then. I think that was probably the case for a lot of the activists," recalls Sam Bell.

I joined the ICC after graduating law school, several months after the case against Harun and Kushayb was announced. My colleagues were talented lawyers from across the globe, but we were all dealing with a gigantic workload within an embryonic institutional structure. Literal screams of exasperation were all too frequent from those around me.

I watched the prosecutor's Security Council presentation via Webstream from my office in The Hague. At the court, the prosecutor would invariably speak at a million miles an hour with a thick Argentinean accent that could render him incomprehensible to those who were not used to it. But before the council he spoke slowly and deliberately. He was informing the council that he would be presenting a second case on Darfur in July. Williamson remembers listening and absorbing the signal the prosecutor was sending: His next case would go up to the very top of the Sudanese state.

Williamson had been invited to the Security Council presentation by Moreno Ocampo three months earlier, when they had met during a conference in Chicago at which they both spoke. At the time, Williamson was not authorized to actually meet with the prosecutor—the Bush administration's agreement to refer Darfur to the ICC had been driven by the need to reach an armistice with the Europeans, not by any particularly warm feelings toward the court itself. But the convener of the conference held a dinner at his house and, with Moreno Ocampo's encouragement, had invited Williamson and Moreno Ocampo to arrive before the other guests.

Williamson says he was open with Moreno Ocampo about his position. "I told him I had not been opposed to the U.S. not signing up to the ICC." Before the other guests arrived the conversation got onto Sudan. "He never said 'Bashir,' but it was clear that was whom he was talking about," says Williamson, who told Moreno Ocampo he didn't think it was a good idea to prosecute the Sudanese president. Nevertheless, Williamson says he found Moreno Ocampo to be "open and a good interlocutor," and as the other guests began to arrive, Williamson agreed to attend the prosecutor's briefing to the Security Council.[3]

GOING AFTER AL-BASHIR

A month after Moreno Ocampo's report to the UN Security Council, journalists from around the world crowded into the media room at the court in The Hague. Moreno Ocampo, overtired and with a speech that had been finalized just minutes beforehand, stood before the mass of cameras and microphones to announce that he would be applying to the Pre-Trial Chamber of the court for an arrest warrant against President al-Bashir for war crimes, crimes against humanity, and genocide.[4]

Working at the court I was feeling disconnected from the actual situations we were dealing with, so two weeks after the prosecutor's announcement I took annual leave and headed to the refugee camps on the long desert stretch of the Chad-Sudan border. I was curious to know what the refugees thought about the indictment but thought that it would draw undue attention to my relationship to the topic if I started asking questions and planned not to do so. As it turned out, I need not have worried. There was not one camp I visited where the ICC was not the first, and in some cases only, topic the refugees wanted to discuss.

Outsiders could be forgiven for thinking that in the middle of the desert, in a place that can only be reached from the capital of Chad by taking two humanitarian AirServe flights, information about the outside world might be short in supply. But Darfuri refugees of all ages are more in touch with global events than most Westerners, largely thanks to BBC radio. Much-prized shortwave radios are present throughout the camps, and refugees listen eagerly for news updates about those seeking to help them.

I met Amira, who was my age but held her sixth child, a 33-day-old baby, on her lap as we sat together under her makeshift shelter at the Oure Cassoni refugee camp, and she told me about the night she found out the ICC prosecutor was applying to have al-Bashir arrested. "We heard the news in the middle of the night. When I heard it, I ran to my neighbors' and we started shouting and laughing," she said, laughing again at the recollection. "We spent the whole night out of our rooms—we gathered all together at my neighbor's. We told others and at first one woman said to me 'no, you're lying'.... She couldn't believe it. And so another woman who had a radio brought it to where we were gathered so she could hear it for herself. When I heard about it, the first thought that came to me was—now there is peace."[5]

Amira's desire for al-Bashir's arrest was repeated by every refugee I spoke with along the border. "When we heard the ICC announcement we were so very very happy. We all went to the television to try and see when they would bring him to justice," I was told at Djabal refugee camp.[6] "Even if I am as old as a table, if I see on television that Omar al-Bashir is arrested, I will dance all the way from the television back to Darfur!"[7] a middle-aged woman at the camp proclaimed. The women around her burst into high-pitched ululation.

President al-Bashir was furious. The secretary-general of the Arab League, Amr Moussa, was the first foreign diplomat to meet with him after the indictment was announced. "He was so angry. So so angry. More angry than I have ever seen him," Moussa recounted to me a year later. "Bashir believes what is happening in Darfur is a mutiny, a little civil war."[8] Moussa says that up until the announcement al-Bashir believed that as president of his country he would not be prosecuted.

On the day of the prosecutor's announcement, the African-based Darfur Consortium advocates were gathered at the Elite Royale hotel in Kampala, Uganda, for their annual strategy meeting. "It was chaotic. Everyone was very thrown, incoherent, all over the place. Every time they tried to talk about other things, the question would arise about how those things might change with the indictment," recalls one of those present.[9] Dismas Nkunda, one of the Darfur Consortium cofounders, found his phone ringing nonstop with journalists seeking a response to the indictment. But there was no consensus from the group on how to respond.

Back in March 2005, the Darfur Consortium, and Nkunda in particular, had been instrumental in convincing African leaders that a referral of Darfur to the ICC would not represent a colonization of justice, and that with more signatories from Africa than any other continent, the ICC was an African court. In the three years since, the clarity of this position had diminished due to events at the court and how they were perceived.

When Darfur was referred to the ICC in March 2005, the court had not yet issued any arrest warrants. By July 2008 the court had issued 12 warrants, all for Africans.[10] This opened the court to charges of bias against Africa. The charge was unfair to the extent that in most of the situations, African states—the Democratic Republic of the Congo, Uganda, and the Central African Republic—had themselves asked the court to assist by investigating the crimes committed in their country. And the situation in Darfur had been given to the court by the Security Council. In contrast, several of the situations that the prosecutor began monitoring on his own initiative were outside Africa, including Afghanistan, Georgia, Colombia, and Palestine.

But the all-African list of indictees was not the only cause of concern. Many in the Darfur Consortium began to mistrust the ICC prosecution after its first case, against Congolese warlord Thomas Lubanga, had almost ended prematurely when the judges stayed the case, blaming the prosecution for failing to disclose certain confidential evidence to the defense, and ordered the release of Lubanga.[11] The order stated that his release was not to take place immediately, and in the end Lubanga remained in custody, the disclosure issues were resolved, and the trial resumed. However, the stress on affected Congolese communities had been great; many of Lubanga's supporters believed that the order for his release indicated his innocence, and many of the prosecution's witnesses feared that if released, Lubanga would retaliate against them.

The Darfur Consortium meeting focused on tensions within the international justice system between those from the "global north" (those working on African issues at Western organizations like Human Rights Watch, who generally favored the indictment), versus those from the "global south" (individuals who worked at organizations based in Africa, who opposed it, or were at least not sure they should be vocal in supporting it). The one strong exception to the geographic breakdown of opinions was from the Sudanese in attendance, all of whom were adamant in their support for an ICC arrest warrant against their president.[12]

Back in Washington, Omer Ismail, now working for the Enough Project, remembers being surprised at how surprised other people were by the prosecutor's announcement. "There was no doubt in my mind, from the first time this went to the court, that eventually they would go up the chain and reach him," he says. Sam Bell remembers that for most U.S.-based Darfur advocates, "the Darfuri community was so clear in their support for the ICC, there really wasn't a debate on whether to take Alex's shtick seriously."

By "Alex's shtick," Bell meant the high-profile critique that Alex de Waal, the Harvard scholar who had been so involved in the Darfur Peace Agreement, had launched against the al-Bashir case. De Waal, along with journalist Julie Flint, had been writing articles criticizing the prosecution ever since Moreno Ocampo began to signal that he would be taking his investigation up to the very top of the Sudanese state.[13] Part of their criticism related to the way the prosecutor had characterized the situation in Darfur. De Waal and Flint didn't disagree that serious human rights violations continued to take place in Darfur, but they did not see these as part of what the prosecutor was describing as a second, more subtle stage of genocide in which the massacres of the 2003-2004 period had been replaced by slower forms of destruction at the displacement camps. Regardless of the way the situation was characterized, they also believed that the prosecutor simply should not be going after al-Bashir—at least not at that particular time.

Their argument was not that al-Bashir was innocent; it was, as they put it in a *Washington Post* op-ed, that while indicting him would be "an immense symbolic victory for Darfurians," what Darfuris really needed was "peace, security and deliverable justice.... And with President Omar Hassan al-Bashir and his men still in power, a high-level indictment would probably damage all these objectives."[14]

PEACE AND JUSTICE

From her home in Boston, Gloria White-Hammond remembers filtering de Waal and Flint's critique through the lens of the civil rights movement. "It helped to draw on the civil rights movement when thinking about, shall we say, 'the Alexes' of the world, who sometimes seem to operate from a paradigm of fear—'We can't do this because of what might the consequences be,'" she says. "People always tell you to slow down. But when people keep putting you down generation after generation, you understand why it is difficult to wait." White-Hammond referred to the letter that Martin Luther King wrote from a Birmingham jail in response to those who called his actions unwise and untimely. King wrote, "Frankly, I have yet to engage in a direct action campaign that was 'well timed' in the view of those who have not suffered unduly from the disease of segregation. For years now I have heard the word 'Wait!'...This 'Wait' has almost always meant 'Never.' We must come to see, with one of our distinguished jurists, that 'justice too long delayed is justice denied.'"[15]

I remember reading articles by de Waal and Flint from my office in The Hague and not doubting they believed that their opposition to al-Bashir's prosecution was in the best interests of Darfuris. The prosecutor, whose approach to these issues had been formed as a young lawyer involved in the politically controversial prosecution of the military junta in his native Argentina, also believed equally strongly that the prosecution was in the best interests of Darfuris. Their sharply divergent conclusions seemed to stem from a fundamental difference in worldview. Some people spend their lives working incrementally to make the status quo a little more humane, and accomplishing just this is hard enough. Others feel that the status quo is so flawed that tinkering around the edges won't do, and that the whole system needs an overhaul.

For time immemorial, the status quo for leaders who commit mass atrocities against their own populations has been to stay in power until they die or to bend to external pressure and agree to step down in return for a guarantee of impunity and a comfortable retirement in exile. Such leaders have sometimes been overthrown militarily, with Saddam Hussein being the most notorious example of recent times. But, as in the Saddam Hussein case, the primary motivation of the invading power is rarely the welfare of the local population. The general rule has been that provided a leader sticks to attacking the citizens of his own country and poses no obvious threat to those outside his borders, he has nothing to fear.

Only with the post–Cold War advent of international criminal tribunals that led to the 1999 arrest warrant for the then-president of Serbia, Slobodan Milosevic,[16] and the 2003 warrant for the then-president of Liberia, Charles Taylor,[17] did this historical trajectory begin to change. The indictment of al-Bashir was another challenge to the tried-and-tested way of ending the rule of a leader who had committed mass crimes against his (the role has historically been played by men) own citizens.

The vision behind the indictment of al-Bashir, indeed behind the ICC, is of a world where there is a third way for external actors to end the rule of leaders who kill their own people—something between military overthrow and impunity-ridden exile. This does not necessarily mean that external actors have to execute the ICC's arrest warrants—although this could happen if an indictee travels to a country that has joined the ICC and taken on the obligation to cooperate with the court. But the more fundamental idea is that an ICC warrant isolates the indictee; it marks them as a fugitive from justice. If those outside the country apply diplomatic and economic pressure in support of the ICC's warrant, it can strengthen the hand of those inside the country who also want to see their leader face justice, eventually leading domestic forces to send their leader to The Hague. "People inside Sudan can affect change but we need governments outside of Sudan to adhere to international law," explains Omer Ismail. The hope is that over time, as more warrants of arrest are successfully executed, a prison cell will become the expected outcome of a presidency characterized by mass atrocities, and such crimes will lose their appeal as a means of attempting to stay in power.

Some critics of the indictment said it would prevent peace and argued that past African conflicts would never have been resolved had there been an ICC pushing for criminal accountability.[18] Indeed, the Comprehensive Peace Agreement, which ended two decades of civil war in Sudan, did not have a criminal justice component, and given the atrocities committed by both the Sudanese government and the SPLA against civilians during the north-south war, it would not have been in the interests of Garang, al-Bashir, or other leaders in their respective ranks to sign it if there had been. But had criminal accountability been pursued for al-Bashir's actions in southern Sudan, he may have been in a prison cell rather than in a position to oversee future atrocities in Darfur. The notion that impunity is a carrot to be held out from the toolbox of incentives and pressures deployed to bring an end to a conflict is an anathema to those, myself included, who want to overhaul the status quo. But it is true that there is a gap yet to be bridged between the ideal of prosecuting leaders for mass crimes and the practice of actually doing so. Until that gap is bridged, there are real costs to real people in attempting these prosecutions.

In the short term, indicting a head of state may indeed delay the resolution of a conflict, relative to an alternative where the head of state is offered impunity to step aside. And there should be no doubt that the cost of such delay is borne by the civilian victims of the conflict. Because of this, the discussion around such indictments is typically framed as 'peace versus justice,' with one coming at the expense of the other. A negotiated settlement or a power transition without any justice component, however, may be more likely to falter over the long term.[19] This risk is rarely discussed by those so ready to talk about the short-term costs to the peace process that can come from pursuing justice. The discussion should perhaps be framed as "short-term peace without justice vs. justice with long-term peace." As Omer Ismail observed in Armenia, anger builds into the future. Subsequent generations see the scars their family members and communities carry, so even those who were not there to feel the original pain are affected. "It transcends the people directly harmed and goes on through the generations. That's the vertical. On the horizontal it destroys communities. Horizontal and vertical—nothing survives that until there is justice and redress," says Ismail.

Such justice and redress need not come from the ICC. Indeed, the far preferable option is for a justice process to be undertaken domestically with the participation of the affected communities. However, the feasibility of such a process is often limited by the very atrocities the domestic system has encountered, which is why the need was seen for an ICC, a court of last resort when local systems are unable or unwilling to handle the situation. Such was the case in Darfur. A statistically rigorous survey of thousands of Darfuri refugees in Chad conducted in 2009 found that while 87 percent of the refugees still believed that their traditional justice mechanisms were important to enable Darfur to live in peace, only 6 percent of them believed that these mechanisms alone could handle what had happened in recent years. Leaders among the refugees reported that not only were their traditional justice mechanisms not designed to deal with these kinds of mass crimes, but also that they weren't designed to deal with crimes involving the government. Almost all (98 percent) of the refugees said they wanted to see Omar al-Bashir tried at the ICC.[20]

Critics of the indictment argued that if the prosecutor had been serious about actually getting al-Bashir arrested, he should have made an application to the court for the warrant to be issued under seal rather than holding a press conference to announce his intention to apply for a warrant.[21] A warrant issued secretly would have meant that al-Bashir would have continued to travel unaware to states more likely to execute the warrant than Sudan. Instead, with the prosecutor's intentions publicly known, al-Bashir could avoid traveling to states that might actually arrest him.

This issue was debated inside the prosecutor's office. In the end the determination was made that it would be irresponsible if al-Bashir left Sudan one day and was extradited to The Hague the next without any prior warning to any of the internal or external actors involved in the daily business of the Sudanese state. The UN, AU, and the Sudanese people would wake up one morning to find al-Bashir gone and no transition plan would be in place. In contrast, signaling the intention to prosecute al-Bashir publicly and well in advance gave time for all the political actors to arrive at a consensus on the need for his arrest and to plan what the next steps would be following his extradition. The theory made sense in the abstract. But there was a vast gap between the theory and the reality, especially given the recent challenges to the court's credibility in Africa. Instead of the indictment becoming a point around which to mobilize consensus for his arrest, it led to division, as justice for Darfur rapidly became the latest flashpoint in the politics of the West versus the global south.

Five days after the prosecutor's announcement, foreign ministers of the Arab League nations convened an emergency meeting in Cairo, at which they rejected the ICC case and affirmed their "solidarity with the Republic of Sudan in confronting schemes that undermine its sovereignty, unity and stability."[22] Two days later in Addis Ababa, members of the AU Peace and Security Council released a communiqué calling on the UN Security Council to suspend the prosecution of al-Bashir, and they also established a high-level AU panel, led by South Africa's president Thabo Mbeki, to make recommendations on peace and justice in Darfur.[23] "I said to Luis [Moreno Ocampo], 'You have done the one thing no one else in the world could have done—united the African Union behind Bashir!'" remembers Williamson.

Conversations I subsequently had with insiders at the AU indicated that not all African states were as unified against the warrant as the AU statement made it appear.[24] Still, this marked the first time in the Darfur crisis that the AU took a clear public stand in al-Bashir's favor.

THE PROSPECT OF SUSPENSION

Article 16 of the ICC's statute includes a provision that enables the UN Security Council to suspend the court's work on a particular case for a period of 12 months, with renewal possible after that.[25] The provision was included in the ICC's founding document by those worried that an investigation or prosecution could disrupt peace negotiations.[26] The provision provides an escape valve, but it is not the same as being able to offer impunity in the way that was previously possible. While the Security Council can suspend an investigation, it cannot cancel it. In theory, a suspension could be renewed indefinitely, but everyone, including the accused, would still know that the prosecution can be resumed at any point in the future. In advance of the 2008 UN General Assembly in September, the AU Peace and Security Council met in New York and issued another communiqué requesting that the UN Security Council suspend the prosecution of al-Bashir.[27]

Darfur advocates swung into action at the prospect of a suspension going through. Until this point there had been very little involvement of mass movement activists in relation to the ICC. At first this was mainly because when the Security Council initially referred Darfur to the ICC back in March 2005, the organizations that would eventually cultivate large constituencies were still in the process of building themselves. Later, it was because of a sense that there was nothing concrete for regular citizens to do in relation to the court. As Bell explains it, "If people are going to rally around something, they need to be able to see it, feel it, know they made a difference. If you can't give that to them, you start losing folks to the 'Is anything I'm doing making a difference?' disease."

It was this kind of thinking that dissuaded GI-Net from spending resources on getting their constituents to call for the United States to provide intelligence to the court, as policy elites had suggested. From Bell's perspective, there would be "no bang for our buck" in getting their constituents to push for this. "There's nothing to advocate for... Cooperation with the ICC is not an event. If it happens, it won't be announced." In contrast, in the face of an attempt to get the case against al-Bashir suspended, it would be a clear victory to share with constituents if the suspension didn't go through. GI-Net mobilized advocates to use the 1-800-GENOCIDE number to call the White House and "urge President Bush to stand up for justice and accountability by opposing Article 16 at the Security Council."[28]

Unknown to advocates, President Bush had decided to oppose a suspension under Article 16 almost a week before GI-Net's action alert went out. On September 11, Williamson had met with the president and his advisers in the Oval Office. "You know Mr. President, you can look at this issue as you don't support impunity or you don't like the ICC," said Williamson, before launching into the history of Bush's engagement on Darfur. "You were the first world leader to call it genocide...you allowed the referral to go forward, and now the prosecutor has taken that and is seeking an arrest warrant for Bashir on the basis of him being a genocidaire. Do you really want to undermine that?" Williamson asked. "No! He's a bad guy," Williamson recalls the president responding. At which point he told Bush that he wanted to signal to the other Security Council members that the United States would veto any resolution suspending the ICC prosecution.

Those listening to the exchange between the president and his envoy pushed back against Williamson's suggestion; by the culture of the Security Council the threat of a veto should be used sparingly. President Bush turned back to Williamson, "What do you think?" he asked. "Let me use the big V word!" said Williamson, gaining the president's seal of approval. I asked Williamson why, after telling Moreno Ocampo he thought that going after al-Bashir was unwise, he nevertheless ended up advocating for the case to go forward. "You must deal with the facts as they are presented and not as you wish they were," he told me. "Luis [Moreno Ocampo] took the steps he felt appropriate given his responsibilities. I respect him for that.... I advocated the path I thought appropriate at the time with the new facts."[29]

The following week, as the UN General Assembly gathered in New York, Williamson set up a series of meetings; the first was with the head of the AU Peace and Security Council, and the next was with the Chinese delegation. In both cases Williamson conveyed the same message: "I looked the president in the eye when he told me to make sure you knew that if you [present] this, we will veto. And if that is what happens, I will go out and give a press conference saying you knew this would happen," Williamson told them. No Security Council member wants to sponsor a resolution that they believe will be vetoed, and in the end no Article 16 proposal to suspend the case against al-Bashir was ever presented.

THE BUSH ADMINISTRATION, which had spent its first term doing all it could to undermine the ICC, was ultimately responsible for ensuring that the court's most high-profile case went forward. Looking at President Bush's decision to let Williamson threaten the use of a U.S. veto, it is tempting to conclude that advocates had no influence; their outcry came after the president had made his decision. But the relationship between advocacy and action cannot be assessed in solely contemporaneous terms.

By 2008 the Darfur movement was organized well enough to ensure that the U.S. government had internalized the need to be seen to support justice on Darfur. As one of the Sudan Program Group officers put it, "Darfur is a domestic issue."[30] The cumulative effect of the previous four years of advocacy efforts must be factored into the president's decision; without years of sustained public action on Darfur, there's unlikely to have been an actor like Williamson to force the issue within the Oval Office, or a president so sensitive to the appeal to his legacy on it.

Over the course of its development the Darfur advocacy community had become much more specific in the policy demands they were making of government, and this improved their ability to measure the impact they were having. But in decisions like this one, the indirect payoff from the purely noise-making function of the mass movement was apparent.

PART IV

DARFUR AND BEYOND

CHAPTER 12

WHILE WE WERE WATCHING DARFUR

When Miriam along with hundreds of thousands of other non-Arab Darfuris fled for their lives in 2003, the international community studiously avoided their plight on the grounds that all Sudan-related energies needed to stay on the Comprehensive Peace Agreement, which promised to end the north-south war and bring about a democratic transformation of Sudan. A few years later, the tables had turned. The massive outcry on Darfur had been enormously successful at changing the agenda of world powers, who had recalibrated their attention toward the atrocities in the west of Sudan. But the pendulum had swung too far, and by 2008 the much-neglected CPA showed clear signs of unraveling.

In late 2007 the SPLM members in Sudan's Government of National Unity had boycotted the parliament, protesting the failure to implement the democratic reforms mandated by the CPA in the nearly three years since the agreement was signed. A national electoral law should have been passed in January 2006 and a national census completed in July 2007 as prerequisites to the national elections scheduled for July 2009.[1] Back in 2003, those who opposed adding the emerging crisis in Darfur into the CPA negotiations had bolstered their position by arguing that the democratic national elections mandated in the CPA would give Darfuris an opportunity to gain power and representation, but by late 2007 this possibility seemed remote. The national security laws that gave the NCP-dominated security services legal cover to detain and torture opponents of the regime had not been reformed, and the laws enabling censorship of the media remained in place.[2]

With the SPLM parliamentary boycott these failures of CPA implementation began to appear on the radar of Darfur advocacy leaders, but their primary focus remained on getting the UNAMID peacekeeping mission into Darfur. They did not undertake a serious campaign to educate their constituents about the problems generated by the failure to adhere to the CPA. "For the movement, I don't think it was even part of the talking points," recalls Sam Bell. "Except for Gloria [White-Hammond]—at every [Save Darfur] board meeting she had been all about 'all-Sudan,' like a broken record. But people would say to her, 'We have to go where the violence is.'" This imbalance between advocacy pressure on Darfur as compared to the CPA was reflected inside the U.S. government; in 2007 the Sudan Programs Group staff estimated they spent 70 percent of their time on Darfur, with the remaining 30 percent spread across the rest of Sudan.[3]

By 2008, with Bush's second term drawing to a close and an upcoming presidential election, Darfur was one of many issues in limbo, waiting to see what the change in administration would bring. "2008 was the wait," says Bell. In some respects the year gave the Darfur advocacy organizations a chance to consolidate. After more than seven months of being led by an acting director, Save Darfur hired Jerry Fowler, from the Holocaust Museum's Committee on Conscience, to replace David Rubenstein. GI-Net began making the institutional changes needed to take on situations like Burma and Sri Lanka, in order to build a reputation as an organization against genocide and mass atrocity no matter where it might occur. The Enough Project increased its field staff, and all three organizations began working together on coordinated campaigns. One was called Ask the Candidates, and its goal was to pressure the presidential candidates to commit to a strong position on Darfur.

Ask the Candidates was the ideal campaign to maintain the engagement of grass-roots activists around the country. Unlike trying to attract China's attention, there were established local forums—town hall meetings, televised and online debates—throughout the year that enabled regular citizens to reach the presidential contenders. And unlike much American political engagement that is centered in the national capital, the presidential contenders tried to engage potential voters countrywide. Turning up to ask questions on Darfur to presidential candidates in Des Moines or Concord, activists in remote areas suddenly had access that was often limited to those who could travel to Washington. The Ask the Candidates campaign was enormously successful at getting presidential candidates to promise they would take strong action on Darfur if elected.[4]

While U.S. attention turned inward, events inside Sudan raised the pressure on Khartoum. On May 10, 2008, the Darfur conflict arrived on Khartoum's doorstep. Hundreds of Darfur rebels from JEM attacked Omdurman, an area separated from al-Bashir's presidential palace by just one bridge straddling the White Nile. It was the threat that the regime feared most, a challenge to the very center of their power. In political terms, JEM had always been of greater concern to Khartoum than any faction of the SLA because JEM had a national agenda. JEM's leader, Khalil Ibrahim, did not just want equality for Darfur; he wanted regime change. He had been one of the authors of the *Black Book*, which had made such an accurate critique of how all wealth and power in Sudan was concentrated in the hands of the riverine Arab elite to which al-Bashir belonged.

During the Darfur peace negotiations in Abuja, the United States had not seriously engaged JEM, which at that time had limited military capabilities. The United States calculated that it was more important to get Minni Minawi's militarily powerful faction of the SLA to sign on the dotted line than to worry about a group that had no leverage on the battlefield. But in the years since, Chadian president Deby's increased support to Khalil Ibrahim had changed JEM's fortunes, and the May 2008 attack on Omdurman showed that JEM's military strength could no longer be dismissed. While the JEM fighters were ultimately repelled, the fact that they had managed to take the long journey across the desert from Darfur and right to the edge of the capital highlighted the vulnerability of al-Bashir's regime.[5]

Just three days after JEM's attack, violence erupted between the SPLA and government soldiers in the north-south border area of Abyei. The area of Abyei represents a microcosm of the north-south struggle for identity in Sudan.[6] Those involved in drafting the CPA had been unable to resolve the question of whether Abyei was part of northern or southern Sudan. So they punted the question forward, creating a separate Abyei Protocol, which specified that on the same day that southern Sudanese would get to vote on whether they wanted independence, the residents of Abyei would have their own referendum on whether to be part of the north or south.[7]

In the borderland of Abyei, southern Ngok Dinka farmers tend their crops, and in the dry season Arab Misseriya nomads graze their cattle near the river that runs south of Abyei town. Historically cooperation between the two groups has been possible at the local level, but since the discovery of oil reserves near the area their coexistence has been jeopardized. The Abyei Protocol required al-Bashir's regime to share oil revenues from Abyei with the southern government and local Abyei residents, and established a special administration for the area. But in 2005 the NCP had rejected a report delineating the borders of Abyei.[8] With Abyei's boundary indeterminate, al-Bashir's regime refused to properly implement these Abyei Protocol provisions.[9] This contributed to the already tense relations between the Sudanese Army and SPLA soldiers in the area.

The violence that broke out in May 2008 had been predicted clearly and specifically by long-time Sudan advocate Roger Winter. Winter had been involved in drafting the Abyei Protocol and had continued to visit the area on a regular basis. He began sounding the alarm about Abyei in January, writing, along with John Prendergast, an Enough strategy paper on the topic, which was distributed throughout the network of citizen activists. After another visit to Abyei, Winter returned with a very specific prediction: "Large scale violence *will* occur within weeks," he wrote in April 2008, drawing attention to the period immediately following the May return migration of the Misseriya.[10]

At the time, Special Envoy Richard Williamson was attending talks with the Sudanese government in Rome, in which the United States once again dangled the carrot of normalization in return for progress in Darfur and the implementation of the CPA.[11] By now, however, the Sudanese government was disbelieving of such promises.[12] Williamson says that Abyei was high on the list of issues discussed in Rome largely because Deng Alor, who had replaced Lam Akol as the Sudanese foreign minister, was from Abyei and so had a personal interest in preventing the outbreak of violence there. At Deng Alor's urging, Williamson pushed for more of the UN peacekeepers already in southern Sudan to move into the Abyei area. Speaking before the Senate Foreign Relations Committee at the end of April, Williamson testified to the urgency of addressing the tense situation in Abyei.[13] However, as Williamson notes, "I didn't have any great insight on how to resolve it."[14]

The fighting that broke out as if to script on May 13 between the Sudanese Army and SPLA soldiers rapidly deteriorated into an assault on civilians. Civilians were not just casualties of cross-fire but were killed deliberately by the Sudanese Army as the town of Abyei was destroyed.[15] Those who could flee did; the UN reported that as many as 50,000 people were displaced.[16] Winter returned to Abyei on May 16, walking through the charred remains of its market and residential area. "The UN had not left the compound [to protect civilians in Abyei] at all during the violence. They had their machine guns manned, their armored personnel carriers…but nobody left the compound," he says.[17]

"These events were predicted, and absent effective word and action, they became inevitable. Somehow, the government of the United States of America missed all the signals—again," Winter wrote on his return to the United States.[18] I put this claim to Williamson. "Was Roger [Winter] or Enough alerting us to things we did not know? Of course not. Yet I failed to stop the violence. I failed. Do I wish I had been successful? Yes." But the failure was not Williamson's alone. The UN troops, actually on the scene and directly responsible for protecting civilians, had not done so.[19]

I asked Winter how he felt, knowing that he had raised the alarm on Abyei so accurately and to so little effect. "I hate to say—partly, I told you so and you should have done something," he began. "But more than that, it was a restatement for me of the long-term deficiencies of American special envoys and the American system itself."[20] In Winter's view, U.S. diplomats have generally been thwarted by their lack of experience with Sudan. So while they might be intellectually aware of a place called Abyei, they don't have "the sense of the vibration necessary to round out factual knowledge."[21] Yet in this particular case Williamson didn't need the intuitive sense that is developed over years of firsthand contact with an area to have absorbed Winter's warnings. His own analysis and Deng Alor's concern had led Williamson to testify to the senate that Abyei was a potential flashpoint. But there were several steps between knowing it was a problem and actually stopping it. Moreover, not all of those steps were under the control of the United States. I asked Winter whether he thought there was anything Williamson could have done with the early warning information to prevent the violence. "Honestly, I don't know. But if our special envoy or our secretary of state or whoever said something in the three years of total neglect of the Abyei Protocol...instead of a flat-line zero of engagement...."[22]

The failure to diffuse the tensions around Abyei for the three years prior to May 2008 can hardly be pinned on Williamson, who only came into the position in January. But it does point to a recurrent problem: Governmental time and resources are only devoted to the problem that is about to explode or, more commonly, has already exploded. Issues that burn slowly rarely make it to the top of a crowded agenda. "My defense, if I need one, is that if you looked at the menu, I had a pretty full plate," says Williamson.[23]

In early June, Williamson visited what remained of Abyei and was taken aback. "It looked like Hiroshima," he told me.[24] Williamson also visited the area where most of Abyei's residents had fled. "It was a mud pit, people sheltering under plastic sheets...the human cost was significant."[25] Williamson had failed to prioritize Abyei before the tensions there came to a head; belatedly he shifted course. Once the fighting began, he urged the parties not to escalate the situation by sending more troops into the area. And in the month following Abyei's destruction, he worked round-the-clock on getting the NCP and SPLM to agree to the Abyei Roadmap, a plan for how to finally resolve the problems that had been festering ever since the signing of the CPA. Finally, the United States seemed to recognize the importance of monitoring and enforcing the earlier peace agreement.

THE PREVENTION PROBLEM

The Enough Project had provided the perfect platform for Winter to get his early warning message out and had ensured that the message was communicated directly to the U.S. special envoy. It was a textbook-worthy performance. Yet Abyei had not been prioritized until after it was too late for some 50,000 people who were displaced. Part of the problem was that there was no obvious policy fix by the time the situation was about to explode.

In his April 28 paper that had warned of violence in Abyei, Winter listed three recommendations. The first was to assign Williamson a full-time diplomat to focus on Abyei. Even if this recommendation had been adopted it would have taken more than the two weeks between then and the outbreak of violence for such a person to be hired, let alone engage substantively with the parties. The second recommendation was to further increase the UN deployment in Abyei. This was something that Williamson had already started facilitating, but it is questionable whether more troops would have helped the situation when even those who were deployed did not act to protect civilians. Finally, Winter urged the United States to signal that there would be accountability for crimes. But while all these may have mitigated the violence in May 2008, the real issue was the parties' failure to agree on the status of the area. And this wasn't something that could be settled in the weeks, or even months, preceding the violence.

Abyei had been subject to a separate protocol in the CPA precisely because the parties could not agree on how to deal with the area, so in order to keep the agreement moving, the drafters punted the problem. This is what the Bush administration continued doing; there was no simple fix, and there were, quite literally, other fires to put out. This is not an excuse. Abyei remains a troublingly acute example of a failure to prevent clearly foreseeable violence. Yet it does, again, illustrate the problem of how to direct resources and attention to second-tier problems far enough ahead of time to prevent them from escalating.

In theory, public pressure might push these second-tier problems up the agenda at an earlier point. But advocates are no less susceptible to the error of prioritizing the urgent over the important than those in government. The leaders of the advocacy movement were aware of the ominous lack of CPA implementation, but they had been unable to engage their constituents on it.

STICKING WITH WHAT YOU KNOW

At the start of 2008, the weekend before Fowler began as head of Save Darfur, he proposed to a group of those most active in the advocacy community that Save Darfur shift its focus from Darfur alone to a whole-of-Sudan picture. No one disagreed, but Fowler says that making the adjustment took longer than he expected. "You have the technicalities of changing the message . . . translating it into messaging in a clear way," explains Fowler. "You are talking about a broad constituency that is not reading books about this, and so you have to communicate in a very efficient way, with lots of repetition."[26]

Without the media reinforcing the message, something they are unlikely to do in the absence of death and displacement, it is an ongoing challenge for those leading a mass movement to get regular citizens interested in situations before they hit a crisis point. In addition, the pull to stay with issues that citizens are already aware of and engaged with is very strong.

Throughout 2008, advocacy movement leaders struggled to shift the focus of constituents away from the demand they were most invested in: the deployment of a protection force in Darfur. "[T]here was a momentum thing—we were obliged to carry on with the things we already had in the fire," says Bell, explaining the continuing interest that advocates showed in seeing UNAMID, the hybrid peacekeeping force, deployed.

Having committed so much to getting authorization for peacekeepers, there was a sound logic to following the process through to implementation. And advocates were not alone in continuing to pursue the deployment of peacekeepers. National Security Adviser Stephen Hadley remembers, "In 2007-2008 I would keep asking [Special Assistant to the President for African Affairs] Bobby Pittman and Jendayi Frazer, 'What is the most useful thing we can do?' They always said, 'Get UN troops on the ground to provide a blanket.'"[27] But the effectiveness of all this effort was disappointing. UN resolution 1769 had authorized the UNAMID deployment, and Sudan, under pressure from China in the buildup to the Beijing Olympics, had finally consented. But its consent was superficial at best, and once the Olympics had passed, China eased off its pressure on Sudan. The result was that the Sudanese government blocked any troops or equipment that would give UNAMID the strength to actually protect civilians.

Part of the legacy of the multiyear efforts of advocates and officials to get UNAMID peacekeepers into Darfur is found on the fifth floor of a 1980s-era shopping complex, on the ring road of a highway in Addis Ababa. It's the sort of building where you are pleasantly surprised to find an elevator, then wonder if the stairs might be the better option. The floor is laid, unevenly, with dusty red carpet, and the paper sign on the door saying "Darfur Desk" is the only indication that this is where a handful of lieutenant colonels are working on one of the world's largest peacekeeping operations.

In August 2009 I did a lengthy interview with the outgoing head of the UNAMID operation, Rodolphe Adada. He asked that almost the entire interview stay off the record, but there was one comment he was happy to associate himself with: "UNAMID is a success, because the biggest challenge we faced was 'Can we be in Darfur?'"[28] I found mere presence to be an odd definition of success for an operation mandated to protect civilians. But going back over the barriers to getting any aspect of UNAMID actually deployed, I could understand how he had come to think this way. Khartoum had used all the bureaucratic obstacles in its arsenal to stall the deployment of the peacekeeping force and to ensure the emasculation of the operation.

"Delay on the hybrid was not the fault of the Sudanese government alone," says Amr Moussa, the head of the Arab League. "There was a hesitation by other states to contribute."[29] His summary is both true and misleading at the same time. The hesitation by other states was, in significant part, a consequence of Sudan's rhetoric against the deployment. China had secured Khartoum's agreement to the resolution, but that didn't mean Khartoum liked it or that it would cooperate in anything that would allow the force to be effective. Former rebel leader Minni Minawi may well have put it the best when he told me that the UNAMID deployment was not "accepted" by the Sudanese government, it was "absorbed" by them.[30]

Two years after the Security Council passed the UNAMID resolution just 69 percent of the authorized troop level had been deployed. And that was the good news. On every other indicator, UNAMID was operating at far less than 69 percent capacity.[31] From one end of the global system to the other, there was a dearth of serious commitment to the operation. For example, the operation has never had the tactical helicopters it requires. "When you have a region like Darfur, with almost no roads, and when it rains you are literally stuck where you are, *and* you have no helicopters...," UNAMID Lieutenant Colonel Stanislas shook his head resignedly in lieu of finishing his sentence.[32]

Globally, there is no shortage of tactical helicopters. A report published a year after Resolution 1769 was passed showed that NATO member states alone had 104 tactical helicopters actively available for deployment, almost six times the 18 helicopters required by UNAMID.[33] Yet none had been offered. Meanwhile, 350 such helicopters were being used in Iraq. Still, even if UNAMID had had the helicopters they needed, this would not have turned them into the protection force that advocates had in mind when they began rallying in Washington, nor that Darfuris themselves expected when they held out hand-written signs saying in English "welcome UN" to any Western delegation that passed through.

Part of the problem was the quality of the troops that Khartoum allowed to be deployed by refusing troops from non-African countries.[34] As one UNAMID planning officer explained it to me, in a NATO deployment a long-haul patrol would mean a mission of several days, whereas for UNAMID troops a long-haul patrol might mean a couple of hours away from the base.[35] "I blame myself for not realizing how much of a negative it is to inherit a force," says Jean-Marie Guéhenno, former head of the UN Department of Peacekeeping Operations. According to UN staff, Guéhenno had in fact been the person who fought hardest against the lowest common denominator compromise that was the hybrid. "I should have fought harder. I should have scared people," he insists. "The Sudanese government used the hybrid concept to exclude armies that had capacities that the AU did not have...."[36]

While I was in Darfur in 2009, a group of fully armed Nigerian peacekeepers handed over their vehicles and their weapons in an ambush. Another contingent set out to investigate a report of violence, but upon being told at a government checkpoint that they could not pass, returned to base without so much as the threat of a warning shot being fired. But the most telling sight I saw of UNAMID's capacity—or lack thereof—was on a visit to their headquarters in el-Fasher. The barbed-wire perimeter of the UNAMID compound was guarded by Sudanese police, who had been sent from Khartoum for the job and were being paid for by UNAMID. "UNAMID troops are IDPs [internally displaced people] in uniform. They cannot protect themselves," a UN official told me.[37]

The perception of the hybrid force as "the grubbiest of compromises" is pervasive within the UN building in New York. I asked one official familiar with the Darfur deployment how, then, it came to pass. His summary was a simple: "The UN Security Council said something has to be done. You couldn't get the U.S. doing an intervention. So it came back to the UN. Sudan didn't want the UN. So the hybrid was the only acceptable option politically."[38] Another high-level UN official summarized the whole endeavor as "a dangerous and flawed compromise to save face for the Sudanese as well as for Western powers—in which the UN lost."[39] Actually, the people of Darfur did.

IT IS EASY TO CRITICIZE advocates for persisting in pushing for the implementation of something that ended up falling so far short of what was needed. But even with less challenging problems, you can never be certain of success in advance; if the threshold for engaging in advocacy was a guarantee of success, then no one would ever try to protect civilians at risk. That said, it makes sense to prioritize the pursuit of policies that have a reasonable likelihood of achieving the end goal.[40] From the outset, Sudan was clear it would not accept an effective peacekeeping force, and the rest of the world was clear it would not back a non-consensual deployment. Given these fundamentals, the likelihood of peacekeepers being able to act effectively in Darfur was minimal. Yet the leading advocates' faith in peacekeeping as a policy response led them to convince thousands of their constituents that this was one of the core components that was needed—and once the mass movement had embraced this policy demand it was hard to shift course, even after leaders of the movement began to appreciate the challenges of peacekeeping in the Darfur context. However, advocates were not alone in harboring high hopes about what boots on the ground could accomplish. On both Darfur and Abyei, there were also government officials and policy experts who had expectations about what the presence of peacekeepers could achieve that were much greater than what the peacekeepers ever delivered. The criticism that can fairly be made of all these actors is that they failed to adequately factor in the impact on a peacekeeping operation when a strong host state like Sudan opposes its deployment.

UNAMID faced overwhelming constraints in terms of troops and equipment. But focusing on these constraints only addresses the symptoms, not the causes, of the operation's failings. The primary determinant of UNAMID's capacity was less about numbers of troops or types of helicopters than it was about the political environment in which the hybrid force was asked to operate. Every arm of the UNAMID operation knew that they could be expelled from Sudanese territory any time Khartoum ordered it; it was this political environment that led Adada to view mere presence inside Darfur as success. Guéhenno summarizes the crux of the problem: "You cannot legislate the consent of a country.... Either it's there or it's not. Everything else is just a distraction."[41]

Advocacy groups demanding that the U.S. government get a protection force on the ground enabled the American politicians to "respond" by calling for a UN deployment. But any slim chance there might have been to get the Sudanese government to genuinely consent to a UN peacekeeping operation would have required unified support from Sudan's strongest allies. Given global perceptions in the aftermath of Iraq, the U.S. government was not well positioned to lead the call on this. And targets like China and the Arab League were difficult for a U.S.-based advocacy movement to reach. The success they had with China in the buildup to the Olympics marks the exception that proves the rule of an overall misalignment between where advocates had most influence and where influence was most needed.

CHAPTER 13

ELECTIONS AND EXPECTATIONS

W hen the Democratic Party's U.S. presidential nomination went
to Senator Barack Obama in August 2008, the Darfur advocacy community was filled with a sense of hope. Not only had
Obama spoken passionately about Darfur back at the April 2006 rally, but
he had remained a consistent advocate on the issue and had hired the movement's guru, Samantha Power, to work with him. Advocates imagined that an
Obama presidency would signal a return to U.S. leadership on Sudan.

The team Obama assembled once he had the nomination was a veritable
wish list for most Darfur advocates. Obama chose Senator Joe Biden to be
his running mate; Biden had long been one of the congressional champions
on Sudan. At the National Jewish Democratic Council forum in April 2007,
Biden had told the audience that if there was no international willingness to
use force in Darfur, then "I'm sending American troops alone."[1] In addition to
seeking advice on his foreign policy positions from Power, Obama had spent
his campaign working closely with Susan Rice, a scholar at the Brookings
Institution, who had repeatedly called for tough action on Khartoum,[2] and
with Gayle Smith, GI-Net's first supporter.

When Barack Obama won the presidential election, he became the first
African American elected to lead the United States. On January 20, 2009, Sam
Bell woke up at 5 a.m. and waited six hours for a spot on the Mall to watch
Obama's inauguration as the 44th president. He and his friends shared peanut
butter and jelly sandwiches with others braving the freezing January tempera-
tures to get a glimpse of their new president. The excitement was palpable as
strangers struck up conversations about how historic an occasion it was.

Beyond the broad significance of the day, Bell also thought expectantly
about the impact that the new president would have on Darfur. "The rap on
Bush wasn't that he didn't care," says Bell. "We thought he cared, but the

Bush administration didn't have any energy or international credibility to take on Darfur in a real way." On inauguration day there was a sense that the new president would come into office with the international leverage that the Bush administration had lost. "I thought he had a real chance to do a bunch of things out of the gate," says Bell.

David Rubenstein, despite no longer having any formal role in the Darfur movement, was thinking along similar lines as he walked from his D.C. neighborhood to the Mall. "My belief at the time regarding his impact on Darfur was that his better attitude toward internationalism would enable him to guide other world leaders to stand up for justice," Rubenstein recalls. Gloria White-Hammond and her husband came down from Boston to witness history in the making. "We thought about the people we wished had lived to see it," she says. Regarding Darfur she remembers, "there was a lot of optimism, almost euphoria."

Omer Ismail watched Obama's swearing in on television at home with his family, alternating his gaze between the television and his children, ages 11 and 12. "It was fascinating to see their eyes fixated. You could see them thinking, 'it is possible for us as well.'" But the occasion was tinged with sadness. "My children have been granted this place, but their cousins who happen to have been born and raised in Sudan may not get that chance."

The victory of Obama's election left Ismail reflecting on election processes more generally: "It's not just about an election. It's about a healing process— that America is coming to grips with its past and its sometimes ugly present." And with that came the inevitable contrast to Sudan where, Ismail feared, the upcoming national elections would not heal but would divide, would "make a winner of an indicted criminal, and legitimize a regime that lives by the gun."

The Comprehensive Peace Agreement, designed to transform Sudan from dictatorship to democracy, first began to veer off course when SPLM leader John Garang died in a helicopter crash just 21 days after he had assumed the vice presidency of Sudan in 2005. Garang had truly believed in the promise of a New Sudan that would bring power to the marginalized people across the country. But for all practical purposes, the vision of a unified, democratic Sudan had died along with Garang. His successor, Salva Kiir, had always been inclined toward southern independence. Moreover, he had neither Garang's skills to handle the political scene in Khartoum nor the same partnership with Vice President Taha that Garang had forged during the course of the CPA negotiations.[3]

Had Garang lived, the ambitious transformation of Sudan that the CPA promised would still have been a challenge of gargantuan proportions. Without Garang, the international community would have needed to commit fully to ensure that each step of the CPA was implemented for the transformation to have had a chance. Instead, and in part due to the international focus on Darfur, deadlines related to the CPA had slipped by without attracting a significant outcry.

ARREST WARRANT

In March 2009, eight months after the ICC prosecutor's indictment of President al-Bashir, the judges of the Pre-Trial Chamber issued their decision on the arrest warrant.

While his colleagues at the Enough Project gathered together around the computers in their D.C. office, live-streaming the announcement from The Hague, Omer Ismail sat alone in his bedroom at home. "I didn't want to be around a lot of people. I wanted to listen to every word. To savor the moment," he recalls. "I thought, from today justice in Darfur will be sought. I thought, one day when my children are old enough—and by that time al-Bashir will be behind bars—I will sit down and tell them the story."

The judges issued an arrest warrant for the Sudanese president, charging him with war crimes and crimes against humanity in Darfur.[4] (The prosecutor's third charge, of genocide, was initially rejected, but the judges subsequently added the genocide charge after the ICC Appeals Chamber found the lower court had used the wrong legal standard to assess the charge.[5])

Just hours after the arrest warrant was issued, al-Bashir ordered the expulsion of 13 international aid organizations from Sudanese territory and disbanded three domestic humanitarian organizations, accusing them of sharing information with the ICC—a claim both the court and the groups denied.[6] The groups' assets were seized by the government, and their foreign staff were forced to leave the country. The office that oversees humanitarian coordination for the UN briefed the UN Security Council that 40 to 70 percent of aid capacity in Darfur would be lost.[7]

The expulsion of the agencies was the most visible obstruction of the humanitarians' work by the Sudanese government to date. Expulsion was something the Sudanese government had either threatened or actually enforced against various aid agencies and their staff since it first let them into Darfur in mid-2004.[8] But the way that al-Bashir linked these latest expulsions to the arrest warrant had a powerful impact at the UN Security Council.

When the United Kingdom and then Japan began circulating a draft presidential statement to express the UN Security Council's "deepest concern" about the expulsions, the Libyan representative on the council tried, again, to get a suspension of the prosecution on the council's agenda. Arguing that the expulsions and the arrest warrant were linked, he said that Libya would only sign onto the statement of concern if it included the AU's latest communiqué requesting the suspension of the al-Bashir case.[9] Again, Western nations opposed this. Neither side budged. The result of the impasse was that al-Bashir got away with expelling key aid agencies, risking up to 70 percent of the operations that served as a lifeline to those stranded in the camps, without being reprimanded by so much as an expression of concern from the UN Security Council.

OBAMA'S SPECIAL ENVOY

On assuming office, the Obama administration initiated a Sudan policy review, led by Michelle Gavin, senior director of African Affairs at the National Security Council (NSC), and Samantha Power, the NSC's senior director of Multilateral Affairs. But when al-Bashir expelled the humanitarians, the administration was caught unprepared; with the review still ongoing, they had neither a policy nor a point person to handle the new crisis.

Advocates created an outcry. Save Darfur organized a sign-on letter calling on President Obama to demand that the agencies be allowed to return.[10] Enough and GI-Net also issued press releases and asked their constituents to call the White House to urge the administration to appoint a high-level envoy for Sudan.[11] Two weeks after the expulsions, Obama announced he was going to do just that. As had been the case since 2006, it was the one advocacy request that the U.S. government was consistently able to meet.

Omer Ismail and Gloria White-Hammond were invited to the White House for the naming of the envoy; they were surprised by the president's choice: Scott Gration. "General Gration was one of the last people that people were talking about to be named envoy," recalls Ismail. "He wasn't in the circles of speculation because people believed he would be named the administrator of [the U.S. space agency] NASA." A retired air force general, Gration was known to have a close personal relationship with President Obama, but he was an unlikely candidate to be the U.S. government's lead interlocutor on Sudan as the country headed toward partition. He had no diplomatic experience. Still, White-Hammond remembers thinking, "With Obama in, and we knew Samantha [Power] was in there—there was a sense that it was going to be okay."

In the announcement of Gration's appointment, much was made of the fact that his first language was Swahili; the son of missionaries, he grew up in Congo. But as Sam Bell remembers thinking, Swahili was not going to be much help in Sudan. "It struck me as weird. Okay, so he's lived in Congo but Africa's not one country." In a reaction akin to White-Hammond's, Ismail says he wasn't too worried who was chosen as the envoy: "I realized the envoy was the messenger. What mattered was the policy. For me the election of Obama was great for the people of Darfur, because we knew Senator Obama and we thought that with him and because of Samantha Power there and Gayle Smith there, what could go wrong?"

Two weeks later, Ismail and John Prendergast were given a meeting with President Obama and his new envoy, which they filmed and posted on the Enough website. Prendergast described Gration as "a thoughtful, committed public servant whose tenure as envoy could be very successful if the president gives him the right policy and tools he needs to succeed."[12] The signs were promising. Unlike Richard Williamson and Andrew Natsios before him, Gration was employed on a full-time basis, and his office was properly integrated into the State Department. Gone were the days of feuding between the special envoy and the assistant secretary for African Affairs. Advocates thought they would soon be getting a new—tougher—policy towards Khartoum.

WORKING WITH KHARTOUM

A few months after he took office, Gration testified before the Senate Foreign Relations Committee—with words that startled many Darfur activists. Like Natsios had done two years earlier, Gration refused to use the word genocide to describe the current situation in Darfur, saying he saw only "remnants of genocide." And going one step further he seemed to indicate that he was ready to recommend the lifting of sanctions on Khartoum: "There's no evidence in our intelligence community that supports [Sudan] being on the state sponsor of terrorism [sic]. It's a political decision."[13] He was not the first U.S. official to think it or even to say it. But he was the first to do so on record. Signs of dissension soon emerged from the Obama administration as it became clear that Gration's approach would differ from the advocates' allies inside government. Susan Rice, now U.S. ambassador to the UN, was celebrated by advocates as she set herself up in public opposition to Gration, pointedly describing Darfur as an "ongoing genocide."[14]

Within days of Gration's testimony, groups of citizen activists across the country issued a statement calling for his resignation.[15] However, the largest Washington-based Darfur organizations, Save Darfur, Enough, and GI-Net, did not join the statement. In fact for the first half of 2009, the major Darfur organizations generally gave the new administration a long leash, so strong was their faith that having human rights allies within the administration would make a difference. Advocacy leaders had far greater access to government insiders than they ever had during the Bush administration. In May, advocacy leaders including Jerry Fowler, Gloria White-Hammond, John Prendergast, and Omer Ismail had met with individuals who Enough described as the "power players on Darfur" inside the administration and emerged confident about Obama's approach.[16]

But as the months continued to pass with the policy review still not complete, these advocates shifted course. At the end of August, Humanity United supported a campaign called Sudan Now: Keep The Promise, a joint project with the major Darfur organizations. In high-profile paid advertising they published the many strong statements on Sudan that Obama had made during his candidacy, challenging him to live up to his word.[17]

Meanwhile, in the continuing absence of a formal, whole-of-government strategy, Gration charted his own course. In his office was a countdown of the number of days until the January 2011 referendum in which southerners would get to vote on independence. He feared that if the referendum did not go forward on time, there would be a resumption of conflict. "If Sudan implodes, the spillover of refugees, the international attention, and the inability to do anything because there's no infrastructure [in the south]. We'd have to airdrop everything," Gration told me.[18]

Gration's belief was that al-Bashir, and al-Bashir alone, could ensure the referendum went forward. This meant that the United States had no option but to work with his regime.[19] As an SPLM member of the Government of National Unity put it, "You can say whatever you want about the NCP, but they are the only people in the history of Sudan that have accepted the southerners right to self-determination, and Gration has come into the situation understanding that fact."[20] But Gration's decision to engage Khartoum, approaching the government with his "hands open,"[21] left Darfuris feeling betrayed.

IT WAS MID-SEPTEMBER 2009 when I returned to Darfur for my second visit in a month, this time accompanying Gration. I had met him in Khartoum the month before, and he had invited me to travel to Darfur with him. At his first meeting in Darfur we were greeted by a group of *omdas* (leaders) from the displacement camps in and around el-Fasher. One of the men, wearing a luggage tag taped over one eye, stood up. "Greetings to Condi Rice...and United States Republicans," said this *omda*. "Greetings to the NCP student," he said to Gration, explaining that he was too frustrated with statements Gration had made recently to look at him with both eyes. "You make a death sentence to me" was the way the *omda*'s words were translated into English.[22]

As Gration's meetings in Darfur soon made clear, it is not only Khartoum that pays attention to the testimony of U.S. officials before congress. Word of Gration's Senate Foreign Relations Committee testimony had quickly spread to Darfuris, who had received the message via cell phone from their friends and supporters in the United States. Gration spent the entirety of his visit to Darfur reiterating the same talking points to every frustrated group of displaced people he met. But in his outreach to Khartoum, he had lost their confidence, and a whistle-stop tour to a few groups of displaced leaders seemed unlikely to make a difference.

At a women's center near Abu Shok camp, one woman told him that since the aid agency expulsions in March, "There is no school, no kindergarten. There is no medical service at all in the camp." Back in June, Gration had told the media that an agreement he reached with Khartoum on readmitting some of the expelled aid groups (albeit without the return of their assets and under new names) had "essentially closed the humanitarian gap" that existed after the expulsions.[23] Presumably believing this, Gration challenged the woman as to whether they really had those services before the expulsions. "Yes," she replied firmly, naming the now-expelled organizations that had been providing health and education.[24]

The impact of the expulsions was something I had been told about repeatedly when I was in Darfur on my own just a few weeks earlier. I was shown empty wooden structures—sturdy by Darfur camp standards—where medical clinics used to operate. Women had been the hardest hit by the expulsions. It was inside these now-empty structures that aid workers had administered medical care, discreetly and free of charge, to women who had been raped.

While direct killing had dropped off since the massacres of 2003-2004, rape had remained prevalent. "Rape here is systematic. I get new reports every day," a UN official responsible for collating incident reports of sexual violence across Darfur in 2009 told me.[25] A network of support services had been built up painstakingly over the previous five years. As a result, women who braved the social stigma associated with reporting rape could receive medical care— from life-saving emergency assistance for injuries sustained during brutal attacks to HIV/AIDS prophylactic treatment and psychological support.

More than any other aspect of the humanitarian operations in Darfur, the agencies that provided these services faced steady opposition from the Sudanese government. At the very top of the state, President al-Bashir denied the reality. "[W]hen it comes to mass rape, there is no document or evidence, just accusations.... The women inside the camps are under the influence of the rebels and some are even relatives of the rebels. That's why they make these claims."[26] Having aid organizations on the ground whose daily experiences contradicted the president's position had never been a comfortable situation, and many of those I spoke with believed the expulsions had targeted the groups that worked with women who had been raped.[27]

It was a very different Darfur that I saw with the U.S. government delegation. Neither the displaced nor the aid workers trusted Gration, and there was no time to build that trust. We traveled from place to place in an armed convoy on a tightly packed schedule that left no room to create the space it takes for people to tell you their fears.

Gration worked day and night. As one of his aides put it, he was doing the job of two full-time envoys: dealing with Darfur, and trying to hold onto what remained of the CPA. Further complicating matters was that in the aftermath of the failed 2006 Darfur Peace Agreement, parallel processes had emerged for negotiating a peace deal for Darfur. By the time Gration became the special envoy, there was a joint UN-AU process, led by Djibril Bassolé, a diplomat from Burkina Faso and hosted by the Qatari government in Doha, and a separate AU panel led by former South African president Thabo Mbeki. In addition, Gration began a new track, focusing on the normalization of relations between Chad and Sudan—something that led to a breakthrough when, in February 2010, Chadian President Deby visited Khartoum for the first time since 2004.[28] With all that was going on, Gration seemed to transfer his personal childhood experiences—of having fled with his parents from Congo into Kenya—onto the displaced population. "I've been through being a refugee. I've been through losing everything…I can empathize," he told me. I wasn't at all convinced that he could empathize with the Darfuris who had not only seen their entire communities destroyed but were, some six years later, still trapped under the rule of the same government that was responsible.

Gration talked about how Khartoum had been under a cloud for a long time and that he wanted to start the relationship anew. "It's very easy to get agreements and very difficult to implement them. We perceive this as them not living up to their commitments, but I'm not convinced the reason has been malicious" he said. "I'm hoping and praying that with incentives we can head toward a lasting peace." In Gration's estimation, changing the relationship would require Washington to change the way it responded to Khartoum. "How well would kids perform if you said, thanks for turning up to school today, now go stand in the corner? Kids, countries, react to gold stars, smiley faces…."

CARROTS AND ~~STICKS~~

The *Washington Post* reporter who was with us on the trip wrote up Gration's gold stars comments in an article that was rapidly circulated among Darfur advocates, and new calls for his resignation emerged. A few days later a group from STAND, the organization that began at Georgetown University but had since been incorporated as the student wing of GI-Net and spread to campuses nationwide, turned up at the Sudanese Embassy in Washington, D.C., to deliver a hastily constructed big cardboard smiley face and a gold star. Filming the stunt, they mockingly tracked it to the Beatles song "We Can Work It Out" and circulated it on YouTube.[29]

When the Obama administration finally released the results of its Sudan policy review on October 19, Sam Bell ran into Gration in the White House conference center. "What's up? What can we do?" he asked. Gration paused. "Just stop shooting at me, Sam," he replied. "It was so sad because part of my job is to shoot, to hold people accountable," says Bell. "We did the gold stars with STAND, and I would 100 percent do it again, but he doesn't get that it's not about him personally."

The protracted period between the initiation of the review and its conclusion some nine months later was the consequence of genuine disagreement between those aligned with Susan Rice, who believed that Khartoum's behavior was best influenced by sticks, and those aligned with Gration, who believed that carrots were the only way forward, and of a president who, in the face of these disputes, chose not to force the review to a conclusion at an earlier point.[30] The long-awaited policy review stated that Darfur, the CPA, and counterterrorism cooperation were three co-equal priorities on Sudan and that a mix of pressures and incentives would be used to get progress on all three objectives.[31] The public commitment not to let Darfur be traded off against cooperation on counterterrorism or be held hostage to the CPA was a welcome sign, acknowledging the risk borne out under the Bush administration that the Sudanese government could play one set of U.S. interests off against another. But it came too late; with Gration's office convinced that al-Bashir's cooperation was essential to the referendum taking place as scheduled and that the referendum was a higher priority than Darfur, the on-paper policy had already been undermined in practice.

The administration told advocates that the specific pressures and incentives, as well as the benchmarks that would be used to measure Khartoum's progress, were in a classified annex. "The fear is that it's a classified annex because they don't really have anything," says Bell, who worried that while carrots were easy to deliver "in some cases with the stroke of a pen," this was not the case with meaningful sticks. After the policy release, Bell told Gration that advocates would be looking to see if the administration was doing the work to build multilateral pressures. "If they don't build the sticks, they don't really have a carrots and sticks strategy, they have a carrots strategy," says Bell.

The classified index has remained classified. And although the benchmarks on which one would have expected progress to be measured—resumption of services for rape victims in Darfur, or genuine reform of the media and of security laws before Sudanese were asked to vote—were not met, there was no sign of any pressure being put on al-Bashir's regime even unilaterally, let alone multilaterally.[32]

SUDAN GOES TO THE POLLS

One of the cornerstones of the Comprehensive Peace Agreement was that Sudan, finally, would hold its first free elections in more than two decades.

The hope had been that if the entirety of Sudanese society felt it had a stake in the government, it would herald the birth of a unified New Sudan, which southerners would not want to secede from. But in the months leading up to the elections the NCP had scuttled any chance of a free vote.

I was in Sudan in the months before the election. I arrived at the dilapidated offices of one of Khartoum's four independent newspapers at 10.30 p.m. on a Friday night. My arrival had been timed to ensure I wouldn't run into one of the censorship officers from Sudan's National Intelligence and Security Services (the NCP-dominated network responsible for the ongoing practice of torturing Sudanese dissidents and known in local parlance simply as "Security"). As it happened, Security had left ten minutes before my arrival, and the journalist I was coming to meet was philosophical about having just been told that two full pages of his copy for the following day's paper would have to be cut. "I'll have to fill up the space with pictures," he said. "This was the reasonable Security guy—at least only two pages were cut. You should see what happens when we get the hardliner." He gave me a wry, tired smile.

Security censors each and every page printed in Sudanese newspapers. Should journalists try to run a story the NCP doesn't like, the officers they have stationed at the printing press itself simply shut down the presses. One of the stories that had been cut that night was a news article reporting that Sudan's beleaguered opposition parties were planning to hold a meeting the following day to strategize on election-related issues.

Pervasive press censorship was just one of the challenges to Sudanese participation in their own elections. At a late-night meeting in a nondescript Khartoum suburb, the acquaintance of an official in Sudan's Central Bureau of Statistics started reading me a list of numbers. I dutifully recorded them in a notebook whose pages were now grainy with dust after a month of interviews in Sudan. The informant summarized, "Between the census conducted in 1983 and the one conducted in 1993, the nomadic population in South Darfur decreased by just over 5.5 percent. This was largely due to the drought, which led to a loss of livestock and forced many nomads into the towns." He resumed his list of numbers before summarizing further. "If we are to believe the recent census, this same nomadic population has increased by 322 percent," he paused for effect, "322 percent since the last census in 1993."

This implausible increase was one of the many anomalies to be found in the census, a nation-wide exercise undertaken to determine how many of the parliamentary seats would be allocated to each geographical area in the 2010 elections. Speculation was rife that figures like these had been doctored in order to allocate more seats to areas that support the NCP. Meanwhile, most displaced Darfuris had refused to participate in the census, fearing that by registering from an IDP camp they would forfeit their residency rights on the land from which they had fled.[33]

In the buildup to the elections pro-NCP billboards with heavily air-brushed images of President al-Bashir in military or religious attire were omnipresent across Khartoum. "Al-Bashir is our dignity!" they claimed. Since the state-run media told citizens the ICC indictment of al-Bashir was an attack on the Sudanese people, voting for al-Bashir was equated to an act of patriotism. It was a far cry from the stigma that the arrest warrant was supposed to bring.

Meanwhile, the man who would be the SPLM's candidate for the Sudanese presidency, Yasir Arman, was under attack for speaking out against the so-called Public Order laws—an NCP version of sharia—that had recently been applied to Christian teenagers from the south who were living in Khartoum. The girls had been flogged for the "crime" of wearing trousers. "Yasir Arman is a prominent figure and they manage to bully him. Imagine what it is like for ordinary people. How can they possibly vote freely?"[34] asked Salih Osman, a Darfur Consortium member who belongs to one of Sudan's opposition parties. "We've been hearing the U.S. government has agreed to donate millions for elections. But elections are supposed to be about the will of the people. To hold an election in this climate...." Osman's voice trailed off in despair.

As election day neared, government agents arrested those who tried to stage opposition protests.[35] A Darfuri student activist in Khartoum was abducted by Security in broad daylight; his dead body was dumped in the neighboring town of Omdurman the next day.[36] Student activists involved in a pro-democracy movement were arrested and beaten.[37] Most of Darfur's displaced population had decided not to vote in an election they viewed as unfair. But even those who did want to vote would have difficulty doing so. Election observers from the European Union pulled their team out of Darfur, saying that the safety of neither the observers nor the voters could be guaranteed.[38]

Policy experts at the International Crisis Group called for the elections to be delayed once again in order for reasonably peaceful and democratic conditions to be created that would, among other benefits, enable displaced Darfuris to vote.[39] But the U.S. government supported the NCP's position that there should be no delay."[40] No longer the dreamed-of climax to a democratic transformation, the elections were now viewed as something of a necessary evil. Al-Bashir wanted them to go ahead so that he could replace the label "indicted war criminal al-Bashir" with "democratically elected al-Bashir."

Gration's office continued to take a better-the-devil-you-know approach, concluding that a flawed election that maintained al-Bashir as president was the best chance of seeing the referendum go forward as scheduled in January 2011.[41] Outweighing any concern about democracy was the overriding fear that if the referendum didn't go ahead on time, southerners would secede unilaterally, and the result would be a resumption of the north-south war.

A few days before polling began, the main opposition parties announced they were boycotting the election,[42] and the SPLM's candidate for president, Yasir Arman, withdrew from the race.[43] It was a vastly different outcome to what John Garang would have imagined back in 2005 when he danced in the streets of Khartoum with the millions of Sudanese who had turned up to welcome a man who promised to represent all the marginalized people of Sudan. In the years since his death, international attention on Sudan's immediate crisis points had overshadowed the longer-term project of the democratization of power in the country.

I was at Omer Ismail's home just outside Washington, D.C., on the day that the Sudanese went to the polls, their first "democratic" election in 24 years. "It is a feeling of someone who has been robbed of something, twice. I was robbed the first time when this cabal came to power and a second time because this is a sham election," he told me. "There are big choices coming up about the future of Sudan. And the Sudanese are supposed to be on the front line to make these choices, but they are not being given the chance." Ismail's phone rang—a cousin in Khartoum. Switching into Arabic, he asked questions about the voter turnout. "I was 10 years old when Nimeiri came to power," he said as he got off the phone. "It was 1969. He was the second dictator. I was born under the first dictator.... By the time I got to vote for the first time, I was 27 years old; so many years had already been robbed...." His phone rang again with more election updates.

"I feel like I never had the chance to contribute along with my fellow Sudanese," Ismail explained after receiving the latest election update. "It is the same for anyone my age. We never had a chance. And now we are going to the twilight of our years, and we cannot even get to have a say in the future for our children and grandchildren. It is as if the whole universe is conspiring to rob us of our right of assembly, opinions, ideas, the freedom of thinking, freedom of voice, and freedom choice." Ismail's voice was right on that thin cusp between anger and sadness. "For all these things we have had to leave our country to enjoy them somewhere else. And even in other people's land, your adopted home, there is a feeling that now this government too is legitimizing this, and not thinking that in doing so, they are robbing the Sudanese people again." He paused. "I deeply regret being excited about Obama coming to the White House."

ANY NEW ADMINISTRATION is constrained by actions of the administration that preceded it. By the time Obama took office, the democratic transformation envisaged in the CPA was already well off course, and prospects for a free and fair election were poor. If the Obama administration had been ready to roll out its Sudan policy on Day One, the 16-month window until the elections would still have been a tight one in which to push for real change. Instead, the administration got bogged down in internal disputes, which ensured that, yet again, the U.S. government was sending mixed signals to Khartoum. Moreover, turning the process around would have required a mix of credible carrots and sticks. And with regard to sticks, the United States had already reached close to the maximum of unilateral pressure it could apply, short of military action, so the only way to build additional pressure was multilaterally.

For the United States to have built a unified multilateral coalition to push for free and fair elections would have necessitated Obama spending a significant amount of the international diplomatic capital he had upon taking office. While statements he had made as a candidate led advocates to believe he would do this, he chose instead to spend his capital on traditional national security interests—putting enormous energy into moving parts of the international system to progress on Israel-Palestine, North Korea, Iran, and nuclear non-proliferation. The consequence was that Gration's all-carrot approach became the policy enacted by default.

As was preordained, the Sudanese elections delivered al-Bashir the presidency. At the time of this writing, the NCP controls more than 80 percent of all the positions in the national government, placing opposition groups in an even more constricted political environment than before the elections. In the grim assessment of one Sudanese civil society organization, "Facilitation of the fraudulent election has assisted the NCP to expand its almost total control of the Sudanese official apparatus, once again reproducing the intensity of the NCP state which was put in place after the June 30, 1989 coup."[44] In a perverse coda to the Darfur crisis, the elections delivered Janjaweed leader Musa Hilal a seat in the national parliament, as a representative of North Darfur.

One of the great ironies of the story of *Fighting for Darfur* is that after the largest citizen outcry for the U.S. government to protect civilians in a foreign land emerged in 2004 and was sustained for an unprecedented number of years, the U.S. government's Sudan policy under Obama in 2010 reverted to what the Bush administration's Sudan policy had been in 2003: Darfur was again sidelined in the service of the north-south problem. Of course there was an important difference: In 2010, thousands of civilians were not being massacred in Darfur. But the basic factors that facilitated the massacres seven years earlier remained unresolved, and the people who were responsible for the massacres remained in power.

From the perspective of short-term U.S. national security interests, there was some logic behind trading off democratic ideals for stability and Darfur for the north-south referendum. And from the perspective of southerners, prioritizing the upcoming referendum also made sense. But for the Sudanese people as a whole, free and fair elections, with the international community standing by the result, would have been the best possible outcome over the long term. As members of Sudanese civil society and opposition groups told me repeatedly in interviews after the elections, the root causes of Sudan's conflicts, whether in Darfur, the south, or elsewhere, can all be traced to governance in Khartoum. Sudanese activists and opposition members say that by just focusing on stopping outbreaks of current or imminent violence, the West keeps getting involved in their country in a piecemeal fashion instead of helping them achieve the redistribution of power needed to address all of Sudan's conflicts.[45]

IF THE 2011 referendum goes forward and southerners are able to freely express their will, there is little doubt they will vote for independence. But the NCP is unlikely to let half of Sudan's territory and the majority of its oil reserves go without a fight. The only real question is whether it will be possible to constrain that fight to the political realm or will there be a return to war.

While a return to the war that has dominated Sudan's post-independence history would be devastating, even the "best-case scenario"—in which the south is granted its independence through a political settlement—will create serious problems. The transition period between the signing of the CPA in 2005 and the referendum in 2011 was supposed to be used to develop the capacity of southerners to govern and to begin implementing basic necessities of education, roads, and other infrastructure. But this kind of development, so long denied to the south, was stymied, in part, due to the global shift in attention to Darfur. Consequently, the prospect of a viable new nation of southern Sudan looks bleak, even if the NCP does not try to stop its secession.

And then there is the situation for northern Sudanese, including Darfuris. In the post-election environment they face rule by a state fully dominated by the NCP. With international attention now back on the south, there is minimal scrutiny of the government's actions in Darfur; at the time of this writing they are conducting aerial bombardments—causing yet more civilian death and displacement—and they have denied both UNAMID and aid organizations access to vast areas of the region without being called to account.[46] In addition, violence between disenfranchised Arab groups in the area is steadily increasing, and, once again, Arab Darfuris are not being adequately represented in the Darfur peace negotiations.[47]

When I tried to get back into Darfur in July 2010, a Sudanese government official told me there was an indefinite ban on foreign journalists being allowed into the region; with no mainstream media coverage, Darfur is becoming a black hole. The cycle is repeating itself: Darfur was initially ignored in favor of the south. Then the situation reversed. Now Darfur is again sidelined.

In 2003 the marginalized Darfuri population agitated for parity when they saw southerners get a political deal giving them a share in the power and wealth of Sudan. In 2011 Darfuris may again look toward the south and wonder, "If they can be independent, why not us too?" And Darfuris are not the only marginalized people in the north. The balkanization of Sudan is a looming threat, and, if it happens, it is hard to imagine it would be peaceful.

20/20 HINDSIGHT

"Looking back, I wish '2005 Sam' was more inquisitive about all Sudan's challenges and not just the ones called genocide," Sam Bell told me in the aftermath of the 2010 election, reflecting back on the dismissive reaction he had some five years earlier to the suggestion that implementing the CPA should have been the highest priority in Sudan. "I think one of the biggest missing pieces for the movement initially was context, understanding the context."

Had this contextual understanding been present from the outset, advocates may not have allowed their focus on Darfur to preclude them from engaging with the whole-of-Sudan picture for so many years. Looking at Darfur in isolation generated solutions weighted heavily towards external actors intervening on behalf of Darfuris who were not in a position to protect themselves. A wider lens would have generated a different analysis. Many of the core problems that led to the atrocities in Darfur are the same problems that, to differing degrees, affect the rest of Sudan's marginalized people. In addition to what was undoubtedly necessary external assistance for Darfuris in the short term, Darfuris and marginalized Sudanese more generally could have been better served had the international community worked to empower citizens inside of Sudan to challenge the core system of governance that makes the crimes like those committed in Darfur possible.

Had advocates had a greater contextual understanding, they might also have appreciated at an earlier point the ability of a strong Sudanese state to undermine the implementation of each and every aspect of international engagement with Darfur. The analogy to Rwanda, so effective at gaining attention to Darfur, did not end up serving Darfuris well when its lessons were carried over into the policy realm because of the very different contexts, both local and international, in which these two manmade tragedies unfolded.

The cautionary tale for the future is not to let the lessons of the Darfur story overdetermine advocacy efforts for the next crisis. Critical reflection on the past is essential, and lessons can and should be learned from the exercise. But the experience in Darfur also reminds us that such lessons must be applied thoughtfully, not dogmatically, and always modified in light of a new context.

CHAPTER 14

CONCLUSIONS

"Let's start by recognizing this truth," Sam Bell began in his address to a conference of Darfur activists at the end of 2009. "We *alone* cannot stop genocide and end atrocities."

Objectively speaking, it was a statement of the obvious. But within the culture of the community Bell was addressing, it had only recently become anything less than a radical admission. It is not much of an oversimplification to say that most of those, myself included, who first got involved in advocacy for Darfur believed that it was our outcry that would mark the dividing line between life and death for Darfuris. Hubristic? Yes. But we humans are apathetic unless we believe that our actions will make the decisive difference.

The birth of the Darfur movement was grounded in a belief in the power of regular citizens to shape the actions of government. The lesson embraced with vigor by the new movement was that "It was in the realm of [U.S.] domestic politics that the battle to stop genocide is lost."[1] Had that lesson been true in the case of Darfur, this would have been a very different book. But with America's standing in the world no longer at the peak of its post–Cold War euphoria, Darfur provided a counternarrative, highlighting the decisive role that global geopolitics play in the battle to stop genocide and mass atrocity.

This is not to say that a domestic outcry is not a necessary component of stopping genocide and other mass atrocities. The fact that the U.S. government sidelined Darfur when there was no public spotlight on the crisis throughout 2003, when so many were being massacred, is a powerful testament to the utility of public action in pushing the government to break from business-as-usual and prioritize human lives. And while it is true that some decisions in the Darfur story took place without any significant pressure from the Darfur movement, we cannot know in advance which situations will benefit from the particular alignment of interests, personalities, or individual convictions that may spur the government to act in the absence of outside pressure. So if the aim is to prevent genocide and mass atrocity in a consistent fashion, across crises, then the only sensible strategy is for the public to make their voices heard. And over time, people inside government may feel an ever-greater need to pay attention to the warning signs that precede such situations, knowing that they can expect a public outcry should they fail to act in time.

The Darfur story, however, shows that this necessary outcry is not sufficient. And while it is frequently argued that stopping genocide requires greater political will,[2] the review of the Darfur advocacy movement identifies a problem that has so far been ignored, namely, that the *way* in which this will is generated matters. Mass mobilization, as successful as it can be at getting a crisis onto the government's agenda and sustaining their attention on it, can also have perverse effects on policymakers and ultimately on the crisis itself, if the mass movement fails to keep up with the evolving nature of the conflict or if their pressure on government to "do something" leads politicians to preference quick and visible actions over actions best suited to resolving the crisis. As activists head into the future, they must carefully manage the ever-present potential for the mass movement approach to do more harm than good, despite the best of intentions. Connecting with people on the ground to be accountable to is the best way to safeguard against this pitfall, and it is an element that has been undervalued by most of the mass movement to date.

The motivation of regular citizens, voluntarily squeezing in advocacy around the demands of daily life, is only sustainable if they believe that their efforts are making a difference. But in challenging situations like Darfur, where the decision makers over whom U.S.-based advocates have the most influence may not be those who have the most influence over the situation, there can be significant periods in which advocates' efforts do not actually make much difference on the ground. In such periods advocates may be tempted to seek "quick wins" that demonstrate their own influence but do not necessarily improve the situation and may even be counterproductive. (On Darfur, the U.S. government's use of rhetoric that was stronger than its actions and the repeated appointment of special envoys provided such examples.) Consequently, leaders of any mass constituency must be consistently attentive to the possibility that success in demonstrating the advocacy movement's influence may not equate to success for those they are supposed to be advocating for.

To be clear, this is not an argument for abandoning the mass movement approach. Having the baseline noise that only persistent public action can generate is a benefit that can outweigh the costs that may be associated with sustaining a mass movement. But the challenge is how to convince citizen activists and the donors who help fund them to value long-term solutions even in the absence of short-term deliverables. "We came into this thinking, 'See something, say something and it will get addressed,'" says Gloria White-Hammond in 2010. "It was a naïve expectation."

The past six years of efforts by Darfur advocates have advanced the way we think about stopping genocide and mass atrocity. No longer do we have to speculate on what might have been if many citizens had raised their voices, persistently and in a politically salient way, to demand that the U.S. government act to protect the lives of those beyond their borders. Until now, the possibility of what a sustained citizen outcry could achieve was confined to the realm of the imagination. The Darfur movement has interjected a dose of reality into this discussion in ways both welcome and not. It has revealed a jarring mismatch between the enormous expectations harbored by those of us who first got involved in creating this outcry and the reality on the ground in Darfur some six years later. But it also gives us a wealth of information about how to do better next time.

ADVOCACY AND ACTION

The U.S. government provided billions of dollars for humanitarian aid and peacekeeping for Darfur, made unusually strong and frequent public statements on the crisis, appointed special envoys, supported UN Security Council resolutions on peacekeeping and sanctions, and maintained and enforced unilateral U.S. economic and diplomatic sanctions. Compared with any other crisis in Africa these actions, taken together, are extraordinary. Looking at events behind the scenes and against the background of the historically weak U.S. engagement in similar situations, these actions can convincingly be attributed to the work of the Darfur advocacy movement.

Advocates took tactics familiar to any organization lobbying congress on a domestic issue and showed they could be successfully applied to the foreign policy arena. They became proficient at organizing large numbers of constituents to visit, call, e-mail, and fax their representatives at short notice, developed working relationships with congressional staffers that facilitated the passage of legislation, and created scorecards to build an accountability mechanism into congressional action on Darfur.

Advocates were also successful at turning the symbiotic relationship between citizens and the media to their advantage. In the past, reporting of genocide or mass atrocity has often been trapped in a vicious cycle: After initial reporting on the crisis, editors don't believe the ongoing situation remains newsworthy because they are not hearing anything about it from the American public; and citizens are not saying anything about it because they are not seeing it covered in the media. This dynamic contributed to the appalling dearth of coverage during the first year of the Darfur crisis. But once the crisis broke through to the mainstream media, Darfur was different; the issue *benefited* from the relationship between the media and public opinion. The American public made visible demonstrations of their interest in the issue, which enabled editors to continue justifying the newsworthiness of the story.

In addition to their impact on the U.S. government and the media, Darfur activists also had a tangible effect on the Chinese government's engagement with Darfur in the 18 months prior to the August 2008 Olympics. The Chinese government appointed a special envoy on Darfur, deployed military engineers to support hybrid AU-UN peacekeeping mission, changed the tone and content of their public statements on Darfur, voted in favor of UN Security Council Resolution 1769 on the hybrid deployment, and agreed to the Security Council's presidential statement supporting the ICC. These actions are particularly noteworthy because they challenge the conventional wisdom that the Chinese government does not respond to "name-and-shame" tactics. There is a caveat, however: The Genocide Olympics campaign only worked because activists could credibly threaten something that the Chinese government cared deeply about, namely, their image as the Olympics' host. Once the Olympics were over, the advocates lost their leverage.

While citizen advocates accomplished a great deal, there were also important points of engagement that cannot be attributed to the Darfur movement. Some decisions, notably Secretary of State Colin Powell's genocide determination and the initial decision of the U.S. government to allow the Darfur situation to go to the ICC, were taken before the mass movement for Darfur was properly organized. In other instances, although the U.S. government ultimately took a course of action that advocates had demanded, the decision was driven as much by other influences on the foreign policy process as by anything advocates themselves did. U.S. government support for a transition from the AU to a UN force is one such example. While advocates had pushed for the deployment of a UN force from early 2006, U.S. government support for the transition was also driven by a desire to alleviate the financial burden on the United States and the other countries that were funding what was seen as a failing AU operation.

IMPACT ON DARFUR

The resilience of the advocacy movement was due to the thousands of ordinary American citizens who wanted to have a positive effect on the lives of ordinary citizens in Darfur. They achieved much in terms of getting the United States to pursue certain actions. But the extent to which this benefited the Darfuri population, which was the ultimate goal, is a separate question.

In terms of funding, the billions spent on humanitarian aid provided substantial benefits to those who survived the attacks on their villages and made it into camps. The significance of the massive humanitarian operation is best illustrated by what happened when humanitarian work was obstructed. Between July 2006 and September 2007, security threats to NGOs coupled with a short-term funding drop led to a sharp decrease in the number of humanitarian staffers in the region. During this period, deaths due to disease in the displaced camps increased by more than 50 percent compared with the 18 months prior, resulting in around 50,000 additional lives lost.[3] In Darfur, the primary constraint on humanitarian operations was obstruction by the Sudanese government and by rebel forces. In contrast, the main constraint on humanitarian operations elsewhere in the world is a lack of funding. Thanks to the efforts of advocates, financing was generally not the main problem for humanitarian efforts in Darfur.

Another repeated achievement of advocates, the appointment of special envoys, did not have such a positive impact. The appointment of a special envoy was a relatively low-cost way for the administration to show it was listening to advocates, and advocates repeatedly understood the appointment of an envoy as a signal that Sudan was being treated as a foreign policy priority. But contrary to advocates' hopes and expectations, the appointment of special envoys generally increased bureaucratic infighting within the Department of State and sent mixed messages to Khartoum. Moreover, the turnover of envoys meant that the diplomatic relationship between the envoy and his Sudanese counterparts began anew almost once a year. In contrast, the same officials in Khartoum had been dealing with the U.S. government for more than 20 years, giving them a distinct advantage that they used to good effect.

Darfur advocates also prompted U.S. officials to take a very strident public line. Strong words were another low-cost way for administration officials (and presidential candidates) to appease the advocacy movement; in a situation where real success was hard to come by, such rhetorical successes as getting administration officials to keep using the word genocide could be used to maintain the morale of the movement. But given that the public and policymakers alike tended to associate the label of genocide with an essentialist genocide like the Holocaust, rather than the kind of instrumentalist genocides in which the perpetrators' behavior might be changed through the application of pressures and incentives, the maintenance of the genocide label over time came to mischaracterize what was happening on the ground and artificially reduced the range of policy options considered, let alone pursued.

At one point, the desire of the Sudanese to normalize relations may have given U.S. officials leverage to get behavioral change from Sudan. But when the promised carrot of normalizing U.S.-Sudan relations after the signing of both the Comprehensive Peace Agreement and the Darfur Peace Agreement was not delivered, Sudanese officials became dubious of future promises. As Sudanese officials understood—and in fact were told explicitly by U.S. officials[4]—the domestic strength of the Darfur advocacy movement and its insistence on a strong public line made it politically untenable for the United States to relax its position on economic and diplomatic sanctions. In effect, the advocacy movement removed the administration's ability to offer the Sudanese any carrots.

But by repeatedly promising tougher action than they delivered, U.S. officials also diminished their ability to credibly threaten the Sudanese government. With no convincing stick to wield, the United States undermined its ability to get behavioral change by pressuring Khartoum. Over time, the result was that the Sudanese viewed both U.S. carrots and sticks with skepticism.

The maintenance of U.S. economic and diplomatic sanctions on Sudan does show the influence of the mass movement; it is no small feat for a new domestic constituency to constrain any foreign policy decision of the U.S. government. But when the question is what impact this constraint had on Darfuris, the victory is not as clear.

We cannot know for sure whether the credible promise of, for instance, removing Sudan from the State Sponsors of Terror list or supporting its accession to the World Trade Organization in return for the arrest of Janjaweed leaders and an end to aerial bombing could have been effective. Certainly Khartoum's poor record in following through on any agreement gives cause for skepticism and points to the need for any such promises to have been tied to verifiable changes on the ground, as opposed to promising normalization in return for merely signing an agreement. But given that the United States was unable to get Khartoum to move through unilateral pressure and was so weakened globally that it could not secure sufficient multilateral pressure, a credible promise of unilateral incentives in return for verifiable behavioral change would have at least been an option to consider. However, there is an important caveat to this: It was vital to many of the displaced Darfuris I spoke with that the United States maintain its strong opposition to the regime that had forced them from their homes and killed so many of their people. Whether Darfuris would have traded this moral support for possible, but uncertain, improvements on the ground is something only they can answer.

ACTIONS NOT TAKEN

Any full review of the advocacy movement must also consider the range of policy responses that advocates asked for and did not obtain or that they never asked for. While the list of U.S. actions on Darfur is impressive, the record of what it did not, and in some cases could not, do is equally telling. Options that were not pursued fall into two broad categories: unilateral and multilateral.

Although the U.S. government applied substantial pressure and exhausted most of its unilateral options, there were two major coercive actions that it did not take. One was any form of military intervention, including steps short of invasion.[5] The other was the implementation of capital markets sanctions—barring foreign companies that did business with the Sudanese government from raising capital in U.S. markets.

The question of military intervention was never seriously considered at the Pentagon. The Pentagon was never ordered to engage militarily in Darfur because President Bush decided that the use of U.S. force would be counterproductive. While such arguments have been used in the past to mask essentially self-serving reasons for not using force, and arguments for inaction based on counterproductivity or the peril of unintended consequences may thus be treated with skepticism, in this case the claim is convincing. Given the Sudanese government's response to a proposed UN deployment, it is reasonable to assume that they would have strongly opposed any presence or operations by a better trained and equipped U.S. (or NATO) force. There is a good chance that any nonconsensual U.S. military activity, even short of an invasion, in a third Muslim country would have been used by the Sudanese to rally aspiring jihadists across the globe into the Darfur region. In an area as large and difficult to traverse as Darfur, with a staunchly opposed national government, fragmented militias and rebels groups, and the prospect of an influx of foreign jihadists, it seems unlikely that even a full-scale U.S. invasion would have succeeded in increasing the security of the civilian population.

The argument against capital markets sanctions is a different story. While certainly no silver bullet, such sanctions could, in contrast to a military intervention, reasonably have been expected to do more good than harm for the people of Darfur. The Genocide Olympics campaign suggests China could be moved by threats to its interests. If access by its major state-owned oil companies to U.S. capital markets was in jeopardy, Beijing may well have viewed pressuring Khartoum as a reasonable price to pay in return for renewed access. But capital markets sanctions were a policy option that Darfur advocates never pushed for, viewing them as politically impossible to achieve after southern Sudan advocates of the Sudan Campaign had failed to secure such sanctions a few years earlier.

Opposition to capital markets sanctions by both the Treasury Department and Vice President Cheney could have been overridden by presidential leadership, but this would likely have had consequences for the stability of the financial system, the U.S.-China relationship, and consequently the U.S.

job market. Thus, the strongest argument against capital markets sanctions comes not from the standpoint of their potential impact on Darfuris, but from the standpoint of other U.S. government interests. The lesson here is that while Darfur was important, it was not important enough to disrupt traditional foreign policy formulation: concern for the material well-being of the U.S. population trumped concern for Darfuri lives.

Turning to the multilateral arena, the effectiveness of U.S. action at the UN Security Council was persistently undercut by the fact that most resolutions did not have unanimous support. Although the United States voted for UN Security Council resolutions on peacekeeping and sanctions, it never got Sudan's allies to actively endorse them. While Darfur sometimes made it onto the talking points that U.S. officials raised with China, it was always secondary to traditional national security interests such as Iran, North Korea, or currency valuation. The result was that resolutions, although formally passed, did not have the unified support of the Security Council. Khartoum read this, correctly, as a signal that it could get away with defying the council.

BEYOND DARFUR

The impact of any advocacy effort cannot be measured or understood in solely contemporaneous terms. Just as when lobbying congress, Darfur advocates stood on the shoulders of groundwork laid by the southern Sudan advocates who came before them, future advocacy campaigns may build on the work done by the mass movement for Darfur. There is certainly much to be done if the concept of "never again" is to be made meaningful.

As the story of Darfur shows, different parts of the U.S. government may have different interests with respect to a foreign government that is committing genocide or mass atrocities. Acting effectively will require a whole-of-government response so that, for instance, a presidential envoy's interest in ending violence in Darfur cannot be traded off against the CIA's interest in counterterrorism cooperation. Political will on the part of those facing the current crisis, and in particular the president, is a piece of that story. But so is establishing, prior to a crisis point, interagency coordination and decision-making systems. Without this, all the will in the world is unlikely to move the many parts of the U.S. government toward the kind of coherent action that can have a meaningful impact on the ground.

Acting effectively will also require a more sophisticated understanding, by advocates and politicians alike, of the available multilateral tools and building their capacity prior to a crisis point. The story of Darfur highlights the gaps with respect to peacekeeping, economic sanctions, and the ICC, which become clear when dealing with a strong state like Sudan.

At the time of this writing, nearly 90 percent of the hybrid AU-UN force's authorized troop level has been deployed. Yet they are frequently unable to protect themselves, let alone civilians. Activists, myself included, approached the Darfur crisis with the notion of a "toolkit"—a list of policy options available to help stop atrocities wherever they occur. The deployment of peacekeepers is a cherished part of the toolkit. But its unquestioningly privileged position needs to be challenged.

Questioning whether peacekeeping is the best response to push for in a particular context does not mean removing peacekeeping as a potential option across the board. Indeed, when you have the scenario that classic peacekeeping was designed for, where peacekeepers are policing a ceasefire between two states or two well-organized belligerents that have agreed to the peacekeeping presence, then peacekeeping can be enormously effective. But when you have a host state like Sudan that actively opposes the deployment, getting peacekeepers on the ground becomes an intensely political undertaking that may ultimately be unattainable.

It is morally satisfying to insist that the consent of the host state is irrelevant when genocide or other mass atrocity crimes are in play. But in a case like Darfur, simply stating such a position does little to advance the protection of civilians on the ground. When the consent of a strong host state is lacking, countries contributing troops will be reluctant to offer their soldiers, and with good reason. Every numbingly repetitive "lessons learned" exercise from failed peacekeeping efforts shows that the consent of the host state is vital to the success of a peacekeeping operation. Darfur is just the latest in the list of cases that prove this point. While U.S. officials have pointed the finger at other countries for failing to contribute troops and equipment to the Darfur deployment, this clouds the real issue; with the Sudanese government opposed to the deployment, peacekeepers were never going to be able to provide the protection that advocates, and Darfuris, had hoped.

Regarding economic sanctions, the U.S. government did increase the sophistication with which it enforced sanctions that it implemented. The enforcement of sanctions against Specially Designated Nationals through the banking system was a useful innovation. But, the ultimate effectiveness of the sanctions was undermined by their unilateral nature. Within six months the Sudanese system had created a work-around for its dependence on the U.S. dollar and shifted its banking into euros. For lasting impact, at a minimum the EU would also have had to take part in the program, again requiring advance coordination and development of the tools to enforce such sanctions, multilaterally.

The ICC represents perhaps the starkest example of the mismatch between ideal and implementation. While the argument that indicting heads of state who commit mass atrocities will help deter future leaders from committing such crimes is logical enough, the argument depends on those indictees eventually being brought to trial.

Unlike domestic systems, the ICC has no police force to execute its warrants of arrest; it relies entirely on the cooperation of states. When the ICC acts with the consent of the state whose nationals it is investigating, the execution of its arrest warrants is less of a problem. But in Sudan, the government was actively opposed to the ICC's involvement. Realistically, this will be the case anytime the ICC investigates crimes allegedly committed by a government that is still in power. If the ICC is ever to fulfill its promise of offering a third way between overthrow and impunity to end the rule of leaders who are responsible for atrocities against their own people, then it will need powerful countries, regional bodies, and international organizations to actively support its actions. Those with most leverage over the country whose officials are indicted by the ICC will have to impose pressures of sanctions and isolation until the cost of defying the ICC becomes too high for the country to bear. And due to a range of geopolitical dynamics, this has not been done with respect to Sudan.

Finally, the effectiveness of any action will often depend upon early engagement. In Darfur, the harsh reality, rarely highlighted in the narrative that has started to be told about Darfur, is that most of those killed through direct violence were already dead by the time the U.S. government began to get involved. Interagency U.S. engagement with Darfur did not really begin in earnest until there was a public outcry, which in turn didn't develop until there was media coverage and a genocide determination. Looking forward, one of the key challenges for citizen advocates is whether it is possible to build an outcry in advance of media coverage and in the absence of an official determination of genocide. For it is in this early-but-quiet window that a wider range of policy responses that stand a greater chance of averting or stopping widespread killings are available. In the case of Darfur, if we look back to the fall of 2003 when the U.S. government first had clear information about what was happening, we see Iraq was not yet the quagmire it subsequently became. It seems possible that a U.S. administration still able to threaten military action with credibility could, at that point, have persuaded Khartoum to pursue an alternative course. Had the Bush administration tackled the Darfur issue when it still had this credible threat in hand, instead of sacrificing Darfur on the altar of a north-south peace agreement and counterterrorism cooperation, its words alone might have convinced Khartoum to adopt a different strategy in Darfur. But by the time the U.S. government was moved to action on Darfur, it had begun to lose its ability to exert unilateral pressure on Khartoum, and the situation on the ground had become much more complex.

As has been clear for some years, and was true in the Darfur case, a lack of information per se is not what accounts for the delay in responding to atrocity situations. The issue is the delay between when citizens and governments have the information and when they act on it—in the first case, by creating political incentives for action, given a crowded agenda, and in the second, by crafting policy responses. At the beginning of my involvement with Darfur advocacy, I believed that if there was a permanent constituency of citizens, with well-rehearsed advocacy strategies at the ready, it would be possible to get ahead of the curve in any given situation by translating early warning information into an outcry before hundreds had already died. Today, I am less hopeful. The same human dynamics that limit the ability of government officials to respond early—prioritizing the immediate crisis over the looming one, attending to what is familiar in preference to learning about a new situation—seem to be present within the advocacy community as well.

The obstacles identified here are formidable. Putting aside the question of whether to act, U.S. officials must do an enormous amount of work to position themselves to save lives if they do decide to act. Darfur was a particularly challenging case for the U.S. government at the multilateral level. But even in a future situation in which the United States has sufficient unilateral leverage to change the behavior of a government committing atrocities, it will not be in a strong position to do so unless U.S. officials have addressed the coordination and capacity deficits within the U.S. government in advance. Many of the current shortcomings were carefully spelled out in a report issued by a blue-ribbon commission, the Genocide Prevention Taskforce, at the end of 2008. The taskforce made specific recommendations, including establishing early warning information as a formal priority for the intelligence community, training foreign service officers on responding to early warning information, and incorporating military guidance on preventing and responding to genocide into Defense Department policies.[6]

The good news is that efforts are now underway, largely as a consequence of the attention on Darfur and with serious donor support, to work on these issues.[7] Indeed, history may show the energy directed to these reforms, rather than any outcome on the ground in Darfur, to have been the real accomplishment of the Darfur movement. The challenge will be how to keep elected officials and political appointees focused on these reforms when the benefits may only be reaped by a future administration. Here, citizens will have a vital role, as they are more likely to see the value in a change that takes ten years to bear fruit than an administration that will be out of office by that time. But it remains to be seen whether the energy generated by an immediate crisis can be harnessed for bureaucratic reform and capacity building.

Then there is a case like Darfur, where the strength of advocates diminished U.S. ability to credibly offer unilateral incentives, and unilateral diplomatic or economic pressure was insufficient. Thus the only way acting alone could be reasonably assured of changing conditions on the ground was through a credible military threat. Absent such a threat, the United States was dependent on the cooperation of at least some other strong countries and/or regional organizations to get change through multilateral diplomatic and economic pressure.

The Darfur crisis unfolded in a multipolar world. The tragedy of the advocacy effort is that the first sustained movement to pressure the U.S. government to fight genocide and mass atrocity arose in response to a crisis where the United States itself became a less influential actor. After the Rwandan genocide, it was generally assumed that if the United States, then the world's lone superpower, would lead the charge to condemn atrocities, its "soft power" could unify the rest of the international community to stop the killing. But by the time of the Darfur crisis, the rise of other countries and regional blocks, combined with the impact of the U.S. invasion of Iraq and associated human rights violations, made this assumption unsustainable.

In theory, it would not have been impossible for the United States to get the international community to move on Darfur. But it would have had to pay hard costs that would have come at the expense of traditional U.S. national security interests, and this level of sacrifice was not one that citizen activists could convince their government to make. Moreover, they are unlikely to have succeeded in this even with an outcry that was 10 or 20 times larger because to challenge the hierarchy of interests underlying traditional foreign policy formulation, advocates on any single issue will struggle to have a decisive impact. There is a much broader, national conversation to be had.

FOR THOSE WHO HOPE to build a world without genocide and mass atrocity, the core question is whether we, and the rest of the citizens to whichever country we belong, are yet willing to internalize the ideal that all human beings are equal. If not, if sacrifices paid by those inside our borders continue to weigh much heavier than the benefits they accrue to people outside our borders, then we do not have the legitimacy to ask China or any other country to disrupt its national priorities to help the citizens of a foreign country. And it makes little sense to speak of the political will of those in power when, as now, the system they are working within is structurally aligned with the idea that the comfort and well-being of people "here" matter more than life or death for people "there."

Looking ahead, though, it is clear that threats to the well-being of citizens in any nation state are increasingly cross-border in nature—from climate change, to disease epidemics, refugee flows, and nuclear terrorism. The idea that any one country can protect the well-being of its own citizens just by focusing on what takes place inside its borders has passed its use-by date. This reality of the interdependency of human life, irrespective of national borders, moves us one step along the road to expanding the concept of the national security interest to the "human security interest"—and in so doing, redefining the way foreign policy is formulated. But our governance systems, the people who operate them, and the public as a whole are only starting to catch up.[8]

There is greater promise for achieving this paradigm shift in the twenty-first century than ever before. Our world is getting smaller. A generation ago, television brought the lives of those outside our borders into our homes. Today, the pace and quantity of information continues to increase; more and more people at different ends of the earth see and interact with each other, in real time. As has always been the case, a sense of community can arise from relationships built over the course of repeated interactions, but no longer does physical proximity dictate the boundaries of these spheres of obligation.

The challenge to traditional notions of the national security interest is coming, but the move toward the *human* security interest will take time and will require the involvement of a much broader constituency than those whose focus is on ending genocide and mass atrocity. As this multigenerational effort moves forward, we will need to recognize that real progress demands not just a battle of domestic politics, or even of global politics, but something much more fundamental: a reckoning with the social and cultural norms around human equality that underpin the formulation of foreign policy.

ACKNOWLEDGMENTS

This book began as a research assignment in a Harvard graduate seminar for the handful of us who were doing a master's in public policy and a law degree at the same time. Without the belief of the seminar's professors, Chris Stone and Phil Heymann, that there was something useful to be gained by pursuing this research further, it might never have gone beyond a class paper. Similarly pivotal at that time was the straightforward "do book" instruction in one of many no-time-for-punctuation e-mails from my overcommitted academic supervisor, Samantha Power. Keeping me going throughout was the sanctuary provided by Jim Cavallaro and Mindy Roseman at Harvard Law School's Human Rights Program. And finally among the early enablers nurturing my interest in these issues were Michael Ignatieff, Richard Goldstone, Jackie Bhabha, Susannah Sirkin, Sifa Nsengimana, Luis Moreno Ocampo, Graham Allison, and the ever-inspiring Martha Minow.

Since then, many others have jumped in at make-or-break points along the way. I'm enormously grateful to the Open Society Institute, which gave me a year of funding to work on this full time, enabling me to expand the book's view to include the perspectives of those in governments and organizations outside of the United States. In a similar vein, my thanks to the New America Foundation for supporting me to see this through to completion. Also vital has been the willingness of the National Security Archive (NSA) to bring this project under its umbrella. My one regret in writing this book so soon (in the historical sense) is that national security restrictions limited my ability to get good documentation on the CIA's relationship with Khartoum and to pin down the extent to which this relationship affected the rest of the U.S. government's approach to Sudan. But I hope that, with the guidance of the incredible staff at the NSA, what I have managed to get declassified to date is just the beginning of efforts that can be built on by others to develop a public file of documents that fully illuminate all aspects of government decision making on Sudan.

This book would not have been possible without the many hours of time given to me by so many government officials, refugees, and activists around the world. In Sudan, Chad, and Egypt, I'm grateful to the many Darfuris who agreed to speak openly with me, despite repeated past instances of sharing their experiences with outsiders to no obviously beneficial effect. In the United States, I owe enormous thanks to Omer Ismail, Sam Bell, David Rubenstein, and Gloria White-Hammond. In addition to their willingness to let me (repeatedly) interrupt their busy schedules, the trust they placed in me to portray their hopes, expectations, and errors along the way was invaluable; I hope this book justifies that trust. Similarly, I hope I have put the knowledge patiently provided to me by various "Sudan gurus" with frequently conflicting views—Suliman Baldo, Alex de Waal, Eric Reeves, Nasredeen Abdulbari, and Ted Dagne chief among them—to good use.

Next comes that category of special people who willingly took on different roles—cheerleader, reality-checker, editor, mentor, and any number of other hats—but who are connected by their unwavering belief in my ability even when I was in doubt: My bestest buddy, Chad Hazlett, who was my original co-conspirator on Darfur activism; Jina Moore, my model for effective and ethical journalism; Hillary Schrenell, for the soundest judgment of anyone on the planet; and Michael Abramowitz, whose combination of whole-hearted support and absolute honesty has been invaluable to the development of this book.

Fighting for Darfur would never have seen the light of day were it not for my agent, Robert Guinsler, at Sterling Lord Literistic, who was willing to jump, both feet first, into a not-obviously marketable project with a first-time author. And then Palgrave Macmillan, which pushed beyond the U.S. publishing industry's wariness of subject matter that seems distant to a domestic audience, to take this on; particular credit here to my editor, Luba Ostashevsky, who persisted in the often-frustrating exercise of getting me to make this material more accessible, Laura Lancaster, for helping me navigate the process, and Donna Cherry, for being willing to go ten-rounds on micro-level changes.

In The Hague I owe much to my international law posse, the Tuesday night crowd, who supported my contextually radical decision to leave proper employment at the International Criminal Court to pursue the distinctly murky path of book-writing, and Danielle Hayaux du Tilly, for making me laugh when I wanted to cry. In Nairobi, Shashank Bengali and Rob Crilly for showing me the ropes. In Washington, Veronica Chau and Mark Morita for the open invitation to occupy their futon while conducting U.S. government interviews, and to Carolina Ventura and Zoe Rosenbaum in New York for the many nights on their unfailingly comfortable sofa while doing UN interviews. In Boston, lifelong indebtedness to Jennifer Leaning, Fernande Raine, and Phil Heymann, for believing in me and standing alongside me when all institutional power thrust in the opposite direction; it is no overstatement to say you saved my life. Back home, Elissa Trafford, Jennifer Hamilton, Chelsea Cameron, and My Bui, whose love and friendship remains constant no matter how many years at a time we spend on different sides of the planet. And globally, my reservoir of strength is consistently replenished by the incredible lives and work of the Young Leaders on Genocide Prevention.

Last but not least comes my family, in all its gloriously unconventional iterations. My mum in New Zealand, Deanne Roberts, whose sheer survival skills are a constant source of inspiration, and who has never doubted that, as far as I am concerned, anything is possible; her wonderful husband, Laurence, who has yet to believe quite how special he is; my beloved big sister, Kara; and my grandma, Nora Cennamo, who continues the cherished weekly letter-writing tradition at age 90. Those I lost too soon: my dad, Eric, who I adored, and though he died when I was nine, had a greater impact on me in those few years than almost anyone since; my grandpa, Morgan, a true gentleman who acted on his belief that if you are good to people they will, in general, reciprocate; and my uncle, JJ, the best of Aussie larrikins who gave me a healthy skepticism for authority. My foster family, the Nortons; Kate and Matt for unreservedly adopting a stranger as a sibling; David, for the openness and generosity required to let the rest of the family convince him this actually was a good idea; and most of all Ewa, for taking a chance on me long before the odds looked any good, and without whom I would never have gone beyond a tenth-grade education. Thank you, thank you, thank you. Finally, the most joyful acknowledgment of all is reserved for the fantabulous Ben Batros, love of my life, who was crazy enough to want to marry me in the middle of my writing this book. I cannot imagine a better life partner—I am so very lucky.

NOTES

PREFACE

1. Henry Morgenthau, *Ambassador Morgenthau's Story* (New York: Doubleday, Page and Company, 1919), 321–322.
2. Elie Wiesel, quoted in *The Courage To Care: Rescuers of Jews During the Holocaust*, eds. Carol Rittner and Sondra Myers (New York: New York University Press, 1986), 125.

CHAPTER 1

1. Miriam (full name withheld), interview with author, Aug. 2008, Oure Cassoni camp, Chad.
2. Ibid.
3. Ibid.
4. Ibid.
5. Francis Deng, *War of Visions: Conflict of Identities in the Sudan* (Washington, D.C.: Brookings Institution, 1995).
6. Robert O. Collins, *A History of Modern Sudan* (Cambridge: Cambridge University Press, 2008), 8. The three ethnic groups are the Ja'aliyyin, to which the current Sudanese president, Omar al-Bashir, belongs; Shayqiyya; and Danaqla. Africa Watch Committee, *Denying "the Honor of Living," Sudan: A Human Rights Disaster*, 1990, 11.
7. See, generally, Collins, 2008; Douglas H. Johnson, *The Root Causes of Sudan's Civil Wars*, 4th ed. (Nairobi: East African Educational Publishers, 2007), 7.
8. Michael Asher, *Khartoum: The Ultimate Imperial Adventure*, 2nd ed. (London: Penguin, 2006), 47–57. (Before the death of the Mahdi, shortly after the fall of Khartoum in 1885, he named 'Abdallahi wad Torshayn, a Darfur nomad who had first supported him, to be his successor. 'Abdallahi led the so-called Mahdist state in Sudan until the British-Egyptian reconquest at the end of 1889. See Asher, 2006, 284.)
9. Collins, 2008, 33.
10. Ibid., 43. In addition to keeping the population subservient, indirect rule was also cost effective; throughout the period the British maintained just 400 British administrators in the entire country. See Collins, 2008, 35.
11. Ibid., 41.
12. Mansour Khalid, *War and Peace in Sudan* (London: Kegan Paul, 2003), 23–25; Johnson, 2007, 17.
13. In a January 1930 memorandum marked "strictly confidential," the British civil secretary ordered British governors in the south that "Every effort should be

made to make English the means of communication...to the complete exclusion of Arabic," even stating that "The use of an interpreter is preferable to the use of Arabic." 1930 Memorandum on Southern Policy, Jan. 25, 1930 (Khartoum), in Mohamed Ismail Beshir, *The Southern Sudan: Background to Conflict* (New York: Praeger, 1968), appendix I; see also Khalid, 2003, 18–23; Collins, 2008, 43.

14. Johnson, 2007, 22; Collins, 2008, 53.
15. Khalid, 2003, 56; Collins, 2008, 62. The change in Egypt's approach came with the Egyptian Revolution of 1952, in which King Farouk, who had wanted Sudan to be united with Egypt, was overthrown by half-Sudanese soldier, General Muhammad Neguib.
16. Gregoria Denk Kir, quoted in Collins, 2008, 65.
17. Johnson, 2007, 28.
18. Ibid.
19. Ibid., 40–41.
20. Ibid., 56.
21. Ibid., 55.
22. Ibid., 56.
23. The manifesto of the SPLM was written in response to the division of the single southern region and announced even before sharia was imposed. Johnson, 2007, 63.
24. Africa Watch Committee, 1990, 65.
25. Johnson, 2007, 69.
26. Collins, 2008, 176.
27. It was in fact the second time that Sadiq al-Mahdi had led Sudan; the first was in 1966. Ibid., 164.
28. Johnson, 2007, 84–85.
29. Al-Turabi had been entrenched in the rule of Sudan for some time, having been the attorney general and guiding hand behind Nimeiri's implementation of sharia.
30. Hassan al-Turabi, interview with author, Aug. 7, 2009.
31. Collins, 2008, 187; "Sudan: Lost sheep," *Economist*, July 22, 1989, 44. In response, the U.S. government withdrew $33 million in aid from Sudan, as required by Section 513 of the Foreign Assistance Act, which prohibits assistance to governments that have overthrown elected leaders. See Africa Watch Committee, 1990, 166.
32. Collins, 2008, 194–195.
33. U.S. Department of State, "Background note: Sudan," 2010, available at http://www.state.gov/r/pa/ei/bgn/5424.htm#relations (last accessed May 30, 2010).
34. UNSC Res.1054, Apr. 26, 1996, S/RES/1054; UNSC Res. 1070, Aug. 16, 1996, S/RES/1070. The sanctions, which called on all states to reduce the number of Sudanese diplomats in their states, restrict travel of Sudanese government officials, refrain from convening any conference in Sudan, and deny landing permission to the Sudanese national air carrier, were removed by UNSC Res. 1372 in 2001 by 14 votes, with the United States abstaining.
35. Collins, 2008, 220. The Sudanese government says it first offered to hand bin Laden over to the United States, but U.S. officials dispute this claim. For details of interactions between the CIA and the Sudanese government during this period, see Steve Coll, *Ghost Wars: The Secret History of the CIA, Afghanistan and Bin Laden from the Soviet Invasion to September 10, 2001* (New York: Penguin, 2004), 319–326.
36. Executive Order 13067, *Federal Register* 62, no. 214 (Nov. 5, 1997).
37. The claim regarding chemical weapons was never proven.
38. See U.S. Department of State, "Background note: Sudan," 2010.
39. David Aikman, "The World's Most Brutal, Least Known War," *Weekly Standard*, June 28, 1999. U.S. congressional activism for southern Sudan had been underway

for some time. In 1989 Democratic congressman Gary Ackerman joined other representatives in a National Day of Concern for Sudan, chastising the administration of George H. W. Bush for its silence. See Seema Sirohi, "U.S. Groups Mobilizing National Day of Concern," Inter Press Service, Mar. 10, 1989.

40. See, generally, Deborah Scroggins, *Emma's War* (New York: Pantheon, 2002); Collins, 2008, 205–6.
41. Collins, 2008, 258.
42. Deng, 1995, 35.
43. See, for example, "War in South Sudan: The Civilian Toll," Africa Watch, Oct. 1, 1993; "Famine in Sudan," Human Rights Watch, Feb. 8, 1998; Collins, 2008; Scroggins, 2002.
44. House Congressional Resolution. 75, 106th Congress, June 16, 1999.
45. Collins, 2008, 140–42.
46. Mansour Khalid, ed., *John Garang Speaks* (London: KPI, 1987).
47. The poem is by Aalim Abbas Mohamed Nour.
48. Mission statement, Darfur Peace and Development Organization website, http://www.darfurpeace.org/about-us/our-mission (last accessed May 30, 2010).

CHAPTER 2

1. Julie Flint and Alex de Waal, *Darfur: A New History of a Long War* (London: Zed Books, 2008), 6.
2. Jérôme Tubiana, "Darfur: A Conflict for Land?" in *War in Darfur and the Search for Peace*, ed. Alex de Waal (Cambridge, MA: Harvard University Press, 2007), 73–75.
3. Mohamed Suliman, "Ethnicity from Perception to Cause of Violent Conflicts: The Case of Fur and Nuba Conflicts in Western Sudan" (conference paper, Institute for African Alternatives, July 1997).
4. Gunnar Håland, "Economic Determinants in Ethnic Processes," in *Ethnic Groups and Boundaries*, ed. Frederik Barth (London: Allen and Unwin, 1969).
5. Sharif Harir, "'Arab Belt' versus 'African Belt': Ethno-political Conflict in Dar Fur and the Regional Cultural Factors," in *Short-Cut to Decay: The Case of the Sudan*, ed. Sharif Harir and Terje Tvedt (Uppsala, Sweden: Nordiska Afrikainstitutet, 1994), 144–85. As in southern Sudan, colonization meant decades of willful neglect; there are just five entries listed in the British government's file on "Economic Development" for Darfur during the entire period of its rule. Flint and de Waal, 2008, 12; see also Gérard Prunier, *Darfur: The Ambiguous Genocide* (Ithaca, NY: Cornell University Press, 2005), 29–31.
6. Anonymous, *The Black Book* (Khartoum, 2000).
7. Ali B. Ali-Dinar, "Between Naivasha and Abeche: The Systematic Destruction of Darfur" (conference paper, Stichting Instituut voor Nieuwe Soedan, Mar. 27, 2004); Saif Elnasr Idris, "Effects of Central Government Policies, Tribal Conflicts, and Civil War in DarFur," *Sudanese Human Rights Quarterly* 8 (July 1999).
8. Douglas H. Johnson, *The Root Causes of Sudan's Civil Wars*, 4th ed. (Nairobi: East African Educational Publishers, 2007), 57; *Denying "the Honor of Living,"* Sudan: A Human Rights Disaster, Africa Watch Committee, 1990, 14.
9. Sadiq al-Madhi's Libyan-sponsored attempt to overthrow Nimeiri failed in 1976, but he went on to win Sudan's 1986 democratic election.
10. Mahgoub El-Tigani Mahmoud, "Inside Darfur: Ethnic Genocide by a Governance Crisis," *Comparative Studies of South Asia, Africa and the Middle East* 24, no. 2 (2004): 5.

11. The colonial boundary between today's eastern Chad and western Sudan was formal-ized in 1923. The border was then, and continues to be, an irrelevance to the ethnic groups that have straddled either side of it for centuries. Chad gained independence from France in 1960, and in an inverted image to what had happened following inde-pendence in Sudan, the southern Chadians gained control of the country with French backing. Much like Sudan's southerners who faced discrimination at the hands of a newly independent northern-led government, Chad's primarily Muslim northern-ers were excluded by their newly independent southern and primarily Christian-led government. It didn't take long for the northern Chadians to form rebel groups, and with the border as arbitrary as it was, many of these groups had bases on the Sudan side of the border in Darfur. See, generally, J. M. Burr and R. O. Collins, *Darfur: The Long Road to Disaster* (Princeton, NJ: Markus Wiener, 2006), 22–54.

12. Helen Young et al., *Darfur: Livelihoods under Siege* (Medford, MA: Feinstein International Famine Center, Tufts University, 2005), 29–30; Musa A. Abdul-Jalil, Adam Azzain Mohammed, and Ahmed A. Yousef, "Native Administration and Local Governance in Darfur: Past and Future" in de Waal, 2007, 50.

13. Harir, in Harir and Tvedt, 1994, 44–85; Young et al., 2005, 29–30; Flint and de Waal, 2008, 22.

14. Interview with Abul Gasim Seif el Din, Aug. 17, 2009.

15. Qaddafi's meddling was not constrained to Sudan. A 1986–87 war between Chad and Libya saw Qaddafi supplement his army's efforts by backing Chadian dissi-dents, who used Darfur as their base. See Flint and de Waal, 2008, 53.

16. Robert O. Collins, *A History of Modern Sudan* (Cambridge: Cambridge University Press, 2008), 154.

17. Jérôme Tubiana, "Darfur: A conflict for land?" in de Waal, 2007, 73–75.

18. Johnson, 2007, 151.

19. Flint and de Waal, 2008, 50; for a slightly different translation, see Gamal A. Adam, "Why Has the Indigenous Population of Darfur Been Exposed to Destruction?" (conference paper, The Current Darfur Crisis, American University, Cairo, 2004, 5).

20. "Qoreish 1," in Flint and de Waal, 2008, 51.

21. 1989 police records from el-Fasher, Harir, in Harir and Tvedt, 1994, 144–85.

22. Speech of the Secretary to the Arab delegation, 1989 el-Fasher reconciliation con-ference, May 29, 1989, translated in Harir, in Harir and Tvedt, 1994, 144–85.

23. Speech of the Secretary to the Fur delegation, 1989 el-Fasher reconciliation con-ference, May 29, 1989, translated in Harir, in Harir and Tvedt, 1994, 144–85.

24. Flint and de Waal, 2008, 56–57. This was not unlike the way that the creation of separate southern states had been used by Nimeiri to undermine the power of the southern region.

25. Burr and Collins, 2006, 287.

26. "Ethnic Cleansing of the Darfur Muslims: The Massaleit," The Massaleit Com-munity in Exile, Egypt, Mar. 2000.

27. Johnson, 2007, 141; Prunier, 2005, 75.

28. "Qoreish 2" in Ali Haggar, "The Origins and Organization of the Janjawiid in Darfur," in de Waal, 2007, 130–133; Flint and de Waal, 2008, 51–52. (Noting that the authorship of the document was never verified, it nonetheless resonated with the young men joining the Arab militias.)

29. See, generally, Suliman, 1997.

30. Anonymous, *The Black Book*, 2000, table 2. The only exception was during Sadiq al-Mahdi's democratically elected term, when this population held 47 percent of the ministerial positions.

31. See Alex Cobham, "Causes of Conflict in Sudan: Testing the Black Book" (working paper, Finance and Trade Policy Research Centre, University of Oxford, Jan. 2005).
32. Flint and de Waal, 2008, 16–17.
33. "Bashir Clips Turabi's Political Role in Sudan," Panafrican News Agency, Jan. 18, 2000.
34. Collins, 2008, 227.
35. Flint and de Waal, 2008, 68.
36. Charles Colson, "Support for Mr. Bush on Sudan Policies," *Washington Post*, Aug. 14, 2004, letters to the editor.
37. "Danforth Named Special Envoy to Sudan," *White House Bulletin*, Sept. 6, 2001.
38. George W. Bush, "Statement by the President in His Address to the Nation," *White House Bulletin*, Sept. 11, 2001.
39. In the final year of the Clinton administration, the Sudanese government had allowed CIA officials to be stationed in Khartoum, but not until after the 9/11 attacks did the Sudanese government begin offering substantial assistance. See Ted Dagne, *The Sudan Peace Process*, Congressional Research Service Report for Congress, June 4, 2003, 5; Ted Dagne, *Sudan: Humanitarian Crisis, Peace Talks, Terrorism, and U.S. Policy*, Congressional Research Service Issue Brief for Congress, Aug. 26, 2005, 13. Nevertheless, the real value of counterterrorism intelligence provided by Khartoum following 9/11 has been subject to debate. See "Sudan/USA: Who's selling who?" *Africa Confidential* 42, no. 20 (Oct. 12, 2001): 4.
40. The negotiations were sponsored by the Intergovernmental Authority on Development (IGAD), a coalition of East African governments originally formed to respond to the horrific drought in the region in the early 1980s. See Collins, 2008, 260.
41. Machakos Protocol, July 22, 2002. While the signing of the protocol was a breakthrough, it left many issues unresolved, including the status of the three areas (Abyei, the Nuba Mountains, and the Southern Blue Nile) on the border between northern and southern Sudan.
42. Collins, 2008, 262.
43. "Bush Signs Sudan Peace Act into Law," AllAfrica.com, Oct. 22, 2002.
44. *Sudan Peace Act*, Public Law 107-245, Sect 2(10), signed into law, Oct. 21, 2002.
45. Ibid., Sect 6.
46. Ted Dagne, e-mail correspondence with author, Feb. 7, 2010.
47. Collins, 2008, 267.
48. Abdel Wahid al-Nur, Letter from Zaleingi, Aug. 9, 2002, quoted in Julie Flint, "Driven to Despair" in *Genocide in Sudan*, U.K. Parliamentary Brief, Special Report, Aug. 2004.
49. Musa Hilal, interview with author, Aug. 14, 2009; Burr and Collins, 2006, 288.
50. Flint and de Waal, 2008, 70.
51. Representative of Tereba village, quoted in Flint, 2004.
52. Gerard Gallucci, interview with author, Jan. 15, 2010.
53. Ibid.
54. Adriaan Koojimans, interview with author, May 1, 2009.
55. Colin Thomas-Jensen, interview with author, Nov. 20, 2009.
56. See "The Situation of Human Rights: June 1-September 30, 2003," *Sudan Human Rights Organization* (Cairo: Oct. 2003), http://www.shrocairo.org/reports/03/october03.htm (last accessed May 30, 2010).
57. "Sudan's Other Wars," *International Crisis Group* (Brussels, June 23, 2003): 16.
58. "Sudan: Humanitarian Crisis in Darfur Caused by Sudan Government's Failures," Amnesty International, Nov. 27, 2003. No other major human rights organization

had researchers on the ground to gather testimony until Human Rights Watch sent a team to the Chad-Sudan border in February of 2004. Their research fed into Human Rights Watch's first report on Darfur, "Darfur in Flames," Apr. 2004.

59. "Sudan: Towards an Incomplete Peace," *International Crisis Group* (Brussels, Dec. 2003): 19.
60. Prunier, 2005, 92.
61. "Sudan: Now or Never in Darfur," International Crisis Group (Nairobi/Brussels, May 2004): 1.
62. Flint and de Waal, 2008, 94.
63. Ibid., 103.
64. "Sudanese Rebels Take Army General Captive," Panafrican NewsAgency, Apr. 28, 2003.
65. Flint and de Waal, 2008, 121.
66. Ibid., 116.
67. Musa Hilal, interview with author, Aug. 24, 2009.
68. Ibid., 54–55.
69. Flint, 2004.
70. Cited in Flint and de Waal, 2008, 37. (Hilal describes the memo as "false." Musa Hilal, interview with author, Aug. 14, 2009.)
71. "Darfur Destroyed," Human Rights Watch (New York), May 2004.
72. See, generally, Report of the International Commission of Inquiry on Darfur to the United Nations Secretary-General, Jan. 25, 2005.
73. Tara Gingerich and Jennifer Leaning, "The Use of Rape as a Weapon of War in the Conflict in Darfur, Sudan," Harvard University, Oct. 2004, 18, available at: http://physiciansforhumanrights.org/library/documents/reports/the-use-of-rape-as-a-weapon.pdf.
74. Ibid.
75. John Hagan and Wenona Rymond-Richmod, *Darfur and the Crime of Genocide* (Cambridge: Cambridge University Press, 2009), 10.
76. Eric Reeves, "Unnoticed Genocide," *Washington Post*, Feb. 25, 2004. The first full article devoted to Darfur in any major U.S. newspaper appeared in January 2004. It included refugee testimony, but noted, "It is impossible to travel in Darfur to verify these claims." See Somini Sengupta, "War in Western Sudan Overshadows Peace in the South," *New York Times*, Jan. 17, 2004.
77. Eric Reeves, interview with author, June 26, 2006.
78. Jean-Marie Guéhenno, interview with author, Feb. 12, 2009.
79. Jan Egeland, interview with author, Jan. 17, 2010.
80. Hussien Adam, interview with author, Aug. 28, 2009.
81. Ibid.
82. Amira (full name withheld), interview with author, Aug. 2008, Oure Cassoni camp, Chad.
83. Deng, 1995, 5.

CHAPTER 3

1. Samantha Power, *"A Problem from Hell": America and the Age of Genocide* (New York: Harper Perennial, 2002), 511.
2. Lorne Craner, interview with author, Mar. 23, 2007. Powell says he was "mindful" of Rwanda but does not recall making this particular statement. Colin Powell, interview with author, Apr. 21, 2009.

3. Lorne Craner, interview with author, Mar. 30, 2007.
4. See, generally, René Lemarchand, *Burundi: Ethnic Conflict and Genocide* (New York: Woodrow Wilson Center, 1994).
5. Lorne Craner, interview with author, Mar. 23, 2007.
6. Bureau of African Affairs, "Background Note: Burundi," U.S. State Department, Dec. 2009.
7. Lorne Craner, interview with author, Mar. 30, 2007.
8. Gerard Gallucci, interview with author, Jan. 15, 2010. Galluci's boss was acting assistant secretary of state for African Affairs, Charles Snyder.
9. "Sudan: Situation in Darfur," U.S. State Department Press Release, Dec. 16, 2003.
10. L. Festinger, *A Theory of Cognitive Dissonance* (Palo Alto, CA: Stanford University Press, 1957).
11. Jim Fisher Thompson, "U.S. Official Cites Possible 'Ethnic Cleansing' in Sudan," Federal Information and News Dispatch, Feb. 26, 2004.
12. Roger Winter, interview with author, Feb. 10, 2010.
13. U.S. State Department official, interview with author, Aug. 27, 2009.
14. Roger Winter, interview with author, Feb. 10, 2010.
15. Report of the International Commission of Inquiry on Darfur to the United Nations Secretary-General ("Report of the International Commission"), Jan. 25, 2005, 88.
16. Julie Flint and Alex de Waal, *Darfur: A New History of a Long War* (London: Zed Books, 2008), 36.
17. Lorne Craner, interview with author, Mar. 23, 2007.
18. Pierre-Richard Prosper, interview with author, Apr. 9, 2007.
19. Lorne Craner, interview with author, Mar. 23, 2007.
20. Nicholas Kristof, "Ethnic Cleansing, Again," *New York Times*, Mar. 24, 2004, 21.
21. Nicholas Kristof, "Will We Say Never Again, Again?" *New York Times*, Mar. 27, 2004, 15.
22. Eric Reeves, "Unnoticed Genocide," *Washington Post*, Feb. 25, 2004; Khadir Haroun Ahmed, "Another Side to the Sudan Story," *Washington Post*, Mar. 11, 2004; "Sudan's Tragedy U.S. Can't Ignore Another Genocide," *Dallas Morning News*, Mar. 29, 2004.
23. Samantha Power, "Remember Rwanda but Take Action in Sudan," *New York Times*, Apr. 6, 2004; "Look Squarely at Genocide," *Los Angeles Times*, Apr. 10, 2004, 23; Richard S. Williamson, "Stop the Genocide in Sudan," *Chicago Sun Times*, Apr. 11, 2004; Frita Ghitis, "We Answer Genocide With Silence, Again," *St. Louis Post-Dispatch*, Apr. 12, 2004; "Another Horror: Reports from Western Sudan Echo Rwanda," *Pittsburgh Post-Gazette*, Apr. 12, 2004; "U.N. Must Assert Itself to Prevent Sudan Genocide," *Chicago Tribune*, Apr. 14, 2004.
24. Power, "Remember Rwanda."
25. Salih Booker and Ann-Louise Colgan, "Genocide in Darfur," *Nation*, July 12, 2004, 27.
26. Power, 2002, 358–64.
27. Samantha Power, "Bystanders to Genocide," *Atlantic Monthly*, Sept. 2001.
28. See Holly Burkhalter, "The Question of Genocide: The Clinton Administration and Rwanda," *World Policy Journal* 11 (1994), 44–54; Philip Gourevitch, *We wish to inform you that tomorrow we will be killed with our families: Stories from Rwanda* (New York: Farrar, Straus, & Giroux, 1998); *Frontline*, "Ghosts of Rwanda," documentary, screened on PBS, Apr. 1, 2004.
29. Statement by President Bush, PR Newswire, Apr. 7, 2004.
30. "Text of Sudanese Peace Agreement," AllAfrica.com, May 28, 2004.

31. Sudanese government official, interview with author, Aug. 2009.
32. General Ismat al Zain, Mar. 2006, as reported in Julie Flint and Alex de Waal, *Darfur: A New History of a Long War* (New York: Zed Books, 2008), 180.
33. UN Integrated Regional Information Networks, "Humanitarian Needs Continue Despite Darfur Accord," AllAfrica, Apr. 15, 2004.
34. "Under-Secretary-General Encouraged by Progress on Ceasefire Negotiations for Darfur," M2 Presswire, Apr. 9, 2004; "U.S. Welcomes Humanitarian Ceasefire in Darfur Region of Sudan," States News Service, Apr. 9, 2004.
35. Hussien Adam, interview with author, Aug. 21, 2009.
36. Jan Egeland, interview with author, Jan. 7, 2010.
37. Ibid.
38. Andrew Natsios, e-mail correspondence with author, Aug. 21, 2010.
39. "Notes from Secretary Powell's June 29, 2004, conversation with Sudanese Foreign minister Mustafa Osman Ismail" (FOIA request from U.S. State Dept.).
40. Marc Lacey, "Sudan Camp is Moved Before UN Visit," *New York Times*, July 2, 2004.
41. Hussien Adam, interview with author, Aug. 21, 2009.
42. Kofi Annan, interview with author, Nov. 27, 2009.
43. Jan Egeland, interview with author, Jan. 7, 2010.
44. Ambassador Richard S. Williamson, "General Statement on Items 3 and 9 on Sudan" (Geneva, Apr. 23, 2004), available at http://geneva.usmission.gov/human rights/2004/statements/0423Sudan.htm (last accessed Mar. 26, 2007).
45. Lisa Schlein, "UN-Sudan," *Voice of America News*, Apr. 23, 2004.
46. Ibid. Australia and the Ukraine abstained.
47. "Rice Asks Arab Listeners to Trust the U.S.," *Birmingham Post*, May 5, 2004.
48. "Sudan; U.N. Passes Resolution," *World News Digest*, May 6, 2004.
49. Colum Lynch, "U.S. Protests Sudan's Election to Human Rights Panel," *Washington Post*, May 5, 2004.
50. Office of the Secretary of Defense, "Secret Discussion Paper: Rwanda," May 1, 1994.
51. Listening to Powell's eventual determination of genocide in September 2004, Under Secretary for Defense Douglas Feith remembers thinking "that's a significant statement that I don't remember being debated." Douglas Feith, interview with author, Mar. 13, 2009.
52. Nina Bang-Jensen and Stefanie Frease from the Coalition for International Justice were the lead NGO collaborators on the project, which also included Human Rights Watch, Crisis Group, and Physicians for Human Rights. Stefanie Frease, interview with author, Jan. 27, 2007.
53. The formation of the teams and their work is well documented in *Genocide in Darfur*, S. Totten and E. Markusen, eds. (New York: Routledge, 2007). See especially the chapter "Creating the ADT: Turning a Good Idea into Reality," Nina Bang-Jensen and Stefanie Frease.
54. See Serena Parker, "Genocide Threat in Darfur," *Voice of America News*, Apr. 26, 2004; State Department, "Sudanese Must Open Darfur to Aid, Says Powell," Federal Information and News Dispatch, June 14, 2004; State Department Press Briefing, "Daily briefing for June 15-transcript," June 15, 2004; Michael Drudge, "Rights Activists, Governments: Should Darfur Crisis Be Classified as Genocide?" *Voice of America News*, Aug. 12, 2004.
55. Charles W. Corey, "U.S. Congress Terms Situation in Darfur 'Genocide'," U.S. State Department press release, July 23, 2004.
56. See Hamilton and Hazlett, in *War in Darfur and the Search for Peace*, ed. Alex de Waal (Cambridge, MA: Harvard University Press, 2007).

57. Donald Steinberg (director of the Joint Policy Council, U.S. State Dept. in 2004), interview with author, Apr. 24, 2007.
58. U.S. State Department official, interview with author, Mar. 6, 2009; confirmed by William Taft, interview with author, May 4, 2009.
59. Colin Powell, interview with author, Apr. 21, 2009.
60. Ibid.
61. Stephen Hadley, interview with author, Dec. 22, 2009.
62. Colin Powell, interview with author, Apr. 21, 2009.
63. Stephen Hadley, interview with author, Dec. 22, 2009.
64. Colin Powell, interview with author, Apr. 21, 2009.
65. Alternative spelling of janjaweed.
66. Colin Powell, testimony before the Senate Committee on Foreign Relations, "The Current Situation in Sudan and the Prospects for Peace," 108th Cong., 2nd sess., 2004, S. Hrg. 108-866:8.
67. Gerard Gallucci, interview with author, Jan. 15, 2010.
68. Amr Moussa, interview with author, June 11, 2009.
69. Salih Halima, interview with author, June 7, 2009.
70. Dawit Toga, interview with author, July 13, 2009.
71. Elghassim Wane, interview with author, July 10, 2009.

CHAPTER 4

1. David Rieff, "The Precarious Triumph of Human Rights," *New York Times Magazine*, Aug. 8, 1999.
2. Samantha Power, *"A Problem from Hell": America and the Age of Genocide* (New York: Harper Perennial, 2002), 509.
3. Ben Bixby, quoted in Rebecca Hamilton and Chad Hazlett, "Not on Our Watch," in *War in Darfur and the Search for Peace*, ed. Alex de Waal (Cambridge, MA: Harvard University Press, 2007), 345.
4. Power, 2002, 350–370.
5. Roméo Dallaire, *Shake Hands With The Devil: The Failure of Humanity in Rwanda* (New York: Carroll and Graf, 2003), 374.
6. "Strategic Plan of the Commission of the African Union. Vol. 2: The 2004–2007 Strategic Framework of the African Union Commission," African Union Commission, May 2004.
7. "Strategic Plan of the Commission of the African Union, Vol. 1: Vision and Mission of the African Union," African Union Commission, May 2004.
8. "Report of the Chairperson of the Commission on the Situation in Darfur," AU Peace and Security Council, 12th meeting, para. 10, July 4, 2004.
9. At the beginning of 2009, the United States had accumulated $174 million in arrears for assessed contributions owed to the UN Peacekeeping budget. "U.S. Debt to the United Nations," Better World Campaign, available at: http://www.betterworldcampaign.org/issues/funding/us-funding-for-the-un-an-overview.html. In June 2009, congressional legislation was signed by President Obama to pay the U.S. outstanding debts to the United Nations. See David Jackson, "House to Cough Up Money U.S. Owes to UN," *USA Today*, June 17, 2009.
10. "A More Secure World: Our Shared Responsibility," A Report of the High-Level Panel on Threats, Challenges and Change, United Nations, 2004, vii.
11. Nicholas Kristof, "Bush Points the Way," *New York Times*, May 29, 2004.
12. Actually, under U.S. taxation law, the museum is prohibited from lobbying activities.
13. Jerry Fowler, e-mail correspondence with author, Aug. 30, 2010.

14. Save Darfur Unity Statement, available at http://www.savedarfur.org/pages/unity_statement (last accessed May 30, 2010).

15. Jerry Fowler, interview with author, Jan. 30, 2010.

16. Ibid.

17. International Commission on Intervention and State Sovereignty (ICISS), "The Responsibility to Protect: Report of the International Commission on Intervention and State Sovereignty," Dec. 2001.

18. Paul Simon on NPR Radio, quoted in Power, 2002, 377.

19. Power, 2002, 509.

20. Fowler, interview with author, Jan. 29, 2010.

21. The approach was hugely controversial, with critics arguing against the practice on both moral and pragmatic grounds. Buying a person, even if only to secure their freedom, meant placing a monetary value on human life. Moreover, Westerners bringing large wads of cash in to redeem slaves simply strengthened the slave trade market, ensuring that slave trading remained profitable and thereby exacerbating the problem over the long term. See Richard Miniter, "The False Promise of Slave Redemption," *Atlantic Monthly*, July 1999. Slave redemption also had strong advocates who argued that the practice of slave redemption is something that local communities were doing anyway, and that the freedom of currently enslaved individuals should not be put on hold until the entire slave trade had been dismantled. See Jok Madut Jok, *War and Slavery in Sudan* (Philadelphia: University of Pennsylvania Press, 2001), 176–79.

22. Gloria White-Hammond, quoted in Bruce Morgan, "The Healer," *Tufts Medicine*, Oct. 4, 2004.

23. Comprehensive Peace Agreement between the Government of the Republic of the Sudan and the Sudan People's Liberation Movement/Sudan People's Liberation Army, Jan. 9, 2005.

24. Gloria White- Hammond, "Keeping Our Sisters Safe," *Boston Sunday Herald*, Feb. 20, 2005.

25. A southern version of the term *muraheel*, meaning "mobile units"; another iteration of government-sponsored irregular militia akin to the *mujahedeen*.

26. Abul Gasim Seif el Din, interview with author, Aug. 17, 2009.

27. Fabio Govoni, "Constitution Signed at Festive Ceremony: Peace Era Starts," ANSA English Media Service, July 10, 2005.

28. Robert Zoellick, interview with author, Mar. 10, 2009.

29. Power, 2002, xviii.

CHAPTER 5

1. Bob Woodward, *State of Denial* (New York: Simon & Schuster, 2006), 230.

2. Farah Stockman, "Rice Takes Oath as Nation's 66th Secretary of State," *Boston Globe*, Jan. 29, 2005.

3. Article 6 provides: "Persons charged with genocide or any of the other acts enumerated in article III shall be tried by a competent tribunal of the State in the territory of which the act was committed, *or by such international penal tribunal as may have jurisdiction* with respect to those Contracting Parties which shall have accepted its jurisdiction." (Emphasis added.)

4. White House press release, "Clinton Statement on Signature of the International Criminal Court Treaty," US Newswire, Jan. 1, 2001: "I will not, and do not recommend that my successor, submit the Treaty to the Senate for advice and consent until our fundamental concerns are satisfied."

5. Carla Anne Robbins, "Disarming America's Treaties," *Wall Street Journal*, July 19, 2002.

6. *Rome Statute*, Art. 13, U.N. Doc. A/CONF.183/9*, 1998.

7. In practice the fear is unlikely to be realized. Under the legal principle of complementarity, the ICC could only prosecute a U.S. suspect if the United States itself could not or would not do so. It is hard to imagine the United States not choosing to do its own prosecution rather than handing the responsibility over to the ICC. Consequently, providing the U.S. proceedings were genuine, the ICC would not be able to intervene. See *Rome Statute*, Art. 1 & 17, U.N. Doc. A/CONF.183/9*, 1998.

8. *American Service Members Protection Act of 2002*.

9. While two other permanent Security Council members, China and Russia, had also not joined the ICC, it was the United States alone that had an active policy of thwarting the court's development.

10. Article 1 provides: "The Contracting Parties confirm that genocide, whether committed in time of peace or in time of war, is a crime under international law which they undertake to prevent and to punish."

11. S.C. Res. 1564, SC/1564 (Sept. 18, 2004).

12. Cable from Ambassador John C. Danforth to Secretary of State Rice, "Peace and Accountability: A way forward," Jan. 7, 2005. (FOIA request from U.S. State Dept.)

13. Cable from Ambassador John C. Danforth to Secretary of State Rice, Jan. 7, 2005. (FOIA request from U.S. State Dept.)

14. John C. Danforth, interview with author, June 1, 2009.

15. Warren Hoge, "U.S. Lobbies Security Council on Darfur Crimes," *International Herald Tribune*, Jan. 29, 2005.

16. Department of State, War Crimes Office document, "Sudan: Accountability for War Crimes," Jan. 28, 2005. (FOIA request from U.S. State Dept.)

17. Sonni Efron, "Dispute over ICC Hampers United Effort on Darfur," *Los Angeles Times*, Feb. 26, 2005.

18. De la Sablière, reading from his journal during interview with author, May 25, 2009.

19. Report of the International Commission of Inquiry on Darfur to the United Nations Secretary-General, Jan. 25, 2005, 5.

20. See, for example, Ewen MacAskill, "Sudan's Darfur Crimes Not Genocide, Says UN Report," *Guardian*, Feb. 1, 2005, 12.

21. Report of the International Commission of Inquiry on Darfur to the United Nations Secretary-General, 5. Genocide scholar Samuel Totten points out that the Commission of Inquiry was not tasked to determine whether the central government alone had genocidal intent, but rather whether genocide occurred. If the commission found that other perpetrators besides the central government, like local officials or Janjaweed, had genocidal intent, this would have enabled them to conclude that genocide had occurred. See Samuel Totten, "The UN International Commission of Inquiry on Darfur: New and Disturbing Findings," *Genocide Studies and prevention*, 4(3)(Winter, 2009).

22. John Ralston, interview with author, Sept. 8, 2009.

23. Report of the International Commission of Inquiry on Darfur to the United Nations Secretary-General, part IV.

24. Neil Henry, "Crash Kills 4 Aid Workers in Sudan," *Washington Post*, Dec. 21, 1989.

25. Peter Biles, "Body of French Charity Worker Explodes at Khartoum Airport," *Guardian*, Dec. 30, 1989.

26. Robert O. Collins, *A History of Modern Sudan* (Cambridge: Cambridge University Press, 2008), 189.
27. Concept paper quotes from State Department Démarche, "Gaining African Support for Sudan Action in the UNSC," Feb. 1, 2005. (FOIA request from U.S. State Dept.)
28. Letter from Senator Patrick Leahey to Secretary Rice, Feb. 4, 2005. (FOIA request from U.S. State Dept.)
29. "Sudan Tribunal Démarche: Senegal," Feb. 11, 2005. (FOIA request from U.S. State Dept.)
30. Brigette Collet, interview with author, July 29, 2009.
31. Ibid.
32. "U.S. Resolution Calls for U.N. Peacekeeping Mission in Sudan," *Washington Post*, Feb. 15, 2005.
33. Zoellick, interview with author, Apr. 3, 2007.
34. On Feb. 7, 2005, the Religious Action Center of Reform Judaism issued an open letter on behalf of "more than 900 congregations across North America encompass[ing] 1.5 million Reform Jews, and the Central Conference of American Rabbis, whose membership includes more than 1800 Reform Rabbis," urging President Bush not to veto a referral to the ICC. Available at: http://rac.org/Articles/index.cfm?id=1074&pge_prg_id=5542&pge_id=1001 (last accessed May 25, 2010).
35. David Rubenstein, interview with author, Apr. 22, 2009.
36. Michael Posner, interview with author, Jan. 26, 2007.
37. Andrew Sniderman's comments, this chapter, e-mail correspondence with author, May 26, 2009.
38. Legislative assistant to Republican "congressional champion" on Sudan, interview with author, Mar. 9, 2007.
39. Jean-Marc de la Sablière, interview with author, May 25, 2009.
40. Philip Zelikow, interview with author, Mar. 26, 2007.
41. Olivia Bueno, interview with author, Dec. 11, 2009.
42. Dismas Nkunda, interview with author, July 9, 2009.
43. Olivia Bueno, interview with author, Dec. 11, 2009.
44. S.C. Res. 1590, U.N. Doc S/RES/1590 (Mar. 24, 2005); Nick Wadhams, "U.N. to Send Peacekeepers to Sudan," *Seattle Times*, Mar. 25, 2005.
45. Jean-Marc de la Sablière, interview with author, May 25, 2009.
46. S.C. Res. 1497, U.N. Doc S/RES/1497 (Aug. 1, 2003), para. 7.
47. Kim Holmes (assistant secretary of state for International Organizations Affairs in March 2005), interview with author, Apr. 10, 2007. See also Warren Hoge, "U.N. Votes to Send Any Sudan War Crime Suspects to World Court," *New York Times*, Mar. 31, 2005.
48. Emyr Jones Parry, interview with author, Oct. 30, 2009.
49. Pierre-Richard Prosper, interview with author, Apr. 9, 2007.
50. UN Security Council press release, SC/8351, Mar. 31, 2005.
51. State Department briefing with Nicholas Burns, Federal News Service, Apr. 1, 2005.
52. U.S. State Department official, interview with author, Mar. 6, 2009.
53. Jean-Marie Guéhenno, interview with author, Feb. 12, 2009.
54. Ken Silverstein, "Official Pariah Sudan Valuable to America's War on Terrorism," *Los Angeles Times*, Apr. 29, 2005.
55. See John Prendergast and John Bagwell, "Why Activism (Still) Matters for Sudan...and What You Can Do," Enough Project report, Mar. 2009: "A major push by activists and congressional allies led the Bush administration to set aside its normal reservations about international justice, and let the referral pass."

CHAPTER 6

1. Senior White House official, interview with author, Sept. 8, 2009.
2. See Benjamin Valentino, *Final Solutions: Mass Killing and Genocide in the 20th Century* (Ithaca, NY: Cornell University Press, 2004), 3. ("Contrary to common perceptions, perpetrators seldom see mass killing as an end in itself.")
3. Hirad Abtahi and Philippa Webb, *The Genocide Convention: The Travaux Préparatoires* (Leiden: Martinus Nijhoff, 2008), 1416–46.
4. A. K. A. Greenawalt, "Rethinking Genocidal Intent: The Case for a Knowledge-Based Interpretation," *Columbia Law Review* 99 (1999), 2259.
5. Abtahi and Webb, 2008, 1440. (In the words of the representative of the USSR, "the majority had adopted an ambiguous definition of genocide.")
6. See Melanie Greenberg, "Crawling Back from the Brink: How conflict resolution can respond to genocide," *How Genocides End*, Social Science Research Council, Dec. 22, 2006. ("In nearly all the cases we reviewed, periods of recognizably genocidal violence alternated with periods of relative peace. This 'sine wave' pattern of violence stands in contrast to the cases that did not step back from the brink (the Holocaust; Rwanda; the Armenian genocide), in which the violence tended to be massive and unrelenting....In Guatemala, the Soviet Union, Sudan, and Biafra, there were points at which the genocidal massacres subsided, before welling up again.")
7. Drake Bearden, "Swarthmore Students Help Bring News of Genocide to Light," *News of Delaware County*, Aug. 11, 2005.
8. Ronald Capps, interview with author, Feb. 23, 2009.
9. African Mission Union in Sudan, "Background and Chronology," http://www.amis-sudan.org/history.html (last accessed May 30, 2010).
10. "African Union Peace and Security Council, Report of the Chairperson of the Commission of the Situation in the Darfur Region of the Sudan," 17th meeting, Oct. 20, 2004.
11. "Communiqué on Enhancement of the AU Mission in Sudan (AMIS)," Apr. 28, 2005 (PSC/PR/2(XXVIII)).
12. Jean Bosco Kazura, interview with author, June 21, 2009.
13. "Genocide Hits Home: Campaign Goal," Genocide Intervention Network, Aug. 2005 (on file with author).
14. "National Day of Action for Darfur Script," Save Darfur Coalition, Sept. 21, 2005 (on file with author).
15. U.S. State Department official, interview with author, Jan. 30, 2008.
16. See Donna Miles, "Airlift Support for Darfur Continues Strong as Rice Visits the Region," American Forces Press Service, July 21, 2005; State Department, "United States Transports Rwandan Civilian Police to Darfur," Federal Information and News Dispatch, Aug. 8, 2005.
17. U.S. State Department official, interview with author, Jan. 30, 2008.
18. Sally Chin and Jonathan Morganstein, "No Power to Protect: The African Union Mission in Sudan," *Refugees International*, Nov. 2005, 2.
19. "AU Security Council Holds Emergency Session on Darfur," AllAfrica, Oct. 4, 2005.
20. Chin and Morganstein, 2005, 2.
21. Stephen Hadley, interview with author, Dec. 22, 2009. All Hadley quotes this chapter from this interview.
22. Jendayi Frazer, interview with author, Mar. 6, 2009.
23. John Bolton, interview with author, Mar. 2, 2009.
24. Senior U.S. Defense Department official, interview with author, Apr. 24, 2009.

25. John Bolton, interview with author, Mar. 2, 2009.
26. Peter Feaver, interview with author, Dec. 19, 2009.
27. Michael Gerson, interview with author, Mar. 12, 2009. All Gerson quotes in this chapter are from this interview.
28. Nicholas Kristof, "Genocide in Slow Motion," *New York Review of Books*, Feb. 9, 2006.
29. Michael Gerson, interview with author, Mar. 12, 2009.
30. "Assisting the African Union in Darfur," http://www.nato.int/issues/darfur/# evolution (last accessed May 30, 2010).
31. David E. Sanger, "Bush Sees Need to Expand Role of NATO in Sudan," *New York Times*, Feb. 18, 2006.
32. Ibid.
33. Alex Meixner, interview with author, Nov. 17, 2009.
34. John Bolton, interview with author, Mar. 2, 2009.
35. Ibid.
36. Judy Dempsey, "Pressure Rises over NATO's Darfur Role," *International Herald Tribune*, Feb. 20, 2006.
37. With the birth of the EU, both the United Kingdom and France wanted to see the new organization "play its full role on the international stage." (Franco-British Summit Joint Declaration on European Defense, St. Malo, Dec. 4, 1998.) This required the EU to have its own military capacity. But as the new century began, one of the key questions was where such capacity would be exercised. NATO already covered the Middle East and the Americas. Any new EU force would need to flex its muscles in Africa—yet, all EU military came from the same pool as NATO's European contributors. The result was a standoff between those European countries that wanted to see the new EU acting in Africa and those that had committed their resources to NATO.
38. Jan Pronk, interview with author, Oct. 14, 2007; U.S. State Dept. official, interview with author, Jan. 31, 2008.
39. African Union Joint Assessment Report, Dec. 20, 2005, para. 55.
40. U.S. State Department official, interview with author, Jan. 30, 2008; Dutch Ministry of Foreign Affairs official, interview with author, Jan. 14, 2008.
41. African Union Peace and Security Council Communiqué, PSC/PR/Comm. (XLV), Jan. 12, 2006, para. 5.
42. "Sudan: African Union Extends Peacekeeping Mandate," *UN IRIN*, Jan. 13, 2006.
43. 45th session of the AUPSC; Jan Pronk, interview with author, Oct. 14, 2007.
44. "Darfur Issue Should Be Solved by Africa's Leaders," Sudanese Media Centre (original in Arabic), Feb. 16, 2006.
45. Jan Pronk, interview with author, Oct. 14, 2007; President al-Bashir, e-mail correspondence with author (through Ghazi Salahuddin Atabani), Sept. 8, 2009.
46. President al-Bashir, e-mail correspondence with author (through Ghazi Salahuddin Atabani), Sept. 8, 2009.
47. Jean Bosco Kazura, interview with author, June 21, 2009.
48. "Sudan's Parliament Rejects Deployment of UN Forces in Darfur," Xinhua General News Service, Feb. 22, 2006.
49. Anoushka Marashlian, "Sudanese Authorities Up the Ante against UN Troop Deployment," *World Markets Analysis*, Mar. 1, 2006.
50. Rebecca Hamilton and Chad Hazlett, "Not on Our Watch," in *War in Darfur and the Search for Peace*, ed. Alex de Waal (Cambridge, MA: Harvard University Press, 2007), 357.
51. Ruth Messinger, interview with author, June 30, 2006.

CHAPTER 7

1. Rebecca Hamilton and Chad Hazlett, "Not on Our Watch," in *War in Darfur and the Search for Peace*, ed. Alex de Waal (Cambridge, MA: Harvard University Press, 2007), 339.
2. Olivia Bueno, interview with author, Dec. 11, 2009.
3. Hussien Adam, interview with author, Aug. 28, 2009.
4. Salim Ahmed Salim, interview with author, July 6, 2009.
5. Ibid.
6. See Jill Savitt, "Pressure on Darfur," May 5, 2006, at http://www.tompaine.com/articles/2006/05/05/pressure_on_darfur.php (last accessed May 30, 2010).
7. See generally Romeo Dallaire, *Shake Hands with the Devil* (New York: Carroll and Graf, 2003); Report of the Secretary General pursuant to Resolution 53/35, "The Fall of Srebrenica," A/54/549, Nov. 15, 1999.
8. UN Department of Peacekeeping official, interview with author, Mar. 17, 2009.
9. Alex de Waal, interview with author, Jan. 11, 2008.
10. Ibid.
11. Alex de Waal, "Darfur Peace Process: Analysis and Prospects, February 2006," Jan. 31, 2006, 2 (on file with author).
12. Michael Gerson, interview with author, Mar. 12, 2009. See also Briefing Memorandum for the Alternate Representative for Special Political Affairs, Apr. 5, 2006 (FOIA request from U.S. State Dept.): "A quick and effective re-hat of AMIS and full deployment of an eventual UN mission to Darfur remains our first priority."
13. Federal Document Clearing House political transcripts, Mar. 9, 2006.
14. Robert Zoellick, interview with author, Mar. 10, 2009.
15. Jendayi Frazer, interview with author, Mar. 6, 2009.
16. Zeid Al Sabban, interview with author, June 12, 2009; Salim Ahmed Salim, interview with author, July 6, 2009.
17. President al-Bashir, e-mail correspondence with author (through Ghazi Salahuddin Atabani), Sept. 8, 2009.
18. Andrew Natsios, interview with author, Nov. 11, 2009; Ghazi Salahuddin Atabani, interview with author, Aug. 9, 2009.
19. Robert Zoellick, e-mail correspondence with author, Aug. 24, 2010.
20. President al-Bashir, e-mail correspondence with author (through Ghazi Salahuddin Atabani), Sept. 8, 2009.
21. Salim Ahmed Salim, interview with author, June 6, 2009.
22. Harry W. Kopp and Charles A. Gillespie, *Career Diplomacy: Life and Work in the U.S. Foreign Service* (Washington, D.C.: Georgetown University Press, 2008), ch. 6.
23. Ronald Capps, interview with author, Feb. 23, 2009.
24. Ibid.
25. Ronald Capps, Dissent Cable, Apr. 28, 2006 (on file with author).
26. Alex Meixner, interview with author, Mar. 6, 2007.
27. "President Meets with Darfur Advocates," Department of the U.S. White House, CQ Federal Department and Agency Documents, Apr. 28, 2006.
28. Ronald Capps, interview with author, Feb. 23, 2009. In 2007, Cameron Hume nominated Capps for the Rivkin Award, which recognizes foreign service officers for "intellectual courage and constructive dissent."
29. Julie Flint and Alex de Waal, *Darfur: A New History of a Long War* (New York: Zed Books, 2008), 162.
30. Jérôme Tubiana, "Land and Power: The Case of the Zaghawa," *Making Sense of Darfur* (Social Science Research Council blog, Alex de Waal, ed.), May 28, 2008,

available at: http://blogs.ssrc.org/sudan/2008/05/28/land-and-power-the-case-of-the-zaghawa/comment-page-1/ (last accessed May 26, 2010).

31. Flint and de Waal, 2008, 163.
32. Jérôme Tubiana, "The Chad-Sudan Proxy War and the 'Darfurization' of Chad: Myths and Reality," *The Small Arms Survey* (Geneva: The Graduate Institute, 2008), 28.
33. Ibid., 32–33.
34. Ibid., 24–25.
35. Ibid., 26–28.
36. Salim Ahmed Salim, interview with author, July 6, 2009.
37. Ibid.
38. Radio France Internationale, "Chadian Rebel Spokesman says 'Capital to fall by end of today,'" via *BBC Monitoring*, Apr. 13, 2006.
39. Al-Ra'y al-Amm, "Chadian Rebels Planning Fresh Attacks," *BBC Monitoring Middle East*, Apr. 15, 2006.
40. Christina Katsouris, "Deby's Dilemmas," *Energy Compass*, Apr. 21, 2006. The French forces in the country also helped repel the rebel attack.
41. Alex de Waal, "Darfur Peace Process: Analysis and Prospects, May 2006," Apr. 27, 2006 (on file with author).
42. Alex de Waal, "Darfur's Deadline: The Final Days of the Abuja Peace Process," in Alex de Waal, ed. (2007), 269.
43. Lydia Polgreen and Joel Brinkley, "Bush Urges Sudan's President to Continue with Peace Talks," *New York Times*, May 3, 2006.
44. Zoellick aide present in Abuja, interview with author, Apr. 21, 2009.
45. Alex de Waal, "Abuja Diary," May 3, 2006 (on file with author).
46. Glenn Kessler, *The Confidante: Condoleezza Rice and the Creation of the Bush Legacy* (New York: St. Martins, 2007), 114.
47. Alex de Waal, in Alex de Waal, ed. (2007), 271.
48. Alex de Waal, "Abuja Diary," May 4, 2006 (on file with author).
49. Alex de Waal, in Alex de Waal, ed. (2007), 274.
50. David Rubenstein, interview with author, Mar. 6, 2009.
51. Zoellick, interview with author, Mar. 10, 2009.
52. White House Briefing, "Remarks by President George W. Bush," *Federal News Service*, May 8, 2006.
53. Geoffrey Mugumya, interview with author, July 16, 2009.
54. Jan Pronk, interview with author, Oct. 14, 2007.
55. Darfuri refugee (name withheld), interview with author, June 2009, Cairo.
56. Minni Minawi, interview with author, Aug. 12, 2009.
57. Secretary Rice, 5434th meeting of the UN Security Council, May 9, 2006.
58. UN Security Council Resolution 1679, S/RES/1679/2006, May 16, 2006.
59. U.S. State Department official, interview with author, Jan. 30, 2008.
60. Jendayi Frazer, interview with author, Mar. 6, 2009.
61. Lam Akol, interview with author, Aug. 15, 2009.
62. Salim Ahmed Salim, interview with author, July 6, 2009.
63. Jan Pronk, interview with author, Oct. 14, 2007.
64. Salim Ahmed Salim, interview with author, July 6, 2009.
65. UN Security Council, S/PV. 55528, Sept. 18, 2006.
66. Ephrem Rurangua, interview with author, June 24, 2009.
67. Ibid.
68. Michael Gerson, interview with author, Mar. 12, 2009.

CHAPTER 8

1. Bridget Moix, interview with author, July 13, 2006.
2. Sudan Emergency Funding letter, June 5, 2006 (on file with author).
3. *Emergency Supplemental Appropriations Act for Defense, the Global War on Terror, and Hurricane Recovery, 2006*, Public Law 109–234, June 15, 2006.
4. U.S. State Dept. official, interview with author, Mar. 6, 2009.
5. Government Accountability Office, "Darfur Crisis: Progress in Aid and Peace Monitoring Threatened by Ongoing Violence and Operational Challenges," Nov. 2006.
6. Allyson Neville, e-mail correspondence with author, Feb. 1, 2009.
7. Recounted in Samantha Power, *"A Problem from Hell": America and the Age of Genocide* (New York: Harper Perennial, 2002), 375.
8. "Capuano Calls on President Bush to Appoint Special Envoy to Sudan," States News Service, July 5, 2006.
9. State Department Press Briefing, Aug. 9, 2006.
10. "Address by H.E. Mr. George W. Bush, President of the United States of America," 61st session, UN General Assembly, Sept. 19, 2006.
11. E-mail from David Rubenstein (Save Darfur) to Darfur activists, Sept. 19, 2006 (on file with author).
12. Nicholas Kristof, "All Ears for Tom Cruise, All Eyes for Brad Pitt," *New York Times*, July 26, 2005.
13. There were just 24 articles on Darfur in U.S. newspapers and wires in the year prior to the April 2004 tenth anniversary of Rwanda, despite the fact that tens of thousands of Darfuris were massacred during that period. LexisNexis, search 04/01/03-04/01/04.
14. The percentage increase was derived from LexisNexis searches by headline "Darfur" for all U.S. newspapers and wires. The absolute numbers are a blunt instrument since, for instance, articles that touch on Darfur may not be catalogued with Darfur headlines in Lexis, and articles appearing in more than one outlet may be double-counted. However, as they are useful for basic comparative purposes, the absolute numbers are (Apr. 2004-Mar. 2005): 1,643; three years later (Apr. 2007–Mar. 2008): 2,447.
15. Alex Meixner, e-mail correspondence with author, Apr. 26, 2010.
16. Form 990 (FY 2007), Save Darfur Coalition, available at: http://darfur.3cdn. net/46600091e09793daea_e8m6b6ncc.pdf (last accessed May 26, 2010).
17. Darfur Peace and Accountability Act, H.R. 3127/S. 1462, signed into law by President George W. Bush on Oct. 31, 2006.
18. U.S. State Dept. official, interview with author, Mar. 6, 2009.
19. Lam Akol, interview with author, Aug. 15, 2009.
20. Jendayi Frazer, interview with author, Nov. 19, 2009. Frazer was not alone in this view. The opening sentence of the Sudan section of the Country Reports on the State Sponsors of Terrorism 2006 states: "The Sudanese government was a strong partner in the War on Terror and aggressively pursued terrorist operations directly involving threats to U.S. interests and personnel in Sudan." ("Country Reports on the State Sponsors of Terrorism 2006," Office of the Coordinator for Counterterrorism.)
21. Home page of www.savedarfur.org on Apr. 3, 2005 (accessed via Internet Archive Wayback Machine, www.archive.org).
22. Home page of www.savedarfur.org on Aug. 14, 2006 (accessed via Internet Archive Wayback Machine, www.archive.org).

23. Taiya Smith, interview with author, Mar. 13, 2009.
24. Blog diary of Kelsey Hoppe, aid worker in Darfur, Dec. 12, 2006, available at: http:// kelseyhoppe.blogspot.com/2006/12/missing-vehicle-club.html (last accessed Aug. 10, 2010).
25. "Darfur: Threats to Humanitarian Aid," Amnesty International, Dec. 2006.
26. Monthly Report of the Secretary-General on Darfur, S/2006/870, para. 26, Nov. 8, 2006.
27. See "Darfur Crisis: Death Estimates Demonstrate Severity of Crisis, but Their Accuracy and Credibility Could Be Enhanced," U.S. Government Accountability Office, Nov. 2006.
28. Oliver Degomme and Debarati Guha-Sapir, "Patterns of Mortality Rates in Darfur Conflict," *Lancet* 375 (2010): 294–300. All figures presented are rounded averages of the 95 percent confidence interval range given by the researchers.
29. Degomme and Guha-Sapir, 2010, 294–300. Figures based on a World Bank baseline mortality rate of .3 deaths per 10,000 people per day. Note: This figure does not include the Darfuri refugee population across the border in Chad.
30. See www.savedarfur.org, Aug. 14, 2006 (accessed via Internet Archive Wayback Machine, www.archive.org). ("Current situation: [P]eople are still dying in large numbers of malnutrition and disease, and a new famine is feared. According to reports by the World Food Program, the United Nations and the Coalition for International Justice, 3.5 million people are now hungry,... [T]he situation on the ground shows a number of negative trends, which have been developing since the last quarter of 2004: deteriorating security; a credible threat of famine; mounting civilian casualties; the ceasefire in shambles; increasing tensions between Sudan and Chad; and new armed movements appearing in Darfur and neighboring states.")
31. Andrew Natsios, "Memo from Andrew Natsios to John Negroponte," Apr. 5, 2007 (on file with author).
32. Ibid.
33. "U.S. Senate Foreign Relations Committee Holds a Hearing on the Situation in Darfur" (transcript), Apr. 11, 2007.
34. Andrew Natsios, interview with author, Nov. 11, 2009.
35. Amira (full name withheld), interview with author, Oure Cassoni camp, Chad, Aug. 6, 2008.
36. Ad hoc tribunals require that a "substantial part" or a "considerable number" are targeted. The murder of approximately 8,000 Bosnian Muslim males in Srebrenica satisfied this standard. *Prosecutor* v. *Krstić*, IT-98-33-T, para. 590, Aug. 2, 2001; *Prosecutor* v. *Bagilishema*, ICTR-95-1A-T, Judgment, para. 64, June 7, 2001; *Prosecutor* v. *Jelisić*, IT-95-10-T, para. 82, Dec. 14, 1999; *Prosecutor* v. *Kayishema and Ruzindana*, ITCT-95-1-T, para. 97, May 21, 1999.
37. Report of the International Commission of Inquiry on Darfur to the United Nations Secretary-General, Jan. 25, 2005, 5.
38. Jerry Fowler, interview with author, Jan. 29, 2010.
39. Sudan was the third largest recipient of U.S. Official Development Assistance (following Iraq and Afghanistan) from 2005 to 2007 (U.S. Official Development Assistance Database). In terms of total humanitarian aid provided by the U.S. government, the figures comparing Darfur, just one region of Sudan (and excluding assistance to Darfuri refugees in eastern Chad) with the entire Democratic Republic of Congo are telling. FY 2004: Darfur, $193.7M (USAID situation report FY04,Sudan–complex emergency ["Sudan sitrep FY04"], Oct. 24, 2004); DRC $65.7M (USAID situation report FY04, Democratic Republic of the Congo-complex emergency ["DRC sitrep FY04"], Aug. 20, 2004) / FY 2005: Darfur, $444.7M (Sudan sitrep FY05, Oct. 14, 2005); DRC, $61.8M (DRC sitrep FY05,

Sept. 30, 2005) / FY 2006: Darfur, $452.2M (Sudan sitrep FY06, Oct. 6, 2006); DRC, $84.6M (DRC sitrep F06, Sept. 29, 2006) / FY 2007: Darfur, $392.7M (Sudan sitrep FY07, Nov. 16, 2007); DRC, $88M (DRC sitrep FY07, Sept. 28, 2007) / FY 2008: Darfur, $508M (Sudan sitrep FY08, Oct. 3, 2008); DRC, $123.3M (DRC sitrep FY08, Oct. 15, 2008).

40. UN DPKO official, interview with author, Mar. 17, 2009.
41. "United Nations Peacekeeping Operations: Principles and Guidelines," UN Department of Peacekeeping Operations, Department of Field Support, 2008, 48–49. ("A United Nations peacekeeping operation is unlikely to succeed when one or more of the following conditions are not in place: A peace to keep; positive regional engagement; full backing of a united Security Council; clear and achievable mandate with the resources to match.")
42. UN DPKO official, interview with author, Mar. 17, 2009.
43. Jean-Marie Guéhenno, interview with author, Feb. 12, 2009. All Guéhenno quotes in this chapter are from this interview.
44. Jendayi Frazer, interview with author, Mar. 6, 2009.
45. U.S. State Department official, interview with author, Apr. 4, 2007.
46. Gal Luft, "Fueling the Dragon: China's Race into the Oil Market," Institute for the Analysis of Global Security, http://www.iags.org/china.htm (last accessed May 30, 2010).
47. Lee Feinstein, "China and Sudan," *TPM Café Talk*, Apr. 24, 2007 (for 2006, 2007, and 2010 oil figures).
48. Hiroyuki Kato, "World Energy Model, 2002," International Energy Agency, Beijing, China, Oct. 2003.
49. $43M worth of small arms and light weaponry was imported from China into Sudan over the period 2003-2008. (The next largest importer of this type of weaponry to Sudan over the same period was Iran at $17.5M.) UN Comtrade, quoted in Mike Lewis, "Skirting the Law: Sudan's post-CPA arms flows," *Small Arms Survey* (Geneva, 2009), available at: http://www.googlesyndicatedsearch.com/u/SmallArms Survey?q=skirting+the+law&sa=go%C2%A0.
50. "Asian Foreign Direct Investment in Africa: Towards a New Era of Operation among Developing Countries" (Geneva: United Nations, 2007), 53.
51. "Sudanese President Inaugurates Merowe Dam on Nile River," Xinhua News Agency, Mar. 3, 2009.
52. The UN Security Council consists of 15 member states at any one time. Ten of those are non-permanent members voted in by their regional bloc for a set period of two years. The remaining five are permanent members: China, France, Russia, the United States, and the United Kingdom (reflecting the power balance at the end of World War II, when the UN was formed). Any Security Council resolution requires nine votes to pass, so even if the permanent five all vote for a resolution, it cannot pass unless at least four of the non-permanent members also vote for it. Any resolution, even one with the support of all ten non-permanent members can fail if just one permanent member votes against it. In other words, the permanent members have the power to veto any resolution.
53. See Feinstein, "China and Sudan."
54. USUN official, interview with author, Nov. 17, 2008.
55. USUN official, interview with author, Nov. 18, 2008.
56. UN Security Council Resolution 1706, S/RES/1706, Aug. 31, 2006.
57. "Sudan Rejects UN Resolution to Control Peacekeepers in Darfur," CBC News, Aug. 31, 2006.
58. "Address by H.E. Mr. George W. Bush, President of the United States of America," 61st session, UN General Assembly, Sept. 19, 2006.

CHAPTER 9

1. Executive Order 13067, Federal Register, vol. 62 (214), Nov. 5, 1997.
2. U.S. State Dept. official, interview with author, Apr. 10, 2007; U.S. State Dept. official, interview with author, Mar. 6, 2009; White House official, Sept. 8, 2009.
3. "Harvard Announces Decision to Divest PetroChina Stock," *Harvard Gazette*, Apr. 4, 2004.
4. "The State of Sudan Divestment: An Overview of States, Cities, Universities, Companies, and Private Pensions Currently Working on Sudan Divestment," Sudan Divestment Task Force, Nov. 19, 2006 (on file with author).
5. Fifteen states has divested by the end of 2007. See National Conference of State Legislatures, "State Divestment Legislation," available at: http://www.ncsl.org/?tabid=13297 (last accessed, May 2, 2010).
6. Nancy Vogel, "State Pension Divestment Bill Signed," *Los Angeles Times*, Sept. 26, 2006.
7. *World Development Report 2007: Development and the Next Generation* (Washington, D.C.: World Bank, 2006).
8. "Blood Money?" *Democracy Now*, Mar. 27, 2006.
9. Pam Omidyar, e-mail correspondence with author, Feb. 14, 2010.
10. Mike Boyer, communications director at Humanity United, e-mail correspondence with author, Aug. 9, 2010.
11. John Norris, "Are Activists to Blame for Darfur?" Center for American Progress, Apr. 23, 2009.
12. Statement by Gareth Evans, "Crisis Group and the ENOUGH Project," International Crisis Group, Sept. 30, 2007.
13. E-mails sent and received by David Rubenstein, Sept. 10, 2004 (on file with author).
14. See Joseph Nye, Jr., *Soft Power: The Means to Success in World Politics* (Washington, D.C.: Public Affairs, 2004).
15. William Iboden, interview with author, Nov. 23, 2009.
16. Peter Feaver, interview with author, Dec. 15, 2009.
17. Ibid.
18. "Congo Named as African Union Head," BBC, Jan. 26, 2006.
19. U.S. (Sudan Programs Group) official, interview with author, Jan. 25, 2007.
20. The following year the same issue arose again, but this time U.S.-based advocates were focused on other campaigns. Ultimately through some quiet back-channel diplomacy from members of the Darfur Consortium, the Tanzanian president was convinced to bid for the position. Dismas Nkunda, interview with author, July 9, 2009; "Tanzania's Kikwete Becomes African Union Chairman," Reuters, Feb. 1, 2008.
21. David Blair, "Darfur Dictator Bans UN Peacekeepers" *Daily Telegraph*, June 22, 2006; "Save Darfur Coalition Responds to Sudanese President's Inaccurate Assertions," AllAfrica.com, June 22, 2006.
22. Ruth Messinger, "Twenty-First Century genocide: The Imperative of a Jewish Response," *Sh'ma: A Journal of Jewish Responsibility*, Oct. 2007, at http://www.shma.com/2007/10/twenty-first-century-genocide-the-imperative-of-a-jewish-response/.
23. Jill Savitt, interview with author, Nov. 16, 2009.
24. Ibid.
25. "Grants List: Africa and Arab World," Save Darfur internal document (on file with author).
26. Nkunda, interview with author, July 9, 2006. All Nkunda quotes, this chapter, from this interview.

27. Olivia Bueno, interview with author, Dec. 11, 2009.

28. Ibid.

29. Kofi Annan, interview with author, Nov. 27, 2009. All Annan quotes, this chapter, are from this interview.

30. John Bolton, *Surrender Is Not an Option* (New York: Threshold Editions, 2007), 358.

31. Andrew Natsios, interview with author, Nov. 11, 2009.

32. Ibid.

33. Lam Akol, interview with author, Aug. 15, 2009.

34. Ibid.

35. Jean Bosco Kazura, interview with author, June 21, 2009.

36. Lam Akol, interview with author, Aug. 15, 2009.

37. Andrew Natsios, interview with author, Nov. 11, 2009.

38. David Blair, "End to Darfur Crisis in Sight, Benn Claims after Troop Deal," *Daily Telegraph*, Nov. 18, 2006.

39. "'Hybrid' Force to Control Darfur," *Weekend Australian*, Nov. 18, 2006.

40. John Prendergast, interview with author, Nov. 30, 2009.

41. Alex Meixner, interview with author, Nov. 17, 2009. (To Meixner's claim, David Rubenstein responds: "Although she was reluctant to take on this unfamiliar job, she acquitted herself well." E-mail correspondence with author, Aug. 20, 2010.)

42. Ibid.

43. There had, however, been some wire reporting of what ended up as Save Darfur's aborted effort to get the Richardson trip to go ahead back in December. See, for example, Felicia Fonseca, "New Mexico Gov. Asked to Travel to Sudan to Help Secure Approval for U.N. Darfur Force," Associated Press, Dec. 18, 2006: "Governor Richardson is very honored by the request of the Save Darfur coalition and he would like to help...."

44. Alex Meixner, interview with author, Nov. 17, 2009.

45. Ibid.

46. Letter from White-Hammond to Rubenstein, Jan. 20, 2007 (on file with author).

47. The television ad can be viewed at http://www.aaiusa.org/press-room/2702/aai-launches-darfur-ads-aimed-at-arabic-speaking-international-community (last accessed May 30, 2010).

48. "Ambassador Andrew Natsios Holds a State Department Press Briefing on Sudan," *Congressional Quarterly*, Nov. 20, 2006.

49. U.S. State Department official, interview with author, Jan. 25, 2007; Natsios, interview with author, Nov. 11, 2009.

50. Andrew Natsios, "Memo from Andrew Natsios to John Negroponte," Apr. 5, 2007 (on file with author).

51. Sean Brooks, interview with author, Nov. 24, 2009.

52. See Julie Flint, "Darfur's Outdated Script," *New York Times*, July 9, 2007.

53. E-mail correspondence from Sam Worthington to David Rubenstein, Feb. 16, 2007 (on file with author).

54. As recounted by David Rubenstein, interview with author, Apr. 22, 2009.

55. Stephanie Strom and Lydia Polgreen, "Advocacy Group's Publicity Campaign on Darfur Angers Relief Organizations," *New York Times*, June 2, 2007.

56. Sean Brooks, interview with author, Nov. 24, 2009.

57. Ben Bixby (STAND cofounder), interview with author, July 21, 2006.

CHAPTER 10

1. Maggie Michael, "George Clooney campaigns in China and Egypt to raise awareness over Darfur conflict," Associated Press, Dec. 13, 2006.

2. Mia Farrow, interview with author, Aug. 12, 2008. All quotes from Farrow, this chapter, are from this interview.
3. Jill Savitt, interview with author, Nov. 16, 2009.
4. Alfred de Montesquiou, "Chinese President Tells Sudan Counterpart He Must Do More for Peace in Darfur," Associated Press, Feb. 2, 2007.
5. Jill Savitt, interview with author, Nov. 16, 2009.
6. Sharon Udasin, "Olympic Gadfly," *Jewish Week*, July 30, 2008.
7. Alexa Olesen, "China: Don't Link Olympics, Darfur," Associated Press, Mar. 29, 2007.
8. In addition to Save Darfur's sponsorship of George Clooney's "celebrity diplomacy" in Beijing, Amnesty International U.S. organized its National Week of Student Action around linking Beijing and Darfur, with rallies across the United States, running, coincidentally, the same weekend that the Genocide Olympics piece was published.
9. "Steven Spielberg Urges China to Act over Darfur," Agence France Presse, May 11, 2007.
10. LexisNexis comparison of headlines linking China and Darfur, Dec. 27, 2006-Mar. 27, 2006 vs. Mar. 28, 2006-June 28, 2006.
11. "Sen. Biden Leads Effort Urging China to Help Stop Violence in Darfur," *U.S. Federal News*, Apr. 30, 2007.
12. "Sudan: U.S. Representatives Send Strong Message to Chinese President on Darfur," *United States Congress*, May 10, 2007.
13. Edward Cody, "Chinese to Deploy Soldiers to Darfur; Engineers to Bolster Peacekeeping Force," *Washington Post*, May 9, 2009.
14. Alexa Olesen, "China Names Special Envoy for Darfur," Associated Press, May 10, 2007.
15. Jill Savitt, interview with author, Dec. 14, 2009. Remainder of Savitt quotes, this chapter, from this interview.
16. Andrew Natsios, interview with author, Nov. 11, 2009.
17. "Remarks on Darfur and Sanctions," States News Service, May 29, 2007.
18. Andrew Natsios, interview with author, Nov. 11, 2009.
19. Andrew Natsios, e-mail correspondence with author, Aug. 20, 2010.
20. Senior Treasury official, interview with author, Jan. 21, 2010.
21. "President George W. Bush delivers remarks on Sudan sanctions," *Congressional Quarterly*, May 29, 2007.
22. Paris-based, B.P.N. Paribus.
23. Senior Bush administration official involved in implementing these sanctions, e-mail correspondence with author, Aug. 16, 2010.
24. Andrew Natsios, interview with author, Nov. 11, 2009.
25. "Sanctions Bite," *Economist Intelligence Unit*, posted by Andrew Heavens, http://sudan-sanctions.wordpress.com/2007/11/16/sanctions-bite/ (last accessed May 30, 2010).
26. See http://www.urgencedarfour.info/.
27. "An Inclusive government; France," *Economist*, May 18, 2007.
28. Mark Oliver, "Brown and Sarkozy Make Darfur Pledge," *Guardian*, July 20, 2007.
29. British official to the UN, interview with author, Nov. 13, 2009.
30. "Daily Press Briefing by the Offices of the Spokesperson for the Secretary-General," *United Nations*, June 18, 2007.
31. British official to the UN, interview with author, Nov. 13, 2009.
32. UN Security Council Resolution 1769, S/Res/1769 (2007), July 31, 2007.
33. USUN official, interview with author, Nov. 17, 2008.
34. Ghazi Salahuddin Atabani, interview with author, Aug. 9, 2009.

35. Nora Boustany, "Symbolic Torch Relay Aims to Shine Light on China, Darfur and Death," *Washington Post*, Aug. 15, 2007.
36. *Dream for Darfur*, "D4D Final Report" (internal document), Oct. 2008 (on file with author).
37. "Mia Farrow and Genocide Survivors from Srebrenica Call for Peace in Darfur," *Bosnia News*, Dec. 8, 2007, http://bosnianews.blogspot.com/2007_12_08_archive.html (last accessed May 30, 2010).
38. "Event Uniting Genocide Survivors Calls for End to Darfur Atrocities," Armenian Assembly of America press release, Sept. 25, 2007.
39. See, generally, James Bryce and Arnold Toynbee, *The Treatment of the Armenians in the Ottoman Empire, 1915-1916* (Princeton, NJ: Gomidas Institute Books, 2000) (unredacted version of contemporaneous documentation of events, first published by the British Government as *The Blue Book* in 1916); Donald Miller and Lorna Touryan Miller, *Survivors: An Oral History of the Armenian Genocide* (Berkeley: University of California Press, 1993) (contains 100 interviews with survivors of the Armenian genocide).
40. See, generally, Ben Kiernan, *The Pol Pot Regime: Race, Power, and Genocide in Cambodia under the Khmer Rouge*, 2nd ed. (New Haven, CT: Yale University Press, 2002); Dith Pran and Kim DePaul, eds., *Children of Cambodia's Killing Fields: Memoirs by Survivors* (New Haven, CT: Yale University Press, 1997) contains 30 interviews with those who were children under the Khmer Rouge.
41. D4D torch relay, Seattle, Nov. 4, 2007, http://www.savedarfur.org/page/content/torchrelay/ny/ (last accessed May 30, 2010).
42. See, for example, Kim Masters, "Hollywoodland: Here Come the Directors," *Slate*, Dec. 18, 2007; "The Challenge to Beijingoism," *Economist*, Dec. 27, 2007; Evan Osnos, "The Glory of Games Is Fraught with Risk," *Chicago Tribune*, Jan. 1, 2008.
43. Michael Abramowitz, "Bush Names Successor as Sudan Envoy Steps Down," *Washington Post*, Dec. 22, 2007.
44. Richard Williamson, interview with author, Dec. 12, 2009; all Williamson quotes, this chapter, from this interview.
45. Jendayi Frazer, interview with author, Apr. 9, 2010.
46. John Prendergast, e-mail correspondence with author, Jan. 14, 2010.
47. Masters, "Hollywoodland: Here Come the Directors."
48. Martin Hodgson, "Spielberg Walks Out on Beijing Games in Protest over Darfur," *Guardian*, Feb. 13, 2008.
49. In the English-language media a LexisNexis search reveals 229 articles on "Darfur" and "Olympics" in the 24 hours following Spielberg's resignation.
50. *Dream for Darfur*, "D4D Final Report," Oct. 2008 (internal document, on file with author). From these meetings, a leadership group (McDonalds, Coca Cola, and General Electric) emerged and began working on a public statement from the sponsors to the UN Security Council calling for the deployment of the hybrid force before the Olympics began. Ultimately the letter did not go forward due to pressure against it from the International Olympic Committee.
51. Ilan Greenberg, "Changing the Rules of the Games," *New York Times Magazine*, Mar. 30, 2008.
52. Sim Chi Yin, "China to Use Its Clout over Sudan, Says Envoy," *Straits Times* (Singapore), Mar. 8, 2008.
53. Costa Rican official to the UN, interview with author, Feb. 12, 2009.
54. Jorge Ballestero, interview with author, Feb. 12, 2009. All Ballestero quotes, this chapter, from this interview.

55. U.S. Senate Foreign Relations Committee Holds a Hearing on the Situation in Darfur (transcript), Apr. 11, 2007.
56. U.S. government official, interview with author, Jan. 21, 2010.

CHAPTER 11

1. Nora Boustany and Stephanie McCrummen, "Sudanese Pair Accused of War Crimes; International Court Names Member of President's Inner Circle, Darfur Militia Leader," *Washington Post*, Feb. 28, 2007.
2. Eric Reeves, "The ICC 'Application' Concerning International Crimes in Darfur," *Sudan Tribune*, Feb. 28, 2008.
3. Richard Williamson, interview with author, Dec. 12, 2009. All quotes from Williamson, this chapter, are from this interview.
4. "ICC Prosecutor Presents Case against Sudanese President Hassan Omar Al Bashir for Genocide, Crimes Against Humanity and War Crimes," States News Service, July 14, 2008. For the prosecutor to request an arrest warrant, the Rome Statute requires he (or she) present evidence to a three-judge Pre-Trial Chamber. If the Pre-Trial Chamber determines there are "reasonable grounds to believe" that a crime within the jurisdiction of the court has been committed by the accused, then they will issue the warrant.
5. Amira (full name withheld), interview with author, Aug. 2008, Oure Cassoni camp, Chad.
6. Hawa (full name withheld), interview with author, Aug. 2008 Djabal camp, Chad.
7. Aziza (full name withheld), interview with author, Aug. 2008, Djabal camp, Chad.
8. Amr Moussa, interview with author, June 9, 2009.
9. Olivia Bueno, interview with author, Dec. 18, 2009.
10. See "Situation in the Democratic Republic of Congo in the Case of Prosecutor vs. Thomas Lubanga Dyilo, Decision on the consequences of non-disclosure of exculpatory materials covered by Article 54(3)(e) agreements and the application to stay the prosecution of the accused, together with certain other issues raised at the Status Conference on 10 June 2008," Trial Chamber I, June 13, 2008.
11. Olivia Bueno, interview with author, Dec. 18, 2009. See "Situation in the Democratic Republic of Congo in the Case of Prosecutor vs. Thomas Lubanga Dyilo, Decision on the release of Thomas Lubanga Dyilo," Trial Chamber I, July 2, 2008.
12. Notes from conference participant, July 14, 2008 (on file with author).
13. See Julie Flint and Alex de Waal, "Justice Off Course in Darfur," *Washington Post*, June 28, 2008; Julie Flint, Alex de Waal, and Sara Pantuliano, "ICC Approach Risks Peacemaking in Darfur," *Guardian* (letters), June 10, 2008.
14. Flint and de Waal, "Justice Off Course in Darfur."
15. Martin Luther King, Jr., "Letter from Birmingham Jail," Apr. 16, 1963.
16. "Prosecutor of the Tribunal vs. Slobodan Milosevic *et al.*" Indictment, International Criminal Tribunal for the former Yugoslavia, May 23, 1999. Milosevic was not arrested until after he had been removed from office by defeat in a democratic election.
17. The indictment was signed by the prosecutor of the Special Court for Sierra Leone on Mar. 3, 1999, but was kept under seal until June 1999. Under pressure from the U.S. government, Taylor resigned control of Liberia and went into exile in 2003, but in 2006 he was arrested while trying to escape from his place of exile. Joe De Capua, "Sierra Leone Welcomes the Capture of Charles Taylor," *Voice of America*, Mar. 29, 2006.
18. See, for example, Mahmoud Mamdani, *Saviors and Survivors: Darfur, Politics and the War on Terror* (New York: Random House, 2009), 285–86.

19. M. Cherif Bassiouni, "Accountability for International Crime and Serious Violations of Fundamental Human Rights: Searching for Peace and Achieving Justice: The Need for Accountability," *Law and Contemporary Problems* 9 (1996): 9–28.
20. "Darfurian Voices: Documenting Darfurian Refugees' Views on Issues of Peace, Justice and Reconciliation," 24 hours for Darfur Project preliminary report (on file with author).
21. Bram Posthumus and Jan Huisman, "ICC—An Asset to International Justice," Radio Netherland, May 6, 2009; Annalisa Ciampi, "The Proceedings against President Al-Bashir and the Prospects of their Suspension under Article 16 ICC Statute," *Journal of International Criminal Justice*, 6 (2008): 886.
22. "Arab League Condemns ICC Prosecutor," UPI, July 20, 2008.
23. African Union Peace and Security Council, 142nd meeting, July 21, 2008.
24. AU officials, interviews with author, Addis Ababa, July 2009. Interestingly, a poll taken of citizens in Kenya and Nigeria at the time suggested that the AU's stated position did not necessarily resonate with regular people either (77 percent and 71 percent, respectively, of those polled said they approved of the ICC warrant for al-Bashir). "Muslim and African Nations on Bashir Indictment and Darfur," *World Public Opinion*, July 16, 2009.
25. *Rome Statute*, Art. 16, U.N. Doc. A/CONF.183/9*, 1998.
26. For details, see Morten Bergsmo and Jelena Pejić, "Article 16: Deferral of Investigation or Prosecution," in Otto Triffterer, *Commentary on the Rome Statute of the International Criminal Court* (Oxford: Hart Publishing, 2008).
27. "African Officials Troubled by Timing of Genocide Arrest for Sudan's President," Voice of America, Sept. 30, 2008.
28. GI-Net e-mail to constituents, Sept. 18, 2008 (on file with author). One hundred and fourteen calls were generated from GI-Net constituents to the White House in the 48 hours following the ICC-related prompt being recorded. Author correspondence with Allyson Neville, Jan. 28, 2010.
29. Richard Williamson, e-mail correspondence with author, Jan. 26, 2010.
30. U.S. official (Sudan Programs Group), interview with author, Jan. 25, 2007.

CHAPTER 12

1. "Factual Report on the status of CPA Implementation 2007," Assessment and Evaluation Commission, Oct. 2007.
2. Ibid.
3. U.S. official (Sudan Program Group), interview with author, Jan. 25, 2007.
4. See, for example, Barack Obama, "Barack Obama Response to AJC Questionnaire," http://www.ajc.org/site/c.ijITI2PHKoG/b.3878133/ (last accessed May 10, 2010). (On Darfur: "The United States needs to lead the world in ending this genocide, including by imposing much tougher sanctions that target Sudan's oil revenue, implementing and helping to enforce a no-fly zone, and engaging in more intense, effective diplomacy to get a political roadmap to peace.... To stop the genocide, the international community needs to deploy a large, capable force with a robust enforcement mandate to protect civilians.") John McCain, "An Enduring Peace Built on Freedom," *Foreign Affairs*, Nov./Dec. 2007. ("The genocide in Darfur demands U.S. leadership. My administration will consider the use of all elements of American power to stop the outrageous acts of human destruction that have unfolded there.")
5. Rob Crilly, "Darfuri Rebels Cross Wilderness to Mount Raid on Gates of Khartoum," *The Times of London*, May 12, 2008.

6. See Francis Deng, *War of Visions: Conflict of Identities in The Sudan* (Washington, D.C.: Brookings Institution, 1995), part 4.

7. Protocol between the Government of the Sudan (GOS) and the Sudan People's Liberation Movement/Army (SPLM/A) on the Resolution of the Abyei Conflict (Naivasha, Kenya), May 26, 2004, sect. 1.3. This marked the second time the people of Abyei had been promised a self-determination referendum. (The Abyei self-determination referendum in the 1972 Addis Ababa agreement was never implemented).

8. The boundary dispute was eventually referred to the Permanent Court of Arbitration, http://www.pca-cpa.org/showpage.asp?pag_id=1306 (last accessed May 30, 2010).

9. "Sudan: Breaking the Abyei Deadlock," *International Crisis Group*, Oct. 12, 2007.

10. Roger Winter, "Sounding the Alarm on Abyei," Enough strategy paper, Apr. 2008.

11. "Position Paper on Normalization of Relations between Sudan and the United States," Feb. 11, 2008 (leaked document, on file with author).

12. President al-Bashir conveyed his skepticism of these U.S. offers of normalization to me via e-mail through Ghazi Salahuddin Atabani in 2009, commenting that: "The same promises regarding sanctions were renewed by then Secretary of State Colin Powell, Assistant Secretary of State at the time, Jendayi Frazer, and then Deputy Secretary of State Robert Zoellick. Now the current U.S. Envoy to Sudan, Scott Gration, reiterates the same promises." Al-Bashir, e-mail correspondence with author, Sept. 8, 2009.

13. Testimony of Richard Williamson, "The Continuing Crisis in Darfur," Senate Foreign Relations Committee, Apr. 23, 2008.

14. Richard Williamson, interview with author, Feb. 25, 2010.

15. "Abandoning Abyei: Destruction and Displacement," Human Rights Watch, July 2008.

16. "Daily Press Briefing by the Office of the Spokesperson of the Secretary-General of the United Nations," *Federal News Service*, May 20, 2008.

17. Roger Winter, interview with author, Feb. 10, 2010.

18. Roger Winter, "Abyei Aflame," Enough strategy paper, May 30, 2008.

19. In responding to the criticism that the UN peacekeepers had hid in their barracks, UN special envoy for Sudan Ashraf Qazi argued that "UNMIS has neither the capacity nor the mandate to militarily intervene." Louis Charbonneau, "UN Report Cites 'Lessons' From South Sudan Attack," Reuters, July 24, 2008. The UNMIS mandate from the UN Security Council authorizes the troops "without prejudice to the responsibility of the Government of the Sudan, *to protect civilians under imminent threat of physical violence*" (emphasis added), S.C. Res. 1590, U.N. Doc S/RES/1590 (Mar. 24, 2005).

20. Roger Winter, interview with author, Feb. 10, 2010.

21. Ibid.

22. Ibid.

23. Richard Williamson, interview with author, Feb. 25, 2010.

24. Richard Williamson, interview with author, Dec. 12, 2009.

25. Richard Williamson, interview with author, Feb. 25, 2010.

26. Jerry Fowler, interview with author, Jan. 29, 2010.

27. Stephen Hadley, interview with author, Dec. 22, 2009.

28. Rodolphe Adada, interview with author, Aug. 9, 2009.

29. Amr Moussa, interview with author, June 9, 2009.

30. Minni Minawi, interview with author, Aug. 12, 2009.

31. UNAMID planning staff, interviews with author, July 2009 (Addis Ababa), Aug. 2009 (El-Fasher and Nyala).
32. Nakaha Stanislas, interview with author, July 14, 2009.
33. Thomas Withington, "Grounded: The International Community's Betrayal of UNAMID," July 31, 2008, available at: www.refugee-rights.org/Publications/2008/UNAMID.073108.pdf.
34. Glen Segell, "The United Nations Africa Union Mission in Darfur," *Strategic Insights*, vol. VII (1), Feb. 2008.
35. UNAMID planner, interview with author, Aug. 21, 2009 (el-Fasher).
36. Jean-Marie Guéhenno, interview with author, Feb. 12, 2009.
37. UN official, interview with author, Aug. 2009 (el-Fasher).
38. UN official, interview with author, Mar. 18, 2009.
39. UN official, e-mail correspondence with author, Oct. 12, 2009.
40. Of course there are times when advocates can play an important role in putting a policy on the agenda that politicians may otherwise rule out prematurely as unachievable, when in actual fact the circumstances can be built up to increase the likelihood of success.
41. Jean-Marie Guehénno, interview with author, Feb. 12, 2009.

CHAPTER 13

1. Joseph Biden, quoted in Shmuel Rosner, "What Would Biden's Middle East Policy Look Like?" *Slate*, Aug. 25, 2008.
2. During an interagency discussion when Susan Rice was the Clinton administration's assistant secretary of state for African Affairs during the 1994 Rwandan genocide, Rice allegedly questioned what the impact would be on the upcoming congressional elections if the administration called what was happening in Rwanda genocide and then did nothing about it. Following criticism of her comments, Rice said, "I swore to myself that if I ever faced such a crisis again, I would come down on the side of dramatic action, going down in flames if that was required." Rice quoted in Samantha Power, "Bystanders to Genocide," *Atlantic Monthly*, Sept. 2001.
3. Alex de Waal, "Sudan's Choices: Scenarios beyond the CPA," in *Sudan—No Easy Ways Ahead* (Berlin: Heinrich Böll Stiftung, 2010).
4. "Warrant of Arrest for Omar Hassan Ahmad Al Bashir," ICC-02/05-01/09, Mar. 4, 2009.
5. "Second Decision on Prosecutor's Application for an Arrest Warrant," ICC-02/05-01/09-94, July 12, 2010.
6. "Sudan to Expel Foreign Aid Groups," Al Jazeera.net, Mar. 16, 2009; "US Envoy Blasts Sudan NGO Expulsion," Voice of America, Mar. 20, 2009.
7. Costa Rican official present at the UN OCHA briefing, interview with author, Mar. 17, 2009.
8. See "UN Denounces Expulsion of Humanitarian Chief," *Miraya FM*, Juba, Nov. 9, 2007, on expulsion of head of UN humanitarian operations for South Darfur state); Ewen MacAskill, "Darfur Relief Operation Weeks Away from Collapse, Warns UN," *Guardian*, Apr. 22, 2006 ("Sudan expelled a Norwegian aid group this month that had been caring for 90,000 people"); "Sudan Threatens to Expel Charity Workers," UPI, Nov. 30, 2004, on Save the Children and Oxfam.
9. Costan Rican official to the UN, interview with author, Mar. 17, 2009.
10. "Darfur Groups Urge Immediate Obama Administration Leadership to Solve Humanitarian Crisis," Save Darfur Coalition, Mar. 11, 2009 (sign-on letter to

President Obama), available at: http://www.savedarfur.org/pages/press/darfur_
advocacy_groups_urge_immediate_obama_administration_leadership_to_so/
(last accessed Aug. 15, 2010).

11. "Enough Project Statement on the NGO Expulsions by Sudan," Enough Project,
Mar. 5, 2009, available at: http://www.enoughproject.org/news/enough-proj-
ect-statement-ngo-expulsions-sudan (last accessed Aug. 16, 2010); "Act Now:
Humanitarian Organizations Expelled from Sudan," Genocide Intervention
Network, Mar. 11, 2009 (e-mail to constituents, on file with author).

12. John Prendergast, "Our Meeting With the President," Enough Project, Mar. 31,
2009, available at: http://www.enoughproject.org/blogs/our-meeting-president
(last accessed Aug. 15, 2010).

13. Testimony of Scott Gration, "A Comprehensive Strategy for Sudan," Senate
Foreign Relations Committee, July 30, 2009.

14. Danielle Kurtzleben, "U.S. officials disagree over Sudan strategy," Inter Press
Service, Aug. 3, 2009.

15. "'Gration Must Go' Say Darfur Activists from Coast to Coast," Pax Communications, June 19, 2009, available at: http://paxcommunications.org/news/2009/06/19/
gration-must-go-say-darfur-activists-from-coast-to-coast/ (last accessed Aug. 15,
2010).

16. "Power Players on Darfur Meet With President Obama: Your Insiders Guide,"
Enough Project, May 7, 2009 (on file with author).

17. John Norris, "Sudan Now," *Huffington Post*, Aug. 26, 2009.

18. Scott Gration, interview with author, Sept. 13, 2009. All Gration quotes, this chapter, from this interview.

19. U.S. State Department official working for Gration, interview with author, Sept.
13, 2009.

20. Luka Biong, Sudanese Minister of Cabinet, interview with author, July 29, 2010.

21. Ginger Thompson, "White House's New Sudan Strategy Fits Envoy's Pragmatic
Style," *New York Times*, Oct. 19, 2009.

22. Darfuri *omda* (name withheld), among a group of *omdas*, Sept. 12, 2009, el-Fasher.

23. "Darfur Rebel Leader Lashes Out at US Envoy over Genocide Statements," *Sudan
Tribune*, June 19, 2009.

24. DPDO Women's Centre, Abu Shok, Sept. 12, 2009.

25. UN official, interview with author, Aug. 2009, el-Fasher.

26. Lindsey Hilsum, "Interview: Omar al-Bashir," Channel 4, Oct. 17, 2008.

27. Aid workers, interviews with author, Aug. 2009, Nyala and el-Fasher.

28. "Chad's leader in Sudan to ease ties," Al-Jazeera, Feb. 9, 2004, available at: http://
english.aljazeera.net/news/africa/2010/02/20102910033222268.html.

29. See http://www.standnow.org/blog/giving-sudan-its-gold-star.

30. With Susan Rice's office not responding to interview requests, I was unable to
get her views on these disputes directly; however, reporting from *Foreign Policy*
indicates that the disagreements between Gration and Rice continued even after
the policy review was released. See Josh Rogin, "As Tensions Boil, Obama's Sudan
Envoy Contemplates Kenya Post," *Foreign Policy*, Aug. 13, 2010.

31. "Sudan: A Critical Moment, a Comprehensive Approach," U.S. Department of
State, Oct. 19, 2009.

32. In September 2009, al-Bashir announced that formal press censorship would end
and be replaced by self-censorship. In making the announcement, he warned journalists to "differentiate between what is patriotic and what is destructive to the
nation," threatening that those who failed to do so would "face severe punishment." (Phone interview with journalist present at the announcement, Sept. 26,
2009.) (Al-Bashir reinstated formal press censorship shortly after his electoral

victory.) In late December 2009, the national security laws were also "reformed." Opposition parties, including the SPLM, voted against the new legislation, but the NCP was able to pass it because of their majority. The "reforms" did not, in any practical sense, limit the ability of security officers to arrest and detain Sudanese citizens incommunicado, and the maintenance of immunity from prosecution for security officials further undermined any notion that the new law would improve accountability for acts of torture committed by security services. ("Sudan ruling party official slams opposition for rejecting new security law," SUNA via BBC Monitoring Middle East, Dec. 22, 2009; [Sudan] National Security Act 2009, on file with author.)

33. "5th Population and Housing Census—An Incomplete Exercise," Darfur Relief and Documentation Centre, Feb. 2010, 19.
34. Salih Mahmoud Osman, interview with author, Aug. 6, 2009.
35. See, for example, "Sudan Says It Will Not Permit Any Demonstrations by Opposition," *Sudan Tribune*, Dec. 17, 2009.
36. Mohamed Musa Abdella Bahraldien was found dead on Feb. 11, 2009 (author confirmation through several eyewitnesses and confirmation sent by Abdelrahman Gasim, Darfur Bar Association).
37. See, for example, "Arrest and Beating of Girifna Members Inspecting Elections," http://www.girifna.com/?p=1458 (last accessed May 20, 2010).
38. Lisbeth Kirk, "EU Election Observers Withdraw from Darfur," EUObserver. com, Apr. 8, 2010.
39. "Sudan, Preventing Implosion," International Crisis Group, Dec. 17, 2009, 1.
40. "'No Delay' for Sudan's National Elections," BBC News, Apr. 3, 2010.
41. U.S. government officials (U.S. State Department and Special Envoys Office), interviews with author, Sept.-Oct., 2009; Sudanese opposition party members, recounting Gration's comments from a meeting held with them at Al-Fatah tower before the elections, interviews with author, July-Aug. 2010.
42. Opheera McDoom, "Sudan Opposition Umma Party Will Boycott Elections," Reuters, Apr. 7, 2010.
43. Scott Baldauf, "President Bashir's Chief Rival Boycotts Election," *Christian Science Monitor*, Apr. 1, 2010.
44. "Sudan's Rigged Elections," Sudan First Democracy Group, May 4, 2010, available at: http://www.sudantribune.com/spip.php?article35003 (last accessed Aug. 10, 2010).
45. Multiple author interviews with members of the People's Congress Party, the Sudan Communist Party and the Umma Party, as well as women's rights groups and the pro-democracy movement, Girifna, conducted in Khartoum, July-Aug. 2010.
46. "Sudan: Blockade of humanitarian aid in Darfur violates international law—another war crime committed by Bashir?" *Relief Web*, Aug. 13, 2010, available at: http://www.reliefweb.int/rw/rwb.nsf/db900SID/MINE-88ALG4?OpenDocument (last accessed, Aug. 25, 2010); "UN relief chief urges unfettered access for aid workers in Darfur," *U.N. News Centre*, Aug. 23, 2010, available at: http://www.un.org/apps/news/story.asp?NewsID=35696 (last accessed Aug. 25, 2010).
47. "Scores Killed in Darfur Clashes," Reuters, June 20, 2010, available at: http://www.france24.com/en/20100620-arab-tribes-scores-killed-deadly-darfur-clashes-sudan (growing clashes between the Rizeigat and Misserya Arabs over access to land); Representative from the Public International Law Group, assisting with the negotiations in Doha, correspondence with author, Apr. 2010 (stating that although some Darfuri Arabs are present at the negotiations, no Darfuri Arab group has representation as a party to the talks).

CHAPTER 14

1. Samantha Power, *"A Problem from Hell": America and the Age of Genocide* (New York: Harper Perennial, 2002), xviii.
2. See, generally, Gareth Evans, *The Responsibility to Protect: Ending Mass Atrocity Crimes Once and For All* (Washington, D.C.: Brookings Institution Press, 2008); Frank Chalk et al., *Mobilizing the Will to Intervene: Leadership and Action to Prevent Mass Atrocities* (Montreal: McGill-Queens University Press, 2009).
3. Olivier Degomme and Debarati Guha-Sapir, "Patterns of Mortality Rates in Darfur Conflict," *Lancet* 375 (Jan. 23, 2010): 298. The study estimates that there were 96,228 "excess deaths" resulting from nonviolent causes for Jan. 2005-June 2006 compared with 146,408 for the period July 2006-Sept. 2007. Note: This figure does not include the Darfuri refugee population across the border in Chad.
4. Lam Akol, interview with author, Aug. 15, 2009; Omar Al-Bashir, e-mail correspondence with author via Ghazi Salahuddin Atabani, Sept. 8, 2009; Jendayi Frazer, interview with author, Nov. 19, 2009.
5. Not only did it not invade, but it also did not take smaller steps, for example, deploying unmanned aerial vehicles to record, and ideally deter, criminal activity. For a comprehensive listing of military interventions that fall far short of boots on the ground, see Sarah Sewall, Dwight Raymond, and Sally Chin, "Mass Atrocity Response Operations: A Military Planning Handbook," Harvard Kennedy School, 2010, Appendix G, Flexible Deterrent Options.
6. Madeleine Albright and William Cohen, "Preventing Genocide: A Blueprint for U.S. Policymakers," Genocide Prevention Task Force, U.S. Holocaust Memorial Museum, 2008.
7. See, for example, Matthew Waxman, "Intervention to Stop Genocide and Mass Atrocities," Council on Foreign Relations, 2009; Victoria Holt and Glyn Taylor with Max Kelly, "Protecting Civilians in the Context of UN Peacekeeping Operations," United Nations, 2009; "Increasing Global Preparedness to Protect Civilians from Mass Atrocities" (workshop), Stimson Center, Sept. 2009; Sewall, Raymond, Chin, "Mass Atrocity Response Operations"; Sandra McElwaine, "Obama Hires a Clooney Confident," The Daily Beast, Apr. 14, 2010 (creating the position of Director for War Crimes and Atrocity Prevention on the U.S. National Security Council).
8. As recently as 2001, genocide prevention was not addressed in the U.S. National Security Strategy (NSS). The 2002 NSS made a passing reference to genocide, saying that it was a goal of the U.S. government to use its influence to make clear that terrorism is illegitimate and should be viewed in the same light as genocide. See National Security Council, "The National Security Strategy of the United States of America 2002," September 2002, Part III. Not until 2006 did genocide prevention merit its own section of the NSS. See National Security Council, "The National Security Strategy of the United States of America 2006," September 2006, Part IV(C)(4). The Obama administration has continued in this vein, with the 2010 NSS recognizing the need to prevent genocide and mass atrocity, and also mentioning the Responsibility to Protect. See National Security Council, "The National Security Strategy of the United States of America 2010," May 2010, 48.

BIBLIOGRAPHY

SUDAN

Asher, Michael. *Khartoum: The Ultimate Imperial Adventure*. 2nd ed. London: Penguin, 2006.

Baldo, Suliman, et al. "Post-2011 Scenarios in Sudan: What Role for the EU?" European Union Institute for Security Studies Report, edited by Damien Helly. Nov. 2009.

Beshir, Mohamed Omer. *The Southern Sudan: Background to Conflict*. New York: Praeger, 1968.

Burr, J. M., and R. O. Collins. *Revolutionary Sudan: Hasan al-Turabi and the Islamist State, 1989-2000*. Leiden: Brill, 2003.

Cobham, Alex. "Causes of Conflict in Sudan: Testing the Black Book." Working paper, Finance and Trade Policy Research Centre, University of Oxford, Jan. 2005.

Collins, Robert O. *A History of Modern Sudan*. Cambridge: Cambridge University Press, 2008.

Deng, Francis. *Frontiers of Unity: An Experiment in Afro-Arab Cooperation*. New York: Routledge, 2009.

Deng, Francis. *War of Visions: Conflict of Identities in the Sudan*. Washington, D.C.: Brookings Institution, 1995.

Johnson, Douglas H. *The Root Causes of Sudan's Civil Wars*. 4th ed. Nairobi: East African Educational Publishers, 2007.

Jok, Jok Madut. *War and Slavery in Sudan*. Philadelphia: University of Pennsylvania Press, 2001.

Khalid, Mansour. *War and Peace in Sudan*. London: Kegan Paul, 2003.

Moorehead, Alan. *The White Nile*. New York: Harper & Row, 1960.

Salih, M. A. Mohamed, and Sharif Harir. "Tribal Militias: The Genesis of National Disintegration." In *Short-Cut to Decay: The Case of the Sudan*, edited by Sharif Harir and Terje Tvedt, 186–203. Uppsala, Sweden: Nordiska Afrikainstitutet, 1994.

Salmon, Jago. "A Paramilitary Revolution: The Popular Defence Forces." *Small Arms Survey*, Dec. 2007.

Tvedt, Terje. *Angels of Mercy or Development Diplomats: NGOs & Foreign Aid*. Asmara: Africa World Press, 1998.

DARFUR

Adam, Gamal A. "Why Has the Indigenous Population of Darfur Been Exposed to Destruction?" Conference paper, The Current Darfur Crisis, American University, Cairo, June 16, 2004.

Burr, J. M., and R. O. Collins. *Darfur: The Long Road to Disaster.* Princeton, NJ: Markus Wiener, 2006.

Darfur: The Responsibility to Protect. Edited by David Mephan and Alexander Ramsbotham. London: IPPR, 2006.

de Waal, Alex, ed. *War in Darfur and the Search for Peace.* Cambridge: Harvard University Press, 2007.

de Waal, Alex. "Tragedy in Darfur: On Understanding and Ending the Horror." *Boston Review,* Oct./Nov. 2004.

Degomme, Oliver, and Debarati Guha-Sapir. "Patterns of Mortality Rates in Darfur Conflict." *Lancet* 375 (2010): 294–300.

Flint, Julie. "Rhetoric and Reality: The Failure to Resolve the Darfur Conflict." *Small Arms Survey,* Jan. 2010.

Flint, Julie, and Alex de Waal. *Darfur: A New History of a Long War.* London: Zed Books, 2008.

Hagan, John, and Wenona Rymond-Richmond. *Darfur and the Crime of Genocide.* Cambridge: Cambridge University Press, 2009.

Hari, Daoud (as told to Dennis Michael Burke and Megan M. McKenna). *The Translator: A Tribesman's Memoir of Darfur.* New York: Penguin, 2008.

Harir, Sharif. "'Arab Belt' versus 'African Belt': Ethno-political Conflict in Darfur and the Regional Cultural Factors." In *Short-Cut to Decay: The Case of the Sudan,* edited by Sharif Harir and Terje Tvedt, 144–85. Uppsala, Sweden: Nordiska Afrikainstitutet, 1994.

Mamdani, Mahmoud. *Saviors and Survivors: Darfur, Politics and the War on Terror.* New York: Random House, 2009.

Prunier, Gérard. *Darfur: The Ambiguous Genocide.* Ithaca, NY: Cornell University Press, 2005.

Reeves, Eric. *A Long Day's Dying: Critical Moments in the Darfur Genocide.* Toronto: Key Publishing House, 2007.

Tubiana, Jérôme. "The Chad-Sudan Proxy War and the 'Darfurization' of Chad: Myths and Reality." *Small Arms Survey,* Apr. 2008.

Tubiana, Jérôme. "Why Chad Isn't Darfur and Darfur Isn't Rwanda." *London Review of Books* 31, no. 24 (Dec. 17, 2009).

Young, Helen, et al., *Darfur: Livelihoods under Siege.* Medford, MA: Feinstein International Famine Center, Tufts University, 2005.

POLICYMAKING, AMERICAN POLITICS, AND FOREIGN POLICY

Almond, Gabriel A. *The American People and Foreign Policy.* 2nd ed. New York: Praeger, 1960.

Bolton, John. *Surrender Is Not an Option: Defending America at the United Nations and Abroad.* New York: Threshold, 2007.

Brysk, Alison. *Global Good Samaritans: Human Rights as Foreign Policy.* Oxford: Oxford University Press, 2009.

Coll, Steve. *Ghost Wars: The Secret History of the CIA, Afghanistan, and Bin Laden, from the Soviet Invasion to September 10, 2001.* New York: Penguin, 2004.

DeYoung, Karen. *Soldier: The Life of Colin Powell.* New York: Knopf, 2006.

Holsti, Ole R. *Public Opinion and American Foreign Policy.* Ann Arbor: University of Michigan Press, 1996.

Kessler, Glen. *The Confidante: Condoleezza Rice and the Creation of the Bush Legacy.* New York: St. Martin's Press, 2007.

Khong, Yuen Foong. *Analogies at War: Korea, Munich, Dien Bien Phu, and the Vietnam Decisions of 1965.* Princeton, NJ: Princeton University Press, 1992.

Kingdon, John. *Agendas, Alternatives and Public Policies*. 2nd ed. New York: Longman, 2003.

Mertus, Julie A. *Bait and Switch: Human Rights and U.S. Foreign Policy*. 2nd ed. New York: Routledge, 2008.

Nye, Joseph, Jr. *Soft Power: The Means to Success in World Politics*. Washington, D.C.: Public Affairs, 2004.

Slaughter, A. M. *A New World Order*. Princeton, NJ: Princeton University Press, 2004.

Walker, Jack. *Patrons, Professions, and Social Movements*. Ann Arbor: University of Michigan Press, 1991.

Woodward, Bob. *State of Denial*. New York: Simon & Schuster, 2006.

Wright, John. *Interest Groups and Congress: Lobbying, Contributions and Influence*. New York: Longman, 2003.

Yetiv, Steve A. *Explaining Foreign Policy: U.S. Decision-Making and the Persian Gulf War*. Baltimore, MD: John Hopkins University Press, 2004.

SOCIAL MOVEMENTS, HUMAN RIGHTS

Anderson, Kenneth. "The Ottawa Convention Banning Landmines, the Role of International Non-governmental Organizations and the Idea of International Civil Society." *European Journal of International Law* 11, no. 1 (2000): 91–120.

Cameron, Maxwell A., Brian W. Tomlin, and Robert J. Lawson, eds. *To Walk Without Fear: The Global Movement to Ban Landmines*. New York: Oxford University Press, 1998.

Cheadle, Don, and John Prendergast. *Not on Our Watch: The Mission to End Genocide in Darfur and Beyond*. New York: Hyperion, 2007.

de Waal, Alex. "Human Rights Organizations and the Political Imagination: How the West and Africa Have Diverged." *Journal of Human Rights* 2, no. 4 (Dec. 2003): 475–94.

de Waal, Alex. "The Problem of 'Evil' in Secular Humanitarian and Human Rights Discourse." Working paper, Social Science Research Council, Sept. 2009.

Glendon, Mary Ann. *A World Made New: Eleanor Roosevelt and the Universal Declaration of Human Rights*. New York: Random House, 2001.

Ignatieff, Michael, ed. *American Exceptionalism and Human Rights*. Princeton: Princeton University Press, 2005.

Kaufmann, Chaim D., and Robert A. Pape. "Explaining Costly International Moral Action: Britain's Sixty-year Campaign Against the Atlantic Slave Trade." *International Organization* 53, no. 4 (Autumn 1999): 631–68.

Keck, Margaret E., and Kathryn Sikkink. *Activists beyond Borders: Advocacy Networks in International Politics*. Ithaca, NY: Cornell University Press, 1998.

Kennedy, David. *The Dark Sides of Virtue: Reassessing International Humanitarianism*. Princeton, NJ: Princeton University Press, 2004.

Klotz, Audie. *Norms in International Relations: The Struggle against Apartheid*. Ithaca, NY: Cornell Studies in Political Economy, 1999.

Smith, Jackie, Charles Chatfield, and Ron Pagnucco, eds. *Transnational Social Movements and Global Politics: Solidarity Beyond the State*. Syracuse, NY: Syracuse University Press, 1997.

Steiner, Henry, Philip Alston, and Ryan Goodman, eds. *International Human Rights in Context: Law, Politics, Morals*. 3rd ed. Oxford: Oxford University Press, 2008.

Tarrow, Sidney. *The New Transnational Activism*. Oxford: Oxford University Press, 2005.

GENOCIDE AND MASS ATROCITIES

Albright, Madeleine, and William Cohen, "Preventing Genocide: A Blueprint for U.S. Policymakers," *Genocide Prevention Task Force*. Washington, D.C.: U.S. Holocaust Memorial Museum, 2008.

Berkley, Bill. *The Graves Are Not Yet Full*. New York: Basic Books, 2001.

Bryce, James, and Arnold Toynbee. *The Treatment of the Armenians in the Ottoman Empire, 1915-1916*. Princeton, NJ: Gomidas Institute Books, 2000.

Chalk, Frank, Roméo Dallaire, Kyle Matthews, Carla Barquerio, and Simon Doyle. *Mobilizing the Will to Intervene: Leadership and Action to Prevent Mass Atrocities*. Montreal: McGill-Queens University Press, 2009.

Egeland, Jan. *A Billion Lives: An Eyewitness Report from the Frontlines of Humanity*. New York: Simon & Schuster, 2008.

Evans, Gareth. *The Responsibility to Protect: Ending Mass Atrocity Crimes Once and For All*. Washington, D.C.: Brookings Institution, 2008.

Gourevitch, Philip. *We Wish to Inform You that Tomorrow We Will Be Killed with Our Families: Stories from Rwanda*. New York: Farrar, Straus & Giroux, 1998.

Hatzfeld, Jean. *A Time for Machetes*. New York: Farrar, Straus & Giroux, 2005.

Keen, David. *Complex Emergencies*. Cambridge: Polity, 2008.

Kiernan, Ben. *The Pol Pot Regime: Race, Power, and Genocide in Cambodia under the Khmer Rouge*. 2nd ed. New Haven, CT: Yale University Press, 2002.

Kuperman, Alan J. *The Limits of Humanitarian Intervention: Genocide in Rwanda*. Washington, D.C.: Brookings Institution, 2001.

Lemarchand, René. *Burundi: Ethnic Conflict and Genocide*. New York: Woodrow Wilson Center Press, 1995.

Melvern, Linda R. *A People Betrayed: The Role of the West in Rwanda's Genocide*. London: Zed Books, 2000.

Miller, Donald, and Lorna Touryan Miller. *Survivors: An Oral History of the Armenian Genocide*. Berkeley: University of California Press, 1993.

Minow, Martha. *Between Vengeance and Forgiveness: Facing History after Genocide and Mass Violence*. Boston: Beacon Press, 1998.

Power, Samantha. *"A Problem from Hell": America and the Age of Genocide*. New York: Harper Perennial, 2002.

Pran, Dith, and Kim DePaul, eds. *Children of Cambodia's Killing Fields: Memoirs by Survivors*. New Haven, CT: Yale University Press, 1997.

Rittner, Carol, John K. Roth, and James M. Smith. *Will Genocide Ever End?* St. Paul: Paragon House, 2002.

Valentino, Benjamin. *Final Solutions: Mass Killing and Genocide in the 20th Century*. Ithaca, NY: Cornell University Press, 2004.

Wyman, David S. *The Abandonment of the Jews: America and the Holocaust, 1941-1945*. New York: Pantheon, 1984.

INTERNATIONAL CRIMINAL LAW

Abtahi, Hirad, and Philippa Webb, eds. *The Genocide Convention: The Travaux Préparatoires*. Leiden: Martinus Nijhoff, 2008.

Ball, Howard. *Prosecuting War Crimes and Genocide: The Twentieth-Century Experience*. Lawrence: University Press of Kansas, 1999.

Bassiouni, M. Cherif. "Accountability for International Crime and Serious Violations of Fundamental Human Rights: Searching for Peace and Achieving Justice: The Need for Accountability." *Law and Contemporary Problems* 9 (1996): 9–28.

Brunk, Darren. "Dissecting Darfur: Anatomy of a Genocide Debate." *International Relations* 22, no. 1 (2008): 25–44.

de Waal, Alex. "Reflections on the Difficulties of Defining Darfur's Crisis as Genocide." *Harvard Human Rights Journal* 20 (2007): 26–33.

de Waal, Alex, and Gregory H. Stanton. "Should President Omar al-Bashir of Sudan Be Charged and Arrested by the International Criminal Court?" *Genocide Studies and Prevention* 4, no. 3 (Dec. 2009): 329–53.

Drumbl, Mark. A. *Atrocity, Punishment and International Law.* Cambridge: Cambridge University Press, 2007.

Feinstein, Lee, and Tod Lindberg. *Means to an End: U.S. Interest in the International Criminal Court.* Washington, D.C.: Brookings Institution, 2009.

Greenwalt, Alexander K. A. "Rethinking Genocidal Intent: The Case for a Knowledge-Based Interpretation." *Columbia Law Review* 99 (Dec. 1999): 2259–294.

Jones, John R. W. D. "Whose Intent Is It Anyway? Genocide and Intent to Destroy a Group." In *Man's Inhumanity to Man: Essays on International Law in Honour of Antonio Cassese*, edited by Lal Chand Vohrah et al., 468–80. The Hague: Kluwer Law International, 2003.

Kress, Claus. "The Darfur Report and Genocidal Intent." *Journal of International Criminal Justice* 3 (2005): 562–78.

Scheffer, David. "The Merits of Unifying Terms: 'Atrocity Crimes' and 'Atrocity Law.'" *Genocide Studies and Prevention* 2, no. 91 (2007).

Smith, Adam M. *After Genocide: Bringing the Devil to Justice.* New York: Prometheus, 2009.

Triffterer, Otto. *Commentary on the Rome Statute of the International Criminal Court.* Oxford: Hart Publishing, 2008.

INDEX